The Shape of Things to Come

Selected Writings & Interviews

J. Sakai

The Shape of Things to Come

Selected Writings & Interviews

J. Sakai

The Shape of Things to Come
Selected Writings & Interviews
By J. Sakai

ISBN 978-1-989701-21-8

Published in 2023 by Kersplebedeb

To order copies of the book:

Kersplebedeb
CP 63560, CCCP Van Horne
Montreal, Quebec
Canada
H3W 3H8

info@kersplebedeb.com
www.kersplebedeb.com
www.leftwingbooks.net

For
Butch Lee
1940–2021
"Best comrade ever"

Contents

The Shape of Things to Come, Part I 5

Beginner's Kata: Uncensored Stray Thoughts on Revolutionary Organization (2018) 45

Notes Toward an Understanding of Capitalist Crisis & Theory (2009) 67

Aryan Politics & Fighting the W.T.O. (2001) 95

The Green Nazi: An Investigation into Fascist Ecology (2007) 115

When Race Burns Class: Settlers Revisited (2000) 147

Stolen at Gunpoint (2003) 175

Beyond McAntiwar: Notes on Finding Our Footing in the Collapsing Stage Set of the u.s. Empire (2005) 196

Theory Mao Tossed to Us (2017) 223

"Pseudo-Gangs" (1983) 233

From South Afrika to Puerto Rico to Mississippi (1983) . . 259

What Happened to the Zimbabwe Revolution (1984) . . . 265

The Shape of Things to Come, Part II 299

Marginalized Notes to The Shape of Things 366

The Shape of Things to Come, Part I

An Interview with J. Sakai, conducted from mid-2020

Kersplebedeb: We've got a lot to discuss! But maybe first some context: Your work is grounded in Marxism, you clearly have some special affection for Mao, and at the same time you have been accused of being an anarchist (amongst other things); how should younger radicals today approach these legacies of politics from the 19th and 20th centuries? What pitfalls should they be looking out for?

J. Sakai: Questions of how to handle inherited ideologies and politics are important now, as a new generation of revs comes onto the torn-up chaos landscape that is our 21st century. It's not so easy to understand as it's supposed to be. And it really is a deeper matter than if you've just joined team New Green Deal or team social democrat.

As a whole, hard-won pieces of knowledge that revs put together in past tides of struggle to scrawl out a strategic map, and then hopefully a tactical guide however tentative, are valuable. Thought-provoking, with interesting hints, both positive and negative, of what was really thought about, really tried. Yet are always being erased and forgotten, because they were never written in permanent ink in the first place. No more than we ourselves can be. Were always just for right then, though women and men never thought so. Are always receding deeper into memory, as generations and the world itself turn.

Even if saved in some unchristian holy text, they can only become gradually distant from their once sensuous context of immediate life-and-death class struggle, and thus are often now too faded to be easily read. That previous scientific knowledge, that theory and practice, is so precious for us precisely because it keeps disappearing and has to be constantly repatterned and stitched together all over again.

Every new generation must learn to apply revolutionary science themselves, rediscovering fire all over again. Which is why the scraps of basic scientific theory we can hold onto against the tidal pull are so practically important. And, yes, those pitfalls ...

Knowledge isn't something academic or abstract and made only by some intellectual elite. Michael Reinoehl died all alone at night in Lacey, Washington, not knowing how to give himself a chance to stay alive against a right-wing u.s. government assassination squad. Yet the revolutionary movement right here has had extensive, painfully learned practical knowledge in living memory on just this bitter-to-swallow situation. But it was scattered and lost to him as though it never had been.

i believe that revolutionaries have to take studying and using theory very seriously, the good and the bad of it. On the deepest level, we all need theory to help give understandable order to the waves of disparate cries and mass explosions streaming across our receivers.

But if revolutionary theory can be an invaluable tool, that doesn't mean that any given practitioner using the tool knows what they are doing. That's two very different things. The best roller chest of chrome Snap-On tools is no help if the mechanic working on your car has only an uncertain idea of what the problem is. Or is just faking it, which is infuriating but happens. Left theorists aren't any more scientific than auto mechanics, you know.

Maybe it would be good to see how that "ideas side" of our struggle has worked here. Or hasn't, because failed left theory isn't rare, either. This is a hard vagabond science to capture in a bottle. It humbles you—or it had better.

An obvious example—one which i have devoted much of my own work to examining—would be the critical question of the class nature of this type of metropolitan capitalist society, our "America," and its settler colonial working class as the once-expected big agent of revolutionary change. Or not so.

Through many lifetimes, the main u.s. left here used to always take pride in the white male industrial working class. Which until very recently they had for whatever reason theoretically positioned inside their class strategy as the largest and most important component of the "united multinational working class" in the u.s.a., or some such abstract formulation.

The majority of white workers were always supposed to be busy gaining consciousness of hypothetical basic class solidarity with their Black and Brown brothers and sisters, and with solid trade union work any old racist rust on them would soon be cleansed away. Or so it was always said by the organized left with their "power of positive thinking" theories. Any day now, the working class would be finally unified under its good white male leaders, and would brush aside "prejudice" of all kinds and overthrow the most powerful capitalist empire in the world—or so their useless white left class theory confidently predicted, generation after generation, century after century. But now time has run out. Their clock itself is dead.

It was in its own way a beautiful picture, though, the soothing lullaby a loyal left made up of the privileged could become very fond of, even addicted to.

Generation after generation, the most respected white left intellectuals across the spectrum, however they differed ideologically, echoed this one "revolutionary" class theory. Whether it was the marxist-leninist Herbert Aptheker, the social democrat Michael Harrington, or the 1960s New Left socialist Howard Zinn. The only problem was that this most fundamental class theory of theirs wasn't in the least bit true. It was a massive fiction, and a corrupt fiction at that. The "internationalism" of revolutionary anti-capitalism's 19th-century founders was only used as a cardboard shield here to hide corrupt oppressor politics.

We know it for a scientific fact, since in 400 years the euro-settler working class has never yet reached a revolutionary thing, and now as a lesser class never will. Much less ever stopped hating New Afrikan, Indigenous, Brown, and Asian workers. Did those respected left theorists forget to tell us that this piece of "Marxist" theory would only work for us once we all died and went to Left heaven?

And now, with the inevitable spread of technology and production overseas, and advanced mechanization at home, the white male working class here is shrinking and desiccating into a distorted husk of its former self. It will never carry out that crackpot white left theory of being anyone's main revolutionary army. Except for our enemy's, perhaps.

It isn't that these popular but badly askew marxist theorists were villains. There are good reasons why they were so respected. Herbert Aptheker's early 20th-century historical work on enslaved revolts was ground-breaking. Mike Harrington foresaw a time when his kind of "democratic socialism" could be a mainstream position for new state reforms to help the very poor. Howard Zinn was a passionate participant in the early anti-Segregation Sit-In protests of the 1960s South, willing to risk his university teaching career in them.

The total misreading of the class nature of the majority of white workers here persisted in the organized left, generation after generation, A to Z, from Communists to anarchists. It can hardly be the individual fault of this single theorist or that one.

The anti-capitalist left in the u.s. empire, started by radical emigrants and left exiles in the 19th century, carried the germ of a completely mistaken idea about the nature of Project America. That new "America" could be a fresh "democratic" society, constructed on an empty stage without any nasty feudal hangovers as in Old Europe. "Democratic" and white from the ground up, they hoped. They didn't get it that this brand-new militarized society with a continent-wide swagger larger than all the nations of Old Europe, was a *settler colonial capitalism.* A conquest and genocide and occupation society from day one, born to be an "infant empire" for capitalism, as one of the early right-wing white militia leaders named George Washington admitted.

Reading today's headlines, it is hard to really grasp how much the young revolutionaries who founded the anti-capitalist Left in 19th-century still-feudal-tinged Europe saw Project America as the hopeful dawn of a democratic future. Karl Marx himself remarked as a matter of fact that "America" was "the most democratic of nations." (He also observed presciently that its 1776 white power settler revolution marked the "rise of the middle classes.") The young blazing rebel against Czarist despotism and serfdom, future anarchist Mikhail Bakunin, angrily denounced the Confederate States rebellion against the Union, because "they nearly overthrew and destroyed the finest political organization that ever existed in history." (Both Bakunin and Marx always added that the blot of New Afrikan slavery had to be abolished, which they both felt it soon would be.)

Remember that the pioneering anti-capitalist radicals like Proudhon, Marx, Engels, and Bakunin weren't making revolution against the developed capitalism we are so accustomed to. They were part of youthful democratic uprisings against lingering *feudalism* and its oppressive structures—with democratic capitalist factions as the wavering allies of the new and radicalized urban working class.

Feudalism wasn't just another word for kings and dictatorship. It was a society owned by the landed hereditary aristocracy, with their own twisted class structure and rigidly hierarchical culture. Young Bakunin had wanted to be a reforming educator but placed too low in the examinations to win a position in the Russian state civil service. As a male member of a minor elite family, he was pledged from birth to compulsory service to his ultimate lord, the Czar. So would-be teacher Bakunin soon found himself in a stiff woolen uniform training for lifelong service ... as an artillery officer, of all things. To the angry Bakunin, that was just a higher rank of serf or indentured servant.

Later in life, when he escaped Siberian penal exile, crossed the Pacific, and landed on the West Coast of "America" on his long way back to Europe, he became famous here. An escaped pro-democracy turncoat Imperial Russian army officer was quite new and glamorous to the literate white public. Bakunin himself was thrilled to be here, where unlike in the Russian Empire any white man could rewrite his identity and status, making his way freely living and working wherever he willed across the conquered continent. Making his own destiny, as settlers just love to say.

In Boston he reunited with his old comrade Louis Agassiz, who had taken part in the German revolution with him in 1848, when Bakunin had been more or less drafted to lead the brave but hopeless military defense of the liberated city of Dresden against the might of the Prussian army. (Marx and Engels and most of young rebellious Europe praised his fight. As did the famed composer Richard Wagner, who supported the democratic revolution, and had to go with the leaders into exile for many years when the end came crashing down.) Agassiz hosted Bakunin in Boston, and helped promote his cause of opposition to Czarist autocracy. Agassiz doubtless was an influence in radical Bakunin's even filling out an initial application for u.s. citizenship.[1]

Of course, Louis Agassiz was equally famous here himself, as the founder of Harvard's department of anthropology, and one of this u.s. empire's foremost early pseudoscientific "experts" on human races. After the Civil War, he helped justify white public opposition to human rights for New Afrikans. They should have recognized non-enslaved status, but without voting or political rights of any kind ever, Agassiz testified before Congress. Since they were by their basic nature as a race, he said, too "subservient" and inferior to be trusted with any weapon of power in a white man's society. Just like women, some manly white men in the debate pointed out negatively. Even way back then abolitionists raised a storm of protest to this kind of Hate ideology.

Right now at Harvard today, Black Lives Matter wants to finally take his dead white name off their anthropology department door. It all comes 'round. To say that the original founders of left European anti-capitalism, whose contributions were great, and their exiles and political explorers over here, were also to a conscious degree eurocentric, is only to say the obvious.

In *Settlers*, i tried to quickly skip trace the genetic roots of where the left's disastrously out-of-the-ballpark class romance with the euro-settler working class here came from. Primarily to show that it's not a question of individual error, but of understanding that a settler colonial occupation society is not going to create working classes out of itself to fill the roles required in times of revolutionary crisis and change. They are if anything *reactionary* classes, fulfilling if anything a rearguard and counter-revolutionary role as they demand more and more subsidies.

Thus did "America" in real life foreshadow and be the later conscious model for both Hitler's early 20th-century European fascism *and* today's trend of traditional industrial classes in the imperial Western metropolis skewing sideways off the turnpike towards far-rightist political movements. Often glibly labeled in the media as "populist nationalism versus globalization." Which is too shallow to be actually true.

Kersplebedeb: We're getting near the end of 2020—it has been quite the year, with the biggest u.s. uprising in my lifetime, and now a chaotic whirlwind of activity and flux, on our side and our enemies'—what do you make of the current situation?

J. Sakai: Think we can scarcely miss what is happening, that right now we live at some turning point. Here the American white right is coming together in now less and less concealed shape, as the popular movement for violent settler colonial rule. To refurbish the lumpy furniture of the white past as our future. While the Trump White House reaches out to become a populist white dictatorship. Just as new George Floyd protests sweep the continent and beyond, city by city, using the name "BLM" or no name at all—simply intense anonymous anger and resistance, pushing angrily back against the lifelong pressure of police terrorism. Marches sometimes edging into night-time crowd attacks on state centers and bourgeois symbols. Contradictions central to actually existing capitalism are growing only sharper, more unresolvable.

Strikingly unlike the 1960s, when whites took part in nonviolent civil rights actions but not in violent so-called "ghetto riots," now even government buildings have been attacked and cops physically confronted with heavy white participation. A future left is starting to stir, different in its own right from all that which went before. In the 1980s–90s transition between old and new, for the first time the public demonstrations of violent u.s. white supremacist groups were physically challenged not just passively accepted, with young anarchists leading the way for everyone. All the time complaining that they were against all leaders. (A resistance culture here in Babylon needs a sense of radical humor.) And now that moment has gone into the possible future.

And at the same time, more and more "Americans" want some version of a social democratic welfare state, desperately hoping that this imperial way of life can be preserved for them in amber.

We can all get it, that everything has somehow changed in this moment. What's difficult is to comprehend it fully. To catch the inner nature and direction of this transformation as it unfolds.

In the past, some revolutionaries asked, *"Can capitalism*

even survive without colonialism?" Now, in this year 2020, on this terrain, the big answer seems to be clearly *"no."* We should take this seriously, because the ramifications are perhaps beyond our present imagining.

Not content to just accept his shock award as imperial president, Trump has had to spend four years openly talking, scheming, and precariously inching towards a euro-settler dictatorship. Whether he ever wins Civil War 2 or ends his days in pathetic exile somewhere as the Bonnie Prince Charlie of white races past, Trump has had to tap the one superpower available to him: coming out as the acid hate-mouthed champion of the white race. Promising a return to the good old days of "great" uncompromised white settler colonial ownership of their "America" and all within it. As a perverted papal celebration of his commitment to White Power, Trump has repeatedly taken within his palms the bloody hands of the far right, the neo-fascists; just as the Republican Party itself has done for many years in stealth seg mode, at the inconspicuous grassroots local, district, and county levels.

Again—whether he wins or loses elections, lives or dies—the jinni is finally out of the bottle. Smallville may look the same, but nothing *is* the same.

After two generations of state-paraded "civil rights" and "equal opportunity" and "integration," the white majority has spoken—it has experienced more "civil rights" than it thought it would ever see, and has come to the conclusion that it wants Hate. It wants White Power and an impossible return to the life of the post-WW2 u.s. empire at its zenith. Many settler men now want a return to full seg, everything short of chattel slavery. With women as largely servers and reproducers of whiteness; with New Afrikans, Latinos, Indigenous, and Asians recolonized and mostly out of white sight. And only a leader who utters Hate, who calls for mocking and attacking other peoples as less than human, can really satisfy their reality show now, after bitter years of white body blows and white diminishment.

None of his many blunders and lies and nazi-ish hints have cost Trump his core support of something close to a majority of the euro-settler population—especially concentrated among small business owners and those blue collar workers. Again, win or lose, it's a fact he's as popular in the polls with white voters as John F. Kennedy was when he ran for president. After all, if you feel that your superior-but-besieged race is in desperate circumstances, and you only have one superpower champion, you'll rush to defend him all the more when he stumbles.

The other part of North America's neo-colonial contradiction unfolding relentlessly this year was the great tidal wave of Black Lives Matter–labeled protests and campaigns. But how different from the now-classic 1960s rebellions these

have been—and in so many ways, both positive and problematic. How right from the start the class contradictions came forward, where the now decaying term "civil rights" no longer has any positive meaning for anyone. But only stands for opposing lies, where both white and Black "Americans" pretend to believe there is some future within sight where they are not enemies.

One part has been the heightened leadership role of New Afrikan women. Starting from the original Ferguson protests in 2014, where inexperienced young Black lesbians were central to the organizing, young leadership and queer leadership has come out. The same new leadership also has more problematic sides, as all things do, much more than just the DeRay McKesson model (which was like my fath-

er's Oldsmobile). We've watched the living dead—only they don't know it themselves—emerge both from the hustle and from professional NGO managers and would-be liberal politicians. By odd coincidence, Black zombies are currently "in" with filmmakers.

As usual, the real changes, the long-range mass transformations, are occurring below the choppy policed surface. Whole cities are packing up and moving. Last year, an acquaintance who casually takes in various New Afrikan women's talk sites remarked to me that the No. 1 subject right then was "Race War"—and that there was both lots of agreement and lots of disagreement, contradictory as that may sound. People are arming up individually, person by person, in an incoming tide, but seem also not finished yet working out what that means.

Also flaring at the edge of vision has been the role of a determined minority of white women in the protest wave. What was particularly visible was their role in less promising places to organize. In the white suburbs and small towns, and even in some klan-friendly white big city neighborhoods. There were over ten demonstrations in predominantly white Chicago suburbs last summer, not just in the city. Mostly small and organized by young white women who were new to this all. In Western Springs, a high school junior organ-

ized a demonstration and march through town; fists held high by other young white women her age, a small but brave group declaring to locally "amplify the voices" of the big city Black marches that seemed so far away.

This chemical reaction isn't a new thing. As every other time that there has been a major wave of Black struggle in the u.s. empire's long history, a white women's struggle has taken up its own feminist politics in a synchronous wave, standing ambivalently next to the light of Black Freedom Now. Because many know that every step ahead for the white far right will produce more and more patriarchal ownership over their own bodies and their own futures. The enemy who wants to gradually reintroduce full colonialism always has to include "their own" women and children. Because women have always secretly been the "first colony."

This isn't only a homebrewed political war of the settler colonial white right versus today's sudden broad liberal democratic coalition, which involuntarily includes the handcuffed left whether anybody likes it or not. This is that, but is also much larger than that.

Both sides know that we are somehow parts of larger global forces which are clashing all over. In a way somewhat like a World War. Maybe that's what we will become.

The largest transnational corporations and capitalist structural institutions are now also present in our backyards. Signaling away, if only in meaningless hand gestures, their "support" for the BLM protests, and implicitly disavowing anyone's right-wing nationalism. Maneuvering to protect the new world-wide culture of cosmopolitan multiculturalism so necessary for the transnational corporations and financiers working in orbit high above our now-parochial passport nations and politics.

On one level, the tsunami panic of transnational capitalists' attempted simultaneous clumsy warding off of and cooptation of BLM had an instant unpleasant taste all its own. Hilarious mixed with ominous. From the cover of *Vogue* magazine to the FedEx corporation to Netflix. While

Facebook's Mark Zuckerburg declaimed in a preposterous lie, *"We stand with the Black community"*; just as Amazon improbably posted a "Black Lives Matter" banner on its home page. The CEO of Coca-Cola said that, *"Companies like ours must speak up as allies to the Black Lives Matter movement,"* while Sprite, which has campaigned to be the soft drink of the world hip hop subculture, announced its "Give Back" program to hand out $300 million to the New Afrikan community. Reconditioned Democratic Party politicians in flocks and all manner of white executives from coast to coast selfied themselves wearing Black Lives Matter t-shirts. And this was a long hesitant minute after the historic Ford and Carnegie Foundations' announcement that they were pledging to raise $100 million for perpetually unspecified Black Lives Matter bribes ... oops, sorry, i mean "activities." Personally, i am waiting for the u.s. army to roll out a new Black Lives Matter heavy tank.

Kersplebedeb: *Settlers* and your work on this question have been attacked in questionable terms like "racist," "defeatist," "dishonest." Not to mention the truly hallucinatory crackpot dismissals circulating, and the weird role this plays as a negative symbol for various flavors of racist white revanchism. Do you think that the significant white vote—including of the white working class—for Trump will temper such bullshit in left circles?

J. Sakai: That would be nice, but i doubt it. Our settler colonialism is not mainly about some crude distant past that now can be taken for granted as a done deal, as is always implied. It can't be dealt with superficially as only some historified "moral debt," in unequal exchange for an unchanging settler colonial totalitarianism of the land. Settler colonialism here is about our very present conflicted lives and about the unseen future hurtling blindly towards us.

This theoretical controversy over the euro-settler working class, which the white elite-centered left always tried to ignore, dodge, or suppress, particularly since *Settlers* appeared in 1983, is in one sense now resolved. Now everything factually is crystal clear. (Not that the multitude of left political trolls and bare-ass preachers will stop yelling insults and complete nonsense, since that is all that they have left to do.)

A hidden aspect of this question is that it *isn't* about the euro-settler working class and its left apologists not being revolutionary enough. That it *isn't* about the euro-settler left trying to do radical class struggle but falling short. The nature of classes isn't about aspirational metrics of improvement, as in Oprah losing weight or Biden hoping to become more presidential than Obama. It's about the fundamental nature of a class and where it finds itself on the firing line of the actually existing class war.

How can any of this be a surprise, unless you stepped into the pitfall of this false working class theory and were completely detached from "America's" everyday reality? That as we talk a real majority of the settler colonial working class here in the 21st century are wearing red caps actual or metaphorical, but not with Lenin's baseball team logo. Voting for far-right hate with worn-out but actually true excuses of forcing "America" into being what it used to be all over again. Even willing to be bloody "deer" hunting buddies with fascism. Which says a lot today.

The euro-settler working class here never hesitated to join the Slave Patrols of the Old South, or their 1776 Revolutionary War counterpart in New England, the white patriotic Committees of Correspondence (which patrolled the night roads to capture and execute New Afrikans trying to escape Northern euro-settler enslavement by reaching the desperate sanctuary of British military lines). Or ever fought against people joining in the local settler colonial men's gangs and militias to raid and rape and loot and try to kill Indigenous people. The euro-settler working class supported every capitalist war of conquest and expansion, from the startup settler invasion colonies to u.s. imperialism raising itself high

"I Could Care Less If They Get The DEATH Penalty"
Reader Aug. 10, 1979
LIES
RACISM
PROSECUTOR BALIUNAS
STOP THE LYNCHING!
FREE THE PONTIAC BROTHERS

above the rest of the capitalist world as the temporary "lone superpower" with military boots of crumbling clay.

The historic u.s. left was always a house built on a foundation of shifting bone fragments and sand, always divided against itself. Trying to live out our beautiful revolutionary dream of replacing the violent exploitation of capitalism with a liberated world which would freely give "to each according to their needs." But at the same moment a settler left that never was willing to face how half-corrupted it was. With taking as the "normal" their lives in and loyalty to a privileged oppressor society, however up or down one's individual lot. This had ramifications so severe that it determined everything.

The established left here, whether communist, socialist, or anarchist, has always fought against being exposed as fronting for settler colonial domination. It is always being implied by them that real change is dependent on winning over the majority. Which happens to mean a pro-settler white majority here, to no surprise.

Anti-war anti-imperialism, Black Power, Indigenous land and treaty rights, Chicano power, counter-culture youth liberation, radical feminism, gay and queer rights—all the great breakouts that came out of that historic '60s wave were very much minority rebellions far outside the boundaries of majority approval. None of them approved of yet, to tell the truth. Coming from the margins and not the center. Ignored or subtly opposed by the dominant u.s. left of that day as too disruptive, too upsetting, too diversionary to the supposedly main task of building a working-class white majority.

Kersplebedeb: I remember you wrote as much—about change coming from the margins, not the bribed majority—in the interview "When Race Burns Class." When i first read you explaining that, it was incredibly encouraging, and that idea has stayed with me over the years. Can you give some concrete examples of how this has played out in your lifetime?

J. Sakai: So, one of the spontaneous white shifts of the 1960s was of a sex quietly leaving the left youth movement; here and there, by the ones and twos, hardly noticed at first. Like the earliest trickling in of a tide.

In one of her frank memoirs, the left intellectual Roxanne Dunbar-Ortiz relates about her life in the first radical feminist women's collective, Cell 16 in Boston. In 1969 she went on a road trip with a close male anti-war comrade, who was on a speaking tour of the GI coffeehouses which the movement had started in Southern military base towns. Financing their organizing tour by selling "women's lib" Cell 16 literature they had piled into the back of their VW "bug" as they went.

Her plan was that while her male comrade would be the official speaker, she would try to informally follow him with an unscheduled talk on the politics of women's liberation. It had to be kind of improvised, because anything like women's liberation was strongly opposed in the actual existing left then.

It seemed to start off okay. At one base the coffeeshop filled with an audience of soldiers that was half Latino and Black, which was definitely unusual for anti-war meetings then, and was promising. After one GI half-jokingly asked, "Do we get free pussy if we desert?"—pointing to a then-popular white anti-war poster on the wall, which read "Girls Say Yes To Boys Who Say No"—the male speaker quickly called on Dunbar-Ortiz to answer.

Standing up and turning around from her seat in the audience, she gave it to them straight.

> "I said to them that underlying support for the war was institutionalized patriarchy, wherein men were told that they must fight to prove their manhood and that if they didn't change their consciousness about their attitudes towards women, they were supporting the war just as if they were there fighting. I told them that women wanted to be free and equal and not just mothers or sex objects, angels or whores.

"The room fell silent as I spoke in my barely audible voice. When I finished the GIs applauded."

Much more important to her was the discussion the audience had about what she said. "... I had never before heard a group of men seriously discussing male supremacy. I was struck by the irony that these young men—black, white, Latino—from poor, rural, and blue-collar backgrounds were more open to women's liberation than the middle- and upper-class men in the anti-war movement." Where it was commonplace for women trying to raise this question to be shouted down, often shunned, or forced out, even with threats of personal violence.

(Everyone back then, including the white explicitly pacifist "peace movement" and mostly Black non-violent civil rights groups, silently condoned movement men hitting "their" women, since that was dismissed as merely "personal problems." It was surreal back then going into a left office in New York, and noticing that the receptionist's face was heavy with makeup inadequately covering the bruises—knowing also that her husband was one of the most important protest leaders in "America." Just as rape between "comrades" was banned as a subject except for private gossip. All dismissed merely as common human failings irrelevant to the struggle for liberation, or as something "nothing can be done about," to be hushed up to save the movement from police intervention and embarrassment.)

Next, Dunbar-Ortiz and her friend went on to one of the main bases training new army recruits just before they shipped out to Vietnam. But at that GI coffeehouse they ran head-first into a stone wall: the director, a strong woman with a record of civil rights and anti-war views going back to high school. "Nobody is going to talk to my boys about women's lib," she insisted. And hours of arguments didn't change her mind. "So we left," Dunbar-Ortiz recalls. But a year later, she adds, that stubborn woman would herself leave to become "a full-time women's liberation organizer in the South."[2]

"FIRST, A GREETING TO ALL MY SISTERS. COURAGE, ESPECIALLY TO ALL OF MY SISTERS UNDERGROUND IN AMERICA. STAY FREE, STAY STRONG. I INTEND TO FIGHT ON IN EVERY WAY AS A LESBIAN, A FEMINIST AND A AMAZON.

THE LOVE I SHARE WITH MY SISTERS IS A FAR MORE FORMIDABLE WEAPON THAN THE POLICE STATE CAN BRING AGAINST US. KEEP GROWING, KEEP STRONG. I AM A FREE WOMAN, AND I CAN KEEP STRONG. PASS THE WORD. I AM UNAFRAID."

—SUSAN SAXE

SUPPORT
PROTECT
OUR SISTERS & BROTHERS
UNDERGROUND

That's what was slowly happening all over the left with many of the most committed women. Starting with handfuls of white women who had caught the spark from working in the Southern civil rights movement daring to oppose the Klan, radicalized white women were raising the question of their own restricted humanity. Even within the very movements putting forth new demands for freedom and justice.

Women had been quietly writing letters and papers about these ideas and sending them to friends, who sent them on into widening circles. In 1968 the first white women's separatist position paper appeared, *Towards a Female Liberation Movement*. Men themselves were being named as the enemy, the sinew and material realization of patriarchy, while women started study groups and consciousness raising groups, women's houses and women's projects outside familiarity and law. This is the well-known and often-told history of a rising which threatened to change absolutely everything, and yet could not grow to fruition within the structures of the modern patriarchal neo-colonialism that eventually reinfected and contained it.

The point here is that to start together for root change, to shake themselves loose to go for liberation from age-old oppression, those women had to get free of their actually existing male left. Had to distance their activities and especially their own women's decision-making. Whether it was the Old Left of marxist parties and small sects, or the New Left of the mass sprawling Students for a Democratic Society and campus-centered anti-war and civil rights struggles, they had to leave. As New Afrikans, Indigenous peoples, Latinos, and other colonially oppressed people had largely left before them.

Fairly openly, rebellious white women were students whose teacher was the constantly transforming Black liberation struggle. White women confronting their own oppression couldn't learn beyond a certain point from their own established settler left, even with all its century of accumulated anti-capitalist theory and teachings. Because that left was itself so corrupted and represented too much of the oppressor mentality that women coming into their own selves had to exclude in order to be free to punch out without reservations.

The oppressed learn their most basic lessons from other oppressed. What is more simple to understand than that for revolutionaries?

Kersplebedeb: Indeed! But i want to stop for a moment: Going back to what you were saying about Roxanne Dunbar-Ortiz and her talk at that anti-war GI coffeeshop. How the GIs—"black, white, Latino—from poor, rural, and blue-collar backgrounds"—were questioning politics together. Weren't young white workers also doing that?

J. Sakai: Sure, but nowhere near enough of them. There were great moments in the 1960s–70s, like sudden lightning strikes and sheets of rain politically, when the long-anticipated political and cultural rebellion turning old imperialist "America" upside down and inside out was being embraced by so many people from every area of society. And yes, for some mostly young white working-class people to turn towards left politics was one real but small stream in that torrent.

i'll never forget anti-war white working-class comrades like young Ed B., a German-American u.s. Marine veteran, a father and a new union construction worker, sitting-in and going to jail with young Black teenagers. Putting his life into their struggle. Nor the militant GI using the pseudonym "Joe Smith," in the "F—ked Up Fourth" in Vietnam.

Or much more famously, Peggy Terry, who ran for Vice-President with Eldridge Cleaver from the Black Panther Party on the Peace & Freedom Party protest ticket in the 1968 elections (and who never left the poor working-class hillbilly community she came from). Whether Cleaver's leap into electioneering was a good or bad move (it was heavily criticized then by many Panther Party members, for serious reasons), Terry was trying to follow Black revolutionaries into a new wider breakout of the struggle. She used to say that she first started figuring out about racism when the Ku Klux Klan showed up to try and terrorize her and other workers when they were organizing a union in their Southern factory.

It's important not to romanticize all that, though, or to take it out of its material context in the class war. When cautiously edging into the middle-class and upper-class left, white working-class men and women could be like pepper in the mix. But later, going back to the euro-settler communities and backgrounds they came from, they were too thin and incomplete a layer to have the same influence then in the mass.

They had also—and this is critical to understand—been politically abandoned by the middle-class and upper-class u.s. left. Mis-taught that the big revolutionary change would finally come when their white working-class majority soon joined us—and then they were left to go back into their conservative settler communities they knew were not going to do anything like that. It wasn't malice or anything deliberate. That '60s young student left that had spontaneously created itself into a mass dissident subculture didn't know any better. No one had anything better than the worn-out old failed theory about the "united working class" or similar such reformist garbage. There's a big price we pay in the real world, as revs, for corrupted revolutionary theory.

But they left their mark, all of them, though we don't see it.

Kersplebedeb: So much seems to have changed since that time. For one, just the idea of that level of sympathetic organizing within the u.s. military ...

J. Sakai: Indeed. While the lingering public impression of military service is still one of poorly paid enlistees from lower working-class and rural backgrounds taking risks for little reward, like in an old Hollywood movie, the reality is that u.s. imperialism's military is now qualitatively different.

Regrown from gene-altered DNA, the u.s. military today is primarily their world mercenary corps. Today there's no universal draft, which turned out to be a two-edged sword for us, too. Instead, they have an all-volunteer, more selective military that tries to be an elite mercenary global intervention force. With special exotic superhero fighting units which are noticeably advertised as almost completely euro-settler in composition. With layers of technology and a shiftier role with which they hope to distance their very costly u.s. soldiers from the point of the spear.

Now you might join the imperialist military to live out single-shooter video games, but more often it's still to try hands-on, paid while you get an education and a new career. Sure, there's many young GI households living by payday loans and food stamps, or being ripped off by a car dealer in the neon McRetail strips outside bases—but then again, that's just blue collar life in "America."

Things have changed from that old movie cliché, however. 21st-century u.s. military recruits don't primarily come from the white working class anymore; the majority are now from the middle classes. And there's a parallel trend: men and women from what are now termed "national security families" tend increasingly to marry persons of the same background, who understand each other's special values and service careers, not "civilians." Almost like in their many millions they would be some embryonic new ersatz loyalist ethnic group for imperialism. Like the old armed frontier settler Cossacks became under the bygone expanding Russian empire of the Czars.

As the wife of one former elite Special Operations battalion commander pointed out (in u.s. army terminology, she was officially the unit's "senior spouse" with serious assigned duties leading other wives, although completely unwaged of course): the average u.s. "warfighter" is better paid than 75% of u.s. civilian government employees with similar experience, and has major other benefits like free health care and PXs comparable to Walmart's with average prices 30% lower

EEEK!! THE LITTLE PEOPLE
MADE WITH THE COOPERATION OF AMRC
ANTI MILITARY BALL
MUZIK by
WIZARD
AND OTHERS WE ARE CONTACTING OTHER BANDS NOW
Sat NOV 10
8 30 pm
100¢
PROCEEDS TO GO TO KARL'S DEFENSE FUND

GREAT HALL

than civilian stores. With a possible paid four years of full tuition and fees for college. By 2020, one million active duty and retired military were using the special "no down payment, low-interest" federal residential mortgages for their home purchases. "Anyone who thinks there's no such thing as socialism in America," she said, "has never spent time on a military base."[3]

There's a good reason this major change was made. "America's" global imperialism was hit by unexpected roadside bombs in the disastrous defeats of the 'Nam era. Not only trend-setting Vietnamese revolutionary military victory, but even more crucial: unprecedented levels of resistance not just at home but even inside the empire's armed forces. The 1960s–70s threat of mass military insurrections, including from even white servicemen, led by the outbreak of Black liberation. That was the crisis that made Washington step back to crazy-glue their iron fist back together again.

All it took to create that one rebel GI coffeeshop night when "women's lib" surprised the audience, was the mass drafting of millions of young men dropped randomly into a demented 1960s Asian land war they knew nothing about and felt they had no stake in.

Involuntarily uprooting even white youth away from their homes, friends, communities, and planned futures. Everything familiar to them. Mashing them into new regimented communities of similarly uprooted and uniformed youth. Sent far away to risk minimum-wage death or permanent disability in meaningless jungle firefights. All inside a big trumpeted war effort the incompetent Washington brass and politicians couldn't even win at. It wasn't much of a gamble to sow seeds of political questioning and resistance on that fertile ground.

So the imperial state learned and adapted. Once burnt, twice shy for them, too. It's actually a good example for us, on a small scale easy to chart, of how late capitalism in its metropolis uses its super-accumulated wealth from all over the world in actual class restructuring at home. Not in any "natural" unmediated way, of course, but by ruling class strategy force-feeding its morphing and reshaping.

As late as the Vietnam War, in the 1970s, the ruling class was still trying to get by with the traditional "citizen-soldier" mass military of temps. Drafted en masse from the working classes, the lower middle classes, and small farming families. To their shock, in 'Nam that broke down utterly. So much so that the Vietnamese communists at the time privately expressed being really disappointed with us young revs over here in "America." They'd seen drug-using, shoulder boombox carrying, soul and rock playing at top volume, u.s. soldiers clumsily penetrating the jungle, who were child's play to dodge as hometown guerrillas. The Vietnamese weren't slow, and had no trouble recognizing many GIs as politically disaffected foreign soldiers who didn't want to fight.

But under a big North Vietnamese infantry ambush trying to overrun them, the same careless u.s. units might suddenly tighten up and become hedgehogs of automatic weapon and mortar fire. Urgently calling in air support like it was their new religion. "FTA" may have been markered onto countless helmets, but as real kids of "America" no one was going to play the part of General Custer in the game.[4]

(Unlike when the Viets were earlier fighting not only regular European French draftees but also French colonial troops from North Africa—who the Vietnamese communists had some success encouraging to surrender or desert—GIs might be enthusiastic in sabotaging the war, but weren't surrendering to anyone. Some GI deserters in Sweden tried to explain it back then to the Vietnamese comrades—the situational difference between South Vietnamese Army puppet troops who fled or surrendered easily, and the wary, much more gnarly GI units themselves—but the Vietnamese representatives in those talks weren't happy about having to report back to Hanoi some stuff pretty negative and unorthodoxy by their soviet socialist standards.)

That same "FTA" do-for-yourself spirit, nonetheless, did lead to men replacing an unsatisfactory officer (like too gung-ho or too rule book) by their own informal "any means necessary." Often grenades rolled under tent flaps late at night. Black soldiers insisted on holding their own marches with banners around camps. More combat companies stopped actually seeking contact—once out of sight they instead relaxed the day away in agreed upon faked "patrol."

One by one, the critical big aircraft carriers carrying much of the air attack over North Vietnam were delayed and then even knocked out by the military anti-war movement. First the *USS Midway,* then the *Ranger,* the *Forrestal,* and then the *Coral Sea,* whose enlisted men and some officers not only forced it to return to San Francisco but held a large "SOS—Stop Our Ship" press conference once dockside. There were repeated sabotage fires on the big ships. In October 1972, the carrier *Kitty Hawk* returning to 'Nam was forced to head back home after Black sailors holding a rebellious meeting fought hand to hand for hours all over the ship against Marines sent to stop them. Then the carrier *Constellation* was forced to return to San Diego after sabotage and growing unrest. Once ashore, sailors mostly white held a demonstration giving the Black Power salute with upraised fists. Many navy ships had their own illicit anti-war newsletters, such as the *Kitty Hawk*'s "Kitty Litter."[5]

As early as June 1971, the end was publicly apparent. That was the month the *Armed Forces Journal* bluntly admitted: "By every conceivable indicator, our army which now remains in Vietnam is in a state of collapse ... dispirited where not near mutinous."

GI resistance to the Vietnam War was an amazing story of mass illegal and violent resistance to imperialism by the very soldiers supposed to carry out its rule. As such, it momentarily rocked the very stability of the capitalist state. Though it is also an important cautionary tale: for looking back at those military service resisters who were white, once they were demobilized and scattered back into settler communities across the span of the American continent, they as a whole became individualized and lost their political momentum.

The surprising strength of the military rebellions was due to how the anger at "Vietnam" had been taken over, overlaid, and deepened by the even more violent and insistent breakout of Black liberation politics becoming part of daily lived culture against imperialism and its settler colonial hegemony. Black liberation in that entire period was the big straw that stirred the drink for everyone who wanted freeing change. It may not be on some other day, but it was then.

So after their shocked post-defeat period of confusion, the capitalist state and its brass went back to work. Replacing part by part, through trial and error gradually remaking their all-important giant military Frankenstein. Of course, as we know from the strange case of America's "Forever War" against Muslim peoples, no matter how well-equipped and trained, there's lots that this costumed superpower military can't do. Like, it doesn't seem able in the final conclusion to win any wars at all. That's an important enigma for us to think about.

Kersplebedeb: We will come back to that question, but right now i want to return again to this thread that keeps on coming up in this discussion, of the role of class in what you are describing. Class features centrally in all of your work; for readers of this interview who may not be familiar with your other writings, how should we understand different classes, and why is it important that we develop analyses of them?

J. Sakai: Once, when i was quite young and even more naive than i am now, i was taking inexpensive night classes at a local college with St. Clair Drake (co-author of the unparalleled 1940s study, *Black Metropolis*, and a small legend for having once been an organizer with an armed New Afrikan tenant farmers' self-defense movement in the segregated terrorist Deep South). Not because i was that interested in studying "introduction to cultural anthropology" or "West

African society," but because i thought just listening to him might open rooms i never knew existed. Which it did.

One night i was amazed to hear him curtly dismiss, as with the back of his hand, E. Franklin Frazier's then controversial study, *Black Bourgeoisie.* Which he said wasn't even social science and shouldn't be read. That book had surprised me—even scared me intellectually—for its cutting dissection of the insular family culture of that era's small Black bourgeoisie and affluent middle class, saying words bordering on the scandalous on topics like the parentally sanctioned customs of their children. Frazier lit up what he regarded as the self-indulgent individualism and consumerism of the "Black bourgeoisie," which he said was only imitating the sickness of white "American" culture. He said that their declared class political strategy, of eventually overcoming Jim Crow by the spread of their small business roles and government positions, was only a self-protective delusion minimizing the deepest evils of the capitalist racism they were caught in.

i went up to professor Drake after that class and complained to him: "But wasn't everything Dr. Frazier wrote

in his book factually true?" (which we both knew it was). Picking up his briefcase, Drake scowled. "That isn't social science, that is just a man trying to break with his class!" And strode away. (A bit of context against misunderstanding: As fellow rebel Black intellectuals, Frazier and Drake were colleagues and friends.)

This subject of class is so basic, but it's really a sleeper. Like it's so vast, "everything" almost. But "basic" isn't the same as "simple," as so many think. Class is deeper and more complex than we can cover right here, on the run as we are in this interview. We all know your damn love life isn't simple, and raising your kids is too fraught and joyful to be simple, so why the hell should something as all-encompassing as class be the only human thing to be simple? Am going to just lay down some road signs and warnings.

Class identity is real, but its reality is more complex and particular than just rote characteristics or obvious roles. Like the dark blue suits of the corporate manager and the crisp denim overalls of the millionaire farmer are more or less true like all capitalist work uniforms, but also front for layers of deeper roles and identities.

Here as much as in any other life-and-death subject, we need a concrete analysis of the concrete situation to analyze any class situation down to its useful conclusions. Class societies like in global capitalism are made out of building blocks of classes, to the overarching structure of a mode of production and distribution. Classes are the collective identities of people bound together by their common roles and interests and lives in economic production and distribution. People fight for advantages within society as classes. Advance or retreat as classes. All the time people leave their old friends or family, but being disloyal to your particular class is so much harder to even think of.

It's important practically to know that there are many different kinds of working classes in the world, not one—just as there are many kinds of capitalist classes. With varying cultures and differing experiences in their class character.

Just as there are different types of lumpen: Marx and Engels thought there were in Old European history even lumpen/aristocracy, not just the usual lumpen/proletariat. Like in our capitalist Babylon of today's mass affluent classes, we find thrown into our mix relatively so many lumpen/petty bourgeois as well as lumpen/capitalists (the one example we all know well of that latter is the Trump family). This is something significant to our practice, but rarely nailed down in print.

Capitalist society is not so eager to show its real decaying face, for all its loud media din and racket. We should keep in mind that classes constantly change. No matter how carved in living stone they seem, capitalist class structures are always evolving, sometimes drastically changing shape, morphing as human life itself surprisingly always does. As quantities of change in any particular aspect of reality continue piling up higher and higher, until finally at a nodal point their relentless accumulation forces its remaking into something completely new. When all that quantitative change topples into higher *qualitative* change, there occurs a transformation in the basic nature of that class, in that part of reality.

The different classes in capitalism are constantly in the process of change whether their individual members understand it or like it or no. The same with our settler colonialism as a specific form of capitalist hegemony.

This may seem at first more confusing than enlightening, but keeping our bookmark on these ideas, of constant motion and quantitative changes becoming qualitative transformations, helps when we analyze specific aspects of today's political global class war.

What is most important here is to avoid treating class in an alienated way, misunderstanding it as something mechanical, which is an error that left vulgar materialism has always been prone to. As though something called "the economy" forms and reproduces pre-packaged "class" as impersonal products over us, uncontrolled and above ordinary human life. Like it is often implied to young radicals by vulgar Marxist ideologues that they have only to wait around and the greedy profit needs of capitalism will inevitably shape and mass produce capitalism's own "hangman," the pre-packaged takeout proletariat ready-made to do the final revolution. Yeah, about when pigs fly by.

As we have said, capitalist society is never eager to show its real decaying face. And it definitely is far from the first society to mask what are to it really classes, but disguised as races or genders or ethnicities or religions. So that for much of "American" history, the main proletariats or lowest working classes were forced from birth to always wear concealing masks:

The mask of race, as though the sweated bloody commodities of their violently enslaved labors were merely some natural by-products of their New Afrikan or Indigenous subhumanity.

And the mask of gender, as though women giving up their physical bodies and minds were only doing what was biological and "natural" for them. Becoming consumed as lifetime parts in the worldwide patriarchal family machinery, as well as bearing the bio-industrial and social reproduction of all necessary labor for the ruling class economy. Taking loving and being loved while in cages to be an eternal suffocating mask supposedly placed on their faces by the false deities "God" and "Nature."

At the same time, the great history-shaping classes, such as the bourgeoisie, have always been in part self-creating, not just passively accepting some given economic or social roles. But fighting and innovating within the limits of material possibility to enlarge and transform themselves constantly. The long revolution to liberate this great humanity can accept being no less than that. And even more.

The book *Settlers* was written starting in 1975, it started out as just a short informal paper to explore a question of mine in this regard; but the work grew and grew following an unexplored path and ended up taking eight years of research and writing and sending texts in and out of the kamps, editing and rewriting by myself and others into underground publication in 1983 for a small outlaw group. It was raw theory sure enough, underdeveloped and wonderfully new-born to us, but not coming from any campus or its universitariat. It all came illicitly from prisons and poor working-class organizing. From solidarity work with guerrilla liberation fighters. Listening to the root understanding of the world held by African and Indigenous militants already at war for their peoples. *Settlers* then was very basic, theoretically simple, almost raw. Maybe now old but serviceable, like a still-loaded rifle from Wounded Knee.

Radicals have now taken the investigative work of settler colonial theory ranging in different ways beyond that book of labor history, of course. Which would have happened whether or not we had ever had the fortunate chance to do our work (so countless many of the oppressed had just this same insight but were silenced, muffled in blood, trampled under, never had the chance to be heard—it was never our unique idea).

So this is a politics that is still an outlaw coming as an outside threat to established reformist oppressor ideology, from the viewpoint of the oppressed. But drawing more attention, as what we're told is the advanced superior capitalist world grows more dysfunctional all the time. Even the term "settler colonialism" has become widely used within progressive circles here in the u.s., not only in books about race politics but even in daily newspapers and classrooms. As the pulsing umbilical cord becomes so visible between the swelling of the violent white far right and the unacknowledged weight of "America's" living dead history. As rebels look further over the devastation for deeper answers.

In that vein, a revealing blog post by the Indigenous revolutionary Rowland "Enaemaehkiw" Keshena Robinson, *"Fascism and Anti-Fascism: A Decolonial Perspective,"* written in the turbulent uncertainty after Trump's naked settler colonial reappearance in 2016, reappraises white left theory

LET GO LET GO LET GO LET GO
GAY
LIBERATION

on fascism in the first light of Indigenous decolonization. Confronting this settler colonial empire on the deceptively camouflaged ground of fascism/antifascism.

Just as there are also voices shining more light on new questions raised in today's recharged white left protest breakouts. Such as Bromma's 2020 interview: *"Decisively breaking with both worker elite mythology and male leftism."* (Incidentally, Bromma's earlier quick essay, *"Notes on Trump,"* analyzing what was behind his rise and the alt-right, is one of the most concise, tough-minded explanations of their place in the world capitalist crisis). So there is still more to do, to deal with taking on the hegemony of entrenched settler colonial capitalism here.

Several examples from young scholars are also significant. In the ground-breaking paper, "The Settler Order Framework: Rethinking Canadian Working Class History," which appeared in the journal *Labour/Le Travail,* Fred Burrill draws the line between the old academic labor history defined as white settler labor and its official capitalist workplace organizations, and the new labor history which opens itself up to the fugitive story of Indigenous and other colonial labor from the margins in the making of Canadian capitalism.

Imaginative and reminding us of settler colonialism's reality in a different-appearing setting, Zachary Samuel Gottesman's "The Japanese Settler Unconscious: Goblin Slayer the 'Isekai' frontier," in the online journal *Settler Colonial Studies,* shows how the colonial invasion and conquest mentality that created what we know as Japan, is reenacted over and over again in surrogate form, in a popular Japanese video game set in the usual male fantasy cartoon universe.

As more and more comrades are taking up the investigating and the teaching which strengthens strategic understanding to bring it back into the struggle again.

Kersplebedeb: In terms of understanding the political moment we are in globally, the main contradiction is often described as being between globalized neo-liberalism and right-wing populist nationalism. Above you criticized this view as being overly shallow …

J. Sakai: Indeed, though certainly that's how journalists and consultants are paid to explain it. So many of us have to follow those loud-speaking establishment guides right now, temporarily while we wait to find out what's going on. That doesn't make it true, though.

Usually contradictions don't only have one outward form, after all. They present their essence in myriad ways, just as a person can wear different clothes. To describe the clothes helps describe the person, but the clothing isn't the person.

It is closer to what's true, to say that the globalized capitalism of the transnational corporations has grown so extremely successful, so vast, that they have begun involuntarily ripping away from and moving above the nations that once birthed them. They no longer fit within them. So nations are in part still ruthlessly needed and in part tossed aside. By no means are they "over"; they are still very necessary but invisibly lessened, coming apart, left with dysfunctional societies and economies no longer corresponding to the lived locations of the old class society that once provided the territory for these capitalist beings in earlier life. If that makes sense.

So when Trump went on his would-be historic tirade or trade war with designated wrestling villain "Kung Flu" China, both sides had an unspoken agreement that many outsized capitalist beings like the Apple corporation or Tesla had to be exempt from the match. Otherwise, that would have merely been a public b.d.s.m. hookup. Since Apple, just for example, may be a world-famous u.s. company, but as we know in its years of global rise its famous iPhones were produced first in its own low-wage, prison-discipline production metropolis in Shenzhen, China, and now also in Shengzhou and other

Chinese industrial cities. Where almost all iPhones still come from, manufactured by Apple's large Taiwanese production partner Foxconn corporation (and their even larger silent partner, the Beijing "Red" state capitalist dictatorship).

Both Chinese and u.s. capitalist empires are gaining a lot from this. And if the u.s.a. is Apple's largest national market, China itself is No. 3 right behind the No. 2 multinational EU. With a value this year reaching $3 trillion and jostling shoulders with Amazon over being the No. 1 corporation in the world, Apple was left to profitably watch the imperialist mud-wrestling match from comfortable Chinese migrant worker–skin seats on the sidelines. It was way too transcontinentally sprawling and too awkwardly shaped, in either side's understanding, to fit inside the ring of their weirdo pointless nationalist trade war.

Will this imperialist flexing and shoving come in some near future to theatrical "conflict," or even some pointless actual miniature war—in one gender of armed activity or another? It's always possible, since "Red" China has always had plastic container take-out military conflicts with many of its smaller or weaker unhappy neighbors. Russia same same. (As one smartass poet once wrote, "Socialism is not a country whose neighbors curse geography.") While the u.s. empire itself hasn't won a real war since 1945 but is still "forever" actively engaged in mini-warfare in dozens and dozens of unknown countries on any given unpublicized day.

In this new neo-colonial period there are no longer clear dividing lines between what is military and what is civilian, between war and peace, commerce and crime, each of which take on the other's properties. Asymmetrical or surrogate military or financial or cultural actions can always happen every day, to gain some advantage or to disadvantage another within the ceaseless "creative destruction" of capitalism.

Any way it goes, it incidentally settles the left controversy of whether the era of imperialism—which began over a hundred years ago at the end of the 19th century and persisted through two devastating world wars—has been replaced by a fabled era of globalization and peaceful world capitalist unification. We still live—no matter how perilous it seems to us all—in the final capitalist period of imperialism and deep national decadence, and its constant fighting between capitalist entities and powers of all sick shapes and kinds.

That's just one of many warning signs that this whole "globalization versus right-wing nationalism" thing isn't what people are assuming it is. It's not like a real fight, but more like a scripted play of capitalism—with real populations forced to act out its stage directions and lines with our lives.

Nor are the political fistfights ripping apart our own society what we are told they are. To a startling degree, we have been talking about contradictions which are developing in unresolvable ways. That grow only sharper but which cannot be resolved anymore within this actually existing capitalism. The fabric of societies themselves are distorted and are stretched to the breaking point—and then an involuntary tug beyond. Here and now. This is the present moment.

the end for just now

A RADICAL INTERNATIONAL

March 4, 2006
Boston, MA USA

A Day of Workshops

A Night of Music

Fighting
Oppression

Manifesting
Solidarity

For more information:
www.larivolta.org

TRIANGLE SHIRT WAISTE FACTO

Beginner's Kata: Uncensored Stray Thoughts on Revolutionary Organization (2018)

"Beginner's mind" is a zen phrase. It reminds us that when we first took this path as beginners, we approached it almost with awe. Self-conscious of knowing so little—knowing nothing, really—we were open for seeing anything. Aware mostly of how unimportant our own little knowledge was. But as we became much more experienced, even became "expert," it was different. We could separate useful from scrap, what we judge is good from bad, so automatically we hardly needed to pause over it. Our journey became a polished routine. And now we sometimes ask ourselves, is it still a journey?

i was reminded of "beginner's mind" all over again once, in a very different context. Accidentally tuning past an ongoing discussion between a few marxists and anarchists about the pros and cons of leninism vs. "horizontal" spontaneity in revolutionary organization. It was like people at a dinner party having a familiar argument across the room from you. You can't catch everything being said, but you know where it's going anyway.

Seems that every culture has strange traditions. Seemingly illogical ritual ways of approaching some things. Guess it's just human. As in the Japanese cartoon world we know as *anime*, the artistic convention is that the characters are pictured as Caucasians, even though the artists and audience are Japanese. (Critics here guess maybe respecting their art's origins in the fandom for imported u.s. comic books during the post-1945 Occupation?)

Our left subculture, like in that discussion on leninism & revolutionary organization, is as strange as that. Instead of centering on actual organizations we ourselves might have experimented with, learned from or fought against, by cultural convention the debate often uses the Russian Revolution of 1917 and the conflicting stalinist and anarchist experiences of the 1936 Spanish Civil War as its framework. So discussions on a key subject are familiarly conducted at a remove—using the puppetry of actors and scenarios from almost a century ago, on a different continent; none of it in our living memory or knowledge. This is still a serious political discussion, just as Paris couture fashions are still seriously-intended clothing. But both are heavily stylized and artificial, for unspoken class purposes.

Someone in that small discussion pointed out that leninism and his kind of command organization had played such a large role to this day in modern revolutionary politics, that whether it was negative or positive, good or bad in someone's opinion, it should be better understood. Unfortunately, put me down as more than skeptical on this.

Only yesterday i had said the exact same thing. But hearing it played back again in someone else's voice, realized that i don't really expect it to happen. Useful idea, abstractly, but the left in this country has never been able to successfully do this one specific thing about understanding revolutionary organization, not in a hundred years. Neither anarchists nor marxists. So why would you expect it to happen now? Is it that we're much smarter all of a sudden? Is everyone *more* interested in leninism now?

(Those words might sound like i'm either dissing Lenin or dissing revs in this country. No, not at all. But his politics have been untranslatable here, because of the complex barrier which divides our realities. Same reason so many people don't understand his Russian predecessor, the anarchist Bakunin. If time allows, we might touch lightly on this at another turn down the road.)

This is a singular moment in the struggle, where the old left from the 1960s–70s has finally gone, and where the wind-shaken leaves of brand new radicalisms have begun to sprout up, fragile yet driven. As generations go on and off stage, and society is transformed once again by the leap in the means of economic production & distribution. This is a space in the transition between different historic epochs, in the simultaneous unnatural flowering/world collapse of capitalist civilization. Still, in a brutal continental u.s. empire of some 325 millions, it is only ordinary that there are numbers of radical people as well as different groups with revolutionary ideas. But if only temporarily, there is no revolutionary organization yet which is strong enough to impress its ideas upon mainstream politics.

Everyone who has been around radical protest activity for awhile has heard left organizational ideas—anarchist, social-democratic, old marxist-leninist, maoist, eco-survivalist, whatever. To me the first question isn't any longer which ideas are "best"—which is how the organization question is usually framed—but how true or useful are the assumptions on which our discussions are based? Where are we really when we start to navigate our course?

What i am trying to do here is not to argue one organizational form or another, but to examine how we *think* about revolutionary organization. What the framework is around everything. To examine how our easy acceptance of so many assumptions could throw us forward or off-track. Because, at least to me, there's a big gap between the reality and our superficial talk about the shape of revolutionary organizations to come.

So how much have we learned about revolutionary organization? In practical terms, in one way personally i know a lot (certainly much more than we would ever want to spill in public), but in another way i don't know near enough. Maybe like the backyard guy you know who fixes cars, but isn't good enough to get a real mechanic's job at the dealership? So, not nearly enough. But here's a handful anyway, right or wrong, tossed into the pot, my share towards what we need for starters.

i know that marxist-leninists here are supposed to know so much about this subject, but don't.

In my political lifetime i've seen what felt like dozens of primarily middle-class, white and asian M-L collectives, organizations and so-called parties started in the metropolis, this u.s. empire, and none of them to my knowledge have been successful. That's a zero. At one point almost the entire ex-college asian-american movement on the West Coast and New York City emptied itself into fiercely warring "Marxist-Leninist-Mao-Tse-Tung-Thought party-building" organizations and collectives of one kind or another. All long gone now. Most 1960s–70s M-L organizations quickly disappeared. A few "Trotskyist" sects unfortunately lasted it felt like forever, like those fabled cockroaches briskly going about their business immune to the glowing levels of radioactivity in a post-holocaust world (when i think of those groups, there's a reason a mental picture of radioactive cockroaches comes into my mind).

If you started early enough way back then, we even saw "pragmatic" social-democratic organizations with their yearning for the wealthy welfare state of nice civilian mice sharing the cheese, come and then go in the blink of an eye. Their coming on in the late 1950s was the little stirring before the much larger wave of radical rebellion in the 1960s. Historically more a European than a u.s. empire phenomena, but with Globalization's merciless neo-liberalism, more and more people are wanting a full frontal welfare state as their best alternative to mass middle-class flight to Canada. In the 2016 "Bernie" breakthrough, that utopian socialist-capitalist reformism became a progressive "happening." Yeah, been there, done that. Although for this particular discussion it actually lies outside our map, outside the actual combat zone of decisions about revolutionary organization.

i think that we all know scraps of things, but in practice today don't know enough to do anything successful about revolutionary organization. Which is one good reason why we aren't doing it.

One big obstacle to us learning more is our habit of covering up our ignorance. Uncle Mao used the term "invincible ignorance" to identify the self-protective reflex of too many leftists. Shying away from bluntly analyzing the political things that they needed to experience. Clinging to the polishing and re-polishing of "classic" politics in order to avoid the humbling uncertainties of the ever-changing struggle.

A typical old example to me was when famous poet Amiri Baraka & Co. formed their would-be "Maoist" party, the LRS (League of Revolutionary Struggle). One of my asian comrades was a member, and pressing me to join up. So i asked her why their would-be "party" would succeed, when Bob Avakian's RCP, and the Beijing-officially-endorsed October League, and most of the other 1970s "Maoist" pre-party groups had fallen face-first into the pavement? (Hard as it may be to believe now, many thousands of young activists had poured into these M-L party-building groups, which had then promptly evaporated in one of the most striking radical happenings of the Sixties generation. i mean, Charles Manson left a bigger footprint.)

"Because they had bad politics and we have good politics," my asian comrade simplemindedly answered me, completely confident. That sort of left me speechless. Is mercy killing allowed in the movement, i wondered? (guess not, or i would have been cold stone buried ages ago.) Sadly, it isn't true that there's a special goddess to protect the clueless.

The old Marxist left here was like an aircraft manufacturer, whose elite, university-educated engineering teams with great theoretical flourish developed 60 or 70 different airplanes. All of them unfortunately crashing on takeoff. Their potential customers have long since split into two feuding camps: the Marxist-Leninists keep insisting, "Our people are so exceptionally experienced, we *must* buy their next airplane." (Anarchists reply: "What this proves is that aviation should be banned, unless travelers going to a destination spontaneously meet and piece together some kind of a 'plane' out of whatever parts are left around airports.")

i also think that "democracy" in revolutionary organizations is highly overrated. At its worst, it's like "patriotism" and "family," being *"the last refuge of scoundrels."*

Democracy in society may be a necessity of community life, but democracy in revolutionary organizations is something else entirely different. Among other things, revolutionary organizations are part of society and also not part of it. In the society and also living antagonistically outside its borders. Subject to different laws of physics. Resulting in different structures.

Most discussions of revolutionary organizations right here in the garden of the imperialist metropolis, assume and insist on some variety of "democracy." It's definitely something sacred. What does this usually consist of? Something learned from our capitalist bosses. Usually something resembling their bourgeois "democracy." In which the marxist or anarchist or socialist group is "democratic" because there are meetings in which all members have the theoretical right to speak, vote, or consent on its politics and activities. Usually, the handful of leaders have met or communicated privately before that meeting, to decide what the members must do. Often, everything is scripted as much as possible.

There's nothing strange about this. It's organizational "democracy" as we know it in the world of the imperialist center, like suburban village government, state-regulated trade union locals, or the bored of trustees for whatever NGO. It's a certain form that comfortably clothes institutions in this decaying capitalist culture. As such, this "democracy" isn't anything that i'm up in arms about, either for or against. Why shouldn't an anarchist organization or a trotskyist "party" operate like the local bridge club if it wants to? It's just our cultural norm.

But the complete absence of this "democracy" isn't necessarily a loss, either.

Sometimes doing away with "democracy" can be even more democratic in real terms. In fact, stripping away unnecessary people and organization has worked better than leftists here like to admit in many situations. One reason that so much of what has worked well are individual or small group projects, seriously committed to getting things done on a particular issue or function.

As one example, i like the old *Prison News Service* (PNS) newspaper project, done in the 1980s–90s by the late Jim Campbell & friends up in Canada. For many years, PNS survived as a very open political forum, primarily written by many, many different prisoners, and read by thousands of prisoners. Particularly for New Afrikan prisoners in the u.s.a., it became a rare meeting place to talk politics with each other, spread news about the ongoing skirmishes between the brothers and sisters versus the prison authorities, and generally make themselves known.

Jim Campbell mostly financed it himself out of his wages, and although he had a handful of co-conspirators on the project, from what i could tell back then Jim basically made most of the decisions. If Jim didn't think that your letter was that important, flip it went into the dusty files (yes, that happened to me, too—have to laugh about it now). Not only was this close to one-man rule, without any "democratic" structure, but it was one-white-man rule to boot. How about that for taboo?

Why should one white anarchist up in Canada de facto control so much of how prisoners of color in the u.s. gulag talked to each other? Because no one else wanted to or could do it. (The black liberation army-coordinating committee, to be sure, had its own quite serious political discussion zine, but it was both closed and more specifically defined.) Truth was, neither Black nationalist organizations nor white M-L groups wanted to have that much to do with prisoners except to exploit a few famous names. Who might have been hailed in speeches but were privately considered too troublesome, too hard to control, and too needy.

During those years, the National Committee to Defend Black Political Prisoners was also a small but useful source of political linkage for some of those inside, but that was really done by one dedicated older Asian woman. Who stayed up late at night licking the stamps and sending out mailings paid for by her thin wages as a waitress in Harlem (she told me she took the job partly so that she could act as a message center, where guys who might be ducking the Enemy could pick up "kites" from comrades—and to slip hamburgers to hungry rads without cash.) So Jim wasn't alone, but was one of a thin line of advanced explorers. An actual modest person-by-person vanguard, if you will, probing the gulags and other human garbage dumps for the future. There are vanguards in the struggle, but maybe they're not what people usually think.

So it was lucky that Jim Campbell identified so personally with the pain and isolation of prisoners, and was so determined to break down the walls to the extent that he and a few other comrades personally could. PNS definitely had the effect of spreading liberation, enabling radical political discussion among some of the oppressed. Which wasn't ideal, sure wasn't everything, but was pretty democratic. The how they did it was less important. Democracy isn't in the ritual forms, in our little rules. It's in the politics of what we do or don't do.

Which brings us to data-mining the past. Taking lessons from the past is inescapable, for me as well as everyone else. But check this out: We "know" a lot from all our snatch & grab at the past that isn't what we think it is.

One immediate suggestion i do have is to take some of the emotion and value judgements out of it. As one of my old martial arts teachers used to say at our annual class evaluations, "Just take it in as information." One by one, we had to step forward onto the floor and go through our moves, and then were critiqued on the spot by classmates and instructors. "Don't think of what you're being told as positive or negative," he advised us. "It's just information." You'll see what i mean by the next story. (Oh, and to prevent miscues—i'm not any martial artist. Any more than when as kids we played pickup football games in the park with much enthusiasm, that didn't make us what everyone means by football players.)

When we look through the past as revolutionaries, there's a natural tendency to focus on examples that verify our existing beliefs. This is a natural but really dangerous habit. For example: for many years i "knew" that Stalin and his damned commissars were responsible for losing the 1936–39 Spanish Civil War to the fascists. The stalinists' violent repression of the anarchists and independent socialists there had stabbed the most militant center of the working class in the back, and thus fatally weakened the groundbreaking class war. i mean, not that i knew much or anything at all about Spanish history, but like so many others i had read George Orwell's moving first-hand account of the war, *Homage to Catalonia*, and it all fit as neatly as a cherry on top of a banana split. A one-book education. i never questioned it.

By karma, back then i knew an older Maoist comrade who actually had been a young soldier with the International Brigades fighting in that Spanish Civil War. Thinking it strange that up to then we'd freely talked about our own confused 1960s movement politics, but he had never brought up his war experiences in Spain, one afternoon i asked him what he thought of Orwell's book. My friend jumped to his feet and started cursing. He thought that Orwell was a dishonest asshole, and his self-serving version of the anti-fascist Civil War a fabric of clever novelistic half-truths and distortions. The way this older comrade described his war came from a completely different angle than any i'd thought of before then. It really took me aback.

He told me: *"In the field hospital I saw wounded die for nothing, freezing to death in the cold overnight without blankets, because someone had fucked up the supply list. Do you think Stalin had blankets withheld to increase his power?"* My Maoist friend's angry sarcasm had a sharp point: that the whole war was fucked. To him the two sides in Spain, fascist-clericalist versus liberal and left Republican, unfortunately were also the militarily competent versus the idealistic but not-yet competent. He said that all the revolutionaries, the socialists and communists no less than the anarchists, were stumbling around trying to learn how to build a new kind of society there for the first time with the clock running. While with the other hand also fighting a new type of total war against an advancing, experienced mercenary colonialist army, with plenty of guns, artillery, and air squadrons.

To him this was a tragic loss in a far deeper way than abstractly our team versus their team. It was his experiences in Spain, my friend said, that made him an early Maoist sympathizer. Since it was a sign of real hope to him and his comrades in Spain that while their flickering progressive Republic was being inexorably crushed by the fascists, in remote regions of China that Red Army was solving the problem of survival in combat against even the largest capitalist armies. No small thing to my friend, after losing so badly, with more real life casualties he knew than he wanted to remember.

He also said that contrary to what Orwell wrote about, anarchism was a real military problem in Spain. To my surprise, he wasn't talking about the Durruti Column or other legendary anarchist workers' formations. He was talking about what he considered latent or basic anarchism within the International Brigades, which was stalinist, remember. Like most wars, that one was fought by the young, in many cases teenagers no older than fifteen or sixteen years old (the Canadian naturalist R. D. Lawrence had enlisted as a Spanish anti-fascist infantryman back then when he was only fourteen. He was so short that his rifle slung over the shoulder kept almost bumping the ground—but as he said, *"no one cared how old you were if you could shoot a gun."*)

Whenever a fascist offensive somewhere would start, many of the eager young volunteers would spontaneously "desert to the Front." Taking their rifle and hitching rides on supply trucks or trains to wherever the most intense fighting was. Abruptly leaving their own units short of soldiers. Training plans and readiness and new moves on its own front upset.

Since it is hard to successfully plan an overall war that way, "deserting to the Front" was quickly banned. Soldiers were talked to about revolutionary discipline, etc. etc. Nevertheless, just like with sex, when romanticism and adrenalin flood the heart, young dudes aren't always thinking ahead to the larger picture. And the men who did this felt that no blame could be attached to any individual who decided to just go off more bravely by themselves into the fighting. Spontaneous soldiering just went on.

Finally, the commanders decided that a sobering line had to be drawn. The next time it happened, a pretty blameless but undisciplined young American revolutionary was selected for charges, court-martialed, and then executed by his own buddies. Their shooting was understandably bad and the condemned comrade was badly wounded, not cleanly killed. So their unit's commissar (a young tough guy from Brooklyn, my comrade recalled) had to step up, draw his pistol and finish him. Then the commissar wrote the soldier's parents a letter of condolence, saying that their son had died bravely fighting the fascists. But when their unit returned home, the working-class stalinist commissar used his pistol once more and committed suicide. The whole thing was hushed up by the movement. Isn't it always? (Yes, i know that there were probably a dozen better ways to handle that problem politically, not by coercive authority, but that's the kind of thing many normally confused macho men did right then—or even now.)

Was that first-hand view all true, or just my friend stretching memories to defend the integrity of the revolutionary band of his youth? He had only one person's experiences, but think he had an important part of the truth, anyway. i don't know about the whole deal, but i do believe that the Moscow-directed repressing of so many of the most militant Spanish workers was textbook stalinist anti-revolutionary maneuver 101. So i'm definitely not going to want any stalinist anything around at the next revolution. But give us a break, that's kind of like, duh. Maybe hot shit as an insight in 1929 or 1939, but pretty small change as a lesson about revolutionary organization now in the 21st century. We should have easily learned that a long time ago, and much, much more.

The question isn't whether the stalinists or the socialists or the anarchists were right or wrong or in what ways in the 1936–39 Spanish Civil War. That's one series of questions, but is that the *main* lesson we can learn from that past? In radical debates things can get pretty black and white awful fast, lots of tunnel vision, i think. But in the actual struggle with millions of real people freeing themselves, rushing around trying to do things they themselves have never seen before, there are always layers of reality. i mean, not just one true thing, but many true factors of varying meaning, shifting in time. To me what my older comrade said struck a note that went towards the practical heart of things.

Sometimes we can be technically right about something—and still miss the main point.

One very smart anarchist comrade that i told this to, about Spain, came back immediately with: *"No, it was the arms. The lack of arms. See, France and Britain wouldn't sell arms to us. And Stalin cut us off. He wouldn't give us enough arms."* Actually, i've heard that line more than once as an explanation. Which only sounds reasonable until you start to think about it, in terms not of liberal "fairness" but of revolutionary organization. This is something my friend was obviously just repeating from someone else, not something he ever had to work out bit by bit for himself.

Let's see, the anarchists and independent socialists back then in Spain were saying that Stalin was running a bloodthirsty dictatorship which needed to be overthrown, with the stalinist sycophants and criminal bureaucrats needing to be put before workers' courts and firing squads? And yet, they really expected that the *same* lumpen Joe Stalin was going to pour shiploads of weapons into *their* hands like the hip-hop Insane Santa Claus? How unreal was that as strategy? That's like some homeless dude sleeping rough under a bridge, but expecting every freezing night that Obama's limo will soon be pulling up to take him to his lush bedroom in the new mansion.

The problem in this kind of thinking goes deeper still than that. Whether the anti-capitalist forces in Spain didn't get enough arms because of Stalin or Wall Street conspiracies or because the boat was late, or whatever, the net practical effect was the same. That the progressive Republic was outgunned by the mercenary forces of General Franco and his eager German and Italian fascist mentors. Skip past the back story and get to where the rubber meets the road. Let's say that they were outgunned two to one, three to one, or even worse. So? What's the big deal? i mean, it's a nice-sounding *civilian* excuse, but it doesn't mean much in terms of revolutionary practice.

We revs are always way outgunned and outnumbered by the mercenary forces of the capitalist state, until the final stages of the struggle. In Old China way back then, the communist Red Army was outnumbered and outgunned more like five or ten to one, by both the rightist Chinese armies and the Japanese invaders, for many harsh years. True everywhere for anti-capitalist guerrillas, too, not just that particular Spain. It's not an excuse, it's just the usual violent environment of capitalist hegemony everywhere that we must to learn to survive in and grow in.

Everything we do, our tactics and strategies, our organizations and subcultures, all assume great imbalances in strength between us and the capitalist ruling class. Whether of mainstream propaganda, numbers, experience, money, guns, whatever. If it were only a contest of morality and justice, the capitalists would have been kicked out long ago. We all know all this, too. We just don't always absorb the full meaning.

The lesson that really strikes home to me from that experience back then was not only the brilliant courage of those people overturning backward oppressive society, but also our own lack of revolutionary development in the broadest sense. And tragically what it meant when we had to put it to the test in real life, in real time, with the lives of millions involved. Right now we are used to laughing at the incompetence of Big Capitalism, reeling from setback to setback, from Trump the Reality TV Government to their hopelessly lost but unbelievably lethal misadventures in the Muslim world.

But we conveniently forget how even this crumbling chunks-falling-off-of-it Big Capitalism has accumulated within its structures centuries of learning-by-experience knowledge of how to run society part by part their way. Too often, we think that criticizing them well is equal to having enough know-how to design up and successfully operate our own oppositional counter-cultures and societies. While in practice these two things are many miles apart.

Acknowledging that we anti-capitalist revolutionaries are only beginners, are in historical terms still a young culture, still just starting to learn how to build, is to me a healthy first step in better revolutionary organizations. (What we now know as industrial capitalism took 900 years, historians tell us, to evolve out into a dominant social system—oh, don't worry, my mom's a dangerously wild driver and we revs are going to take a much shorter route.)

One thing that i learned the last time around is never to expect evolution to just repeat itself. In the early 1960s, what was that era's old left and new left overlapped briefly, and the disarray was tragi-comical.

Still active veterans of the great 1930s industrial unionism battles in workplaces and factories, watched with bewilderment as 1960s kids staged small, really personal rallies in the middle of a campus, to support a fellow college student holding up and then burning his draft card. Reading aloud his own individual statement of rejecting the draft and the Vietnam War. And accepting soon going into federal prison. Meanwhile, we marched proudly out of Black communities, crossing borders now not as friends but as reluctant enemies, bitterly into the hate-filled euro-settler working-class neighborhoods. The old left veterans from the 1930s were horror-stricken, since they had always believed in the revival of mass euro-settler industrial unionism as the central event in radical social change, like in their own idealistic youth way back when dinosaurs roamed the earth. We felt so sorry for them, because they didn't get it that our future would never look like them. We knew instinctively what Dylan was singing about: *"You don't know what it is, do you, Mr. Jones?"*

But for everyone now, too, the fault lines have shifted once more. The passing of the old euro-colonial economies and the thermal fusing of national imperialisms have been as tectonic plates, grinding deep underneath the earth. Reshaping the political surface into a surprising geography

It Is Not Enough To Be Healthy...

We Must Be Free

Young Patriots Organization

which brings the labor of massive Chinese and Mexican proletariats popping right up into every neighborhood. While the great archipelago of the New Afrikan major cities, built up by accretion like coral reefs during the 20th century, is being physically pounded down and broken up, one after another. As New Afrikans of the "dangerous class" are forced to disperse, to keep moving, keep moving, once again. Many to the prison kamps of the u.s. empire's vast gulag, while others to the isolated suburban exile townships.

When we first took this path, when we joined our lives with the struggle, we were conscious of knowing so very little. One good reason we were so attracted to this revolutionary organization or that one. Not only to find rads we could run with, but to find mentors and a busy hive of experience we hoped to take cues from. *What never occurred to us is that those organizations might know next to nothing, too.*

Here's a cellphone snapshot that comes to mind: One of the liveliest cultural gate-crashers of the 1960s was the sudden popularity of Eastern philosophy and arts. Which was a lot more than the Beatles going to India to try out meditation. The most nitty-gritty among that being the craze for the Eastern martial arts. Even before Bruce Lee's great *Enter the Dragon*, young guys Black and Latino as well as Asian were haunting the cheap rerun movie theaters that showed the Hong Kong martial arts flicks. My dumpy baby sister became a changed teenager, as angular and menacing as the Praying Mantis forms she would train at day after day. All good.

This enthusiasm swept through revolutionary organizations and protest movements as well. Whether it was the desire to help protect our marches from street attacks by the white racists, or just the pull of wanting to be strong physically in the struggle, this was something everyone understood. It was a pretty pathetic new revolutionary organization which didn't have its martial arts class on the side. Or at least its favorite local dojo where its people tended to go. i knew it was really cresting when an enthusiastic white friend told me he had decided to join a rapidly growing local Marxist group, "because their karate class is so good! You should come and try it out!!"

You get the contradiction, the slightly crooked picture. On the one hand, we had so many young revolutionaries sworn to tear down the old American way of life, and most especially all the old left crap. Pushing forward with new radical organizations that were formed next to spontaneously, on the fly, shaped by the dynamite blast of the latest page in the struggle. Often more or less blessed only by a quick papal reading of some "heavy" left text or another. It didn't matter which one, really, since most of us hardly understood any of them.

But when it came to *serious* business, to being *personally* able to really fight, many of the same youth eagerly embraced the legendary training of Eastern martial arts. Which is more traditional and top-down in its teaching than death, with students in the dojo learning forms and sparring painstakingly developed and then tested over generations. Overseen and directed by the black-belt instructor, whose every decision was law on the class floor. Nothing spontaneous or doing whatever-new-you-felt-like there.

To me the double message was definitely signaling something. While youth were in revolt against old oppressive authority, we were hungry for authority in the other sense. For finding *empowering* knowledge that came from the doing. Learning from those who had actually done it and learned to do it well. Like, you wouldn't want to learn plumbing from a person who read to you out of some textbook, but who themselves had never picked up a wrench or gotten shit all over themselves.

One thing was for sure. Since there were no already worked out blueprints for organizations back there and then, we had to borrow from incomplete old histories, from any dusty zombie organizations still stumbling about, and mostly from our own imaginations to improvise organizations best we could (pretending, naturally, that we knew much more than we did). To predictable good and not so good results: neat breakthroughs and equally mass running out of gas and abandoned cars scattered on the freeway.

There were hundreds of thousands of people improvising, trying on and remaking and breaking radical organizations of all kinds in the 1960s–70s New Left. From GI antiwar newspapers and off-base coffee shops to the usual mass protest coalitions owned by nationally famous ministers and charismatic male lumpen hustlers. There were countless local student radical groups running on the horizontal principle of "participatory democracy," as well as at least one nationwide underground of thousands also trying to grow itself by spreading "participatory democracy" local groups well into armed struggle. There were study groups and informal self-defense circles everywhere, way too many to ever keep track of.

There were socialists replacing their college dormitories with a "party" form in which they rented large apartments together in inner city neighborhoods, functioning as community activists together while using their group homes as busy political theory schools. And always there were new seemingly spontaneous grassroots direct actions happening. From mass walkouts closing entire city public school systems (covertly guided in at least one major city by New Afrikan revolutionary nationalist cells quietly working with major youth "gangs") to the "leaderless resistance" of one hundred anti-war firebombings of Bank of America branches by primarily white youth in California, to the many lumpen militant street organizations. To say nothing of the background murmur of various Old Left "parties" or their copycats trying to carry on traditional euro-agendas.

(It goes *almost* without saying that a disproportionate number of the most dramatic breakthroughs in the 1950s–70s here came from the u.s. empire's inner colonies—called the ghetto, inner city, rez, barrios or communidad.)

Looking back, the rich diversity of mass organizational experience was too large to easily describe. Little of which was analyzed or passed on as learning experiences. That's how disorganized and uneducated we were, despite the university intellectuals who composed much of the movement's leadership. Hope comrades doing lift-off now do much better at that.

Here's a thought to share: People sometimes talk about revolutionary organizations as if they were all varieties of one thing, like different gasoline engines to drop under the hood of your same compact car. V6 or straight 4? Which they aren't. There are broadly two very different types of what we mean when we say "revolutionary organizations." The most familiar is like the small left collective or intellectual journal or zine. Sometimes in the outward form of a local anti-war group or whatever. Like an antifa group or like one of the "parties" keeping alive the flicker of someone's ideas. Or it could be the local radical caucuses in the teachers union. And so on.

These are what we are used to seeing sprouting here in the garden of the imperialist metropolis. In other words, meaning "revolutionary organization" as an *organization of revolutionaries,* promoting anti-capitalist ideas and activity. To help people survive or reinforce protest movements. Usually pretty public and acting more or less legally or with official tolerance, since why not? Such organizations are by their nature transitory, and any one will probably be long gone by the time capitalism is overthrown. There is nothing wrong with this, obviously.

That's *not* an organization that actually makes a revolution itself, though. Overthrowing the old society and its state. While there have been many Marxist "parties" here (put this in quotes because they are free to call themselves anything they like, but most here haven't met the real definition of a party) claiming that they were going to carry on and on forever until someday they would overthrow capitalism, revs can safely assume that this stuff is largely delusional.

The other kind of revolutionary organization is simply, directly that. Engaged to actually *make* the revolution against capitalism and its state. To carry out revolutionary transfer of power. These organizations are by their fundamental nature illegal and usually clandestine instruments of warfare. Always popping up from the lower depths, always being repressed and hunted. They are widely present though with different results in the developing neo-colonial periphery, from Mexico to India, but real examples are scarce here in the imperialist metropolis, for obvious reasons, except among the oppressed neo-colonies. Don't think i need to explain that.

One thought that keeps coming up in every generation, is to narrow the gap between these two kinds of organizations. Exploring just how much terrain,

of what kinds, revolutionaries could take over and remake now in daily life in the structures of capitalist society.

Like all complex mechanisms, like a hospital emergency room or a tank brigade, *actual* revolutionary organizations are super high maintenance. If you've never been in one, know that they are a big pain in the ass to keep going. They are also obviously highly dangerous, more dangerous than sex work is or a contract firefighting crew is, or being a clueless u.s. army private somewhere. For sure. So they had better be worth it.

In this violent capitalist end zone of unlimited war and repression, the question of organization suddenly becomes drastically changed for us. Because there you cannot be an individual revolutionary in any meaningful sense. There a lone revolutionary is like being a lone firefighter. You can be as good as you can be, but you are outclassed by the scale of events. Then it is only complex revolutionary organization that lets our full political thoughts and intentions become sails full of reality. This is often lost right now in the garden of the imperial metropolis, where middle-class people so easily deceive themselves that agreeing with this radical idea or that one, makes you a revolutionary. No, it only makes you someone who likes ideas. (And as that lesbian philosopher once said: "Theories are like assholes, everybody has one.")

This has just been an initial re-examination; a walking over of the uneven ground that structures might be built on. There are obviously tons of critical stuff, most things, really, on anti-capitalist organization that i never got around to here. So take this as a restart button. A beginner's mind isn't a bad thing to have.

Notes Toward an Understanding of Capitalist Crisis & Theory (2009)

> *"Dope will get you through times of no money better than money will get you through times of no dope."*
> *F. Franklin*

This was written because several comrades who didn't know anything about it, asked me if marxist theory explains the world capitalist crisis or not? This is such a good question that i found myself pulling together these notes for them. And for myself, it turned out. i don't have any brilliant thoughts here. Compared to some other papers on the crisis this is pretty simple. But if it only opens a door, that is good enough.

The world capitalist crisis has produced many radical papers analyzing the 2007–08 Crash from widely different points of view. There are also many new voices among them. This is definitely healthy, starting a discussion that has not been routine for anyone. One interesting side of these radical papers is the role of theory. Some papers confront the crisis ad hoc, as it were, using little theory besides the bare recognition that there is a class antagonism in society. Others, both liberal and leftist, explain the crisis as one of the business supply-demand cycle, which even Bush's former treasury secretary and federal reserve chairman conceded is part of the basic nature of the capitalist market. Some papers make passing reference to the law of value or the crisis of over-accumulation, but don't explain just how this marxist theory relates to their analysis of the Crash. And while some writers boldly predict the final end of capitalism in this crisis, others more cautiously see the full cyclical recovery of capitalism but with sharply reduced working-class living conditions paying for the recovery.

What i want to do here is to explore how useful anti-capitalist theory is to us in lighting the path ahead.

"Twilight capitalism" is an expression common on the Left now. Even as vanilla a social-democrat as Cornell West speaks of our "twilight civilization." But what does it mean? Do we use it just to reassure ourselves at a time when the Left in the metropolis has weakened so greatly? Is this crisis a stage in the protracted fall of capitalism as a world system? We will come back to this.

To start, we should keep in mind Marx's comment that there really is no such thing as "economics." There are only human beings working to sustain themselves, tied in daily life to each other through social relationships of production and distribution. Capitalism alienates this activity from its living matrix, and calls the object "economics" ...

Capitalism's top economists and corporate managers could not predict this present general crisis. Those who mocked Marxism for not being able to predict crisis well enough, proved themselves far more clueless. It isn't just that the well-funded, full-time economics departments at Harvard and Yale failed to see this crisis coming (just as they also famously failed to do in 1929). Economist James Galbraith of the University of Texas says that of 12,000 professional economists in the u.s. today, only "ten or twelve" predicted this crash. Perhaps for the same reasons that fish canneries and supermarkets can't predict when massive overfishing will create "marine deserts" out at sea?

The loudest liberal criticisms of Wall Street and its obedient government regulators conceal within them new untruths, which only disorient people all over again. One is the often-heard, Barney Frank line that speculation—financial gambling—is at the center of the crisis. But looking at it another way, speculation wasn't so much Wall Street's problem, but Wall Street's attempt at a solution. The other misunderstanding being peddled is that the 2007–2008 collapse of the biggest world financial centers proves the failure of conservative economics. It is understandable to believe that, but what this general crisis really proves is the failure of Keynesian economics.

This brings us to the area of anti-capitalist theory.

Our political toolboxes are jumbled with theoretical tools old and new. Some we don't use because they appear nonfunctional, obsolete now if they ever worked. Many of us don't use theoretical tools at all, approaching politics with bare hands, because we have been taught to distrust tools in general. But it's basic that a tool has to be grasped the right way—which is another way of saying that perhaps our cultural "handle" is wrong. That the approach we use on radical theory like Marx's on capitalist crisis is wrong. Not so much the theory but how we take it.

Marx is a big case in point, usually exceptionalized either as some improbable thinker far above us or dismissed as a monumental relic, another piece of dour Victorian mental furniture. In the first case he is like a genius too complex to be understood by the rest of us, and in the second case he is someone to be politely ignored lest we set off his worshipers. He is rarely accepted as just another revolutionary against capitalism, with his own contribution, albeit one shaped by a different time than ours. To me, it is better to simply take his analysis of capitalist crisis as the insights good and bad of another revolutionary. Like the thoughts our own contemporaries exchange right now, it may be wrong in ways but still give us an unexpected insight into the crowded reality of capitalism.

The question of capitalist crisis is bound up with that of business cycles, of boom and bust. Cycles that we are used to without even thinking about them, as an inescapable part of capitalist life. Bush's last Treasury Secretary Henry Paulson even admitted that he personally expects such economic downturns "every five to ten years. I don't think any regulatory system is going to change that." Unconsciously echoing what Marx wrote long ago: "The characteristic life course of modern industry, which takes the form of a ten-year period of moderate activity, feverish production, crisis and stagnation ..."

This cycle comes from a basic imbalance between business production and consumer production. Between supply and demand. It isn't what kind of product that determines this, but to which side of the economy it belongs. For instance, a power drill owned by a home-remodeling company is part of business capital, while an identical model power drill owned by a consumer as part of their hobby equipment is a part of consumer production.

During the boom upsurge of the business cycle, both production for business growth (new factories and mines, full inventories, expanded transportation, research and development, etc.) and production for mass consumption are growing side by side. But at a certain point, business expansion has reached the limits of the current market (or beyond—for example, for years automobile industry financial analysts have been warning that global truck & auto production capacity is at least one third more than the number of vehicles that can actually be sold). Soon capital investment in new production slackens, which inevitably leads to lower levels of employment & income, leading to a lessening of capital investment in consumer production and distribution. Consumer demand declines in a downward spiral with falling employment and income. This crisis manifests itself on the surface then in the form of a crisis of insufficient demand.

Which is why the "search for the holy grail" of capitalist economic planning is the Keynesian belief in "fine-tuning" the economy. In which state intervention alternately cools down or adds economic demand to a rocketing or stalling economy. In reality, at least since the Reagan administration, conservatives no less than liberals have acted not only by fiscal measures (raising or lowering bank interest rates and the money supply) but by Keynesian massive state deficit spending to boost economic demand. One telling fact is that during the Bush-Cheney regime of 2000–2008, the government share of the national economy was over one-third larger than under the Roosevelt New Deal of the 1930s. Like prezzy Nixon declared back in 1971: "We are all Keynesians now."

That the Republicans wanted to massively deficit finance new high-tech militaries and ruling class personal spending, rather than the new highways and larger police forces that the Democrats prefer, makes a big difference socially but not to the blind maw of the capitalist economy.

Their problem is that despite the near-religious belief in it by liberals, there is no evidence that state "fine-tuning" can work in the long run. Even for the world's most prosperous, high-technology societies. During the past twenty years much of Western Europe has been governed by social-democratic parties, and the level of Keynesian social welfare spending has been high by any past standards. And yet, the current crash has swept Western Europe no less than the u.s.a. and the rapidly rising "BRIC" economies (Brazil, Russia, India, China) that are said to be the new capitalist centers of the future.

During the Great Depression, u.s. unemployment was still officially at over 14% in 1940, after eight years of the Democratic Party's Keynesian deficit spending policies. And real u.s. unemployment was over 30% for that period. It wasn't until the Total War economy of World War II kicked in that the u.s. Depression disappeared. As in 1944, when there was effectively no u.s. unemployment and government spending was 70% of the total u.s. economy. Just as German capitalism couldn't shake off its even-worse economic crisis until Nazism had fully transformed society into a slaughterhouse.

Which raises certain questions about the post-modern capitalist future.

Marx theorized that beneath the easily visible cycle based on the dis-synchronization of supply and demand, which even the capitalists can now see, there exists another imbalance pulling on cycles of capitalist production and distribution. A second, longer kind of economic cycle.

To correctly scan this, we have to capture Marx's background in the dawn of the first industrial capitalist society. Where "science" was a hot word, and people were trying to explain things in the new scientific way as parts of entire systems which governed how they developed. The most sensational example of this, Charles Darwin's theory of evolution, had just simultaneously exploded old ideas of both the biblical and biological worlds. (Marx himself was very impressed by this theory of evolution, and even wrote Darwin a letter seeking his permission to dedicate the first volume of *Capital* to him. Darwin wrote back that he was honored, but felt that he must refuse in order not to shock his still-religious family by association with Marx's well-known radical atheist beliefs.) Of course, the science of that time was often wrong just like ours is. Marx, for instance, was also a convert to phrenology, the theory that the shape of people's skulls indicated their mental tendencies and talents. He would examine the bare heads of young workers who had volunteered to help him in his endless research, to try and see if they had the requisite mental abilities.

(The following nine paragraphs are an unauthorized supersimplification of one part of Marx's big, big blueprint of how capitalism works. If you've read the paperback or seen the movie, feel free to skip down.)

Industrial capitalism was the world-shaking phenomenon of that time, and Marx searched for an understanding of it as an entire system. What unified its structure, inner workings, and the laws of its motion and evolution. Much as 19th-century European scientists tried to discover what the basic stuff of the physical universe was. In his investigation, Marx joined the path already broken by the classical capitalist economists of the 18th century, notably Adam Smith and David Ricardo (whose writings are still read in petrified universities today as significant knowledge). None of this matters now, except to show that Marx's elaborate theories about the capitalist economic system didn't just pop up in his mind. It was part of the whole intellectual fabric, the cultural approach of his time & place.

The classical capitalist economists had already dispelled the primitive belief that there was some inherent value in specific money or precious metals. As one society may use sea shells or bits of copper as a currency, while other societies may judge these items worthless. Still other societies use livestock or printed pieces of paper. David Ricardo posited that the value in all commodities or products in the capitalist marketplace really came from the human labor that went into their making. The young Marx and Engels were also inspired along this line by the idiosyncratic French anarchist pioneer Proudhon, whom they praised in this regard: "Proudhon makes the human element decisive, while in the previous political economy this role is given to the material power of capital and of landed property." From this starting point, Marx developed his economic theories.

In Marx's analysis the exchange of commodities is the fundamental relationship in capitalist society. The term "commodity" is used by Wall Street today to mean raw materials or products contracted for in undifferentiated bulk lots, such as wheat, ore, or beef carcasses. In Marx's terminology, however, a commodity is anything that has both use-value (that fulfills a human want or need) and exchange-value (is a product of human labor for the marketplace). So the life-giving oxygen we breathe every minute has use-value but no exchange-value, since we take it ourselves from the atmosphere. But the same oxygen in a medical oxygen mask has been separated, compressed, packaged, and transported by human labor, and is very definitely a commodity. The most important commodity of all is the labor-power of workers, which is the commodity which more than reproduces itself once in the hands of the capitalist.

This value of commodities eventually expresses itself indirectly on the workaday surface of capitalist life as price. While that share of value which is neither consumed in production of the commodities nor returned to the workers as wages to sustain or reproduce their labor-power, is termed surplus-value, which eventually surfaces as capitalist profit. Marx cautions that there is no direct, one-to-one correlation between the value and surplus value created by a given worker or even a certain factory, and the amounts of prices and profits that result. The process is more indirect and averaged out. To Marx this was not the kind of discovery to predict the stock market with, but a tool to radically understand the inner workings of the system's dynamic.

It's tempting to compare Marx's concept of value & surplus-value to the invisible particles and matter that have conveniently filled in theoretical niches in the history of the European physical sciences. Once, centuries ago, European scientists theorized that a transparent substance that they named "ether" must fill in the vast stretches of the universe between the stars and planets and other solid heavenly objects. Or today it is accepted in physics that there are many sub-atomic particles—often given whimsical laboratory names such as "gluons" or "right-handed snarks"—which are not only necessarily invisible but in some cases only exist as a useful piece of theory without any scientific proof of existence. To a degree, Marx's invisible "particles" of value & surplus-value might be thought about like that.

Marx specifically says that value & surplus-value are not material properties of commodities, but rather properties of the social relationships that really constitute capitalist economics. Which our daily life of the constant exchange of commodities dialectically both manifests and conceals under frenzied and fetishistic activity. (A fetish is a non-living object that is thought of as having living characteristics, the typical examples of which are voodoo charms or the wafer and wine at Catholic communion services.) In Marx's cultural criticism, the dead objects which are exchanged in the market, like money, real estate, or corporations, are given life-like power and vitality under capitalism; while the people whose work produced them are not only subordinated to commodities but are also forced to take on themselves the aspects of non-living things.

This is frustrating to many readers, because it's so elusively non-material. Marx is saying that value & surplus value are essential parts of everything economic from syringes full of penicillin to automobile tires, but don't have any definite, fixed quantitative form in or attached to these things. They don't even have any physical existence you can find, but seem to exist in ... like, a dimension of philosophical reality. Which Marx says is more real than what we appear to see. Since value & surplus-value are supposedly aspects of the social or societal relationships that are production & distribution. It may be strange to just ride with this, but it's easier to not worry temporarily about whether it's true and just follow its logic step by step.

The central pivot comes from the dis-equilibrium in commodity production between the increasing role of mechanization versus the production of human labor-power. This to Marx was the second type of contradiction, beneath the more surface one of supply and demand.

Both aspects of production, both that of machine technology and that of human labor-power, churn out commodities and thus capital. But in Marx's insight only the part coming from human labor-power produces surplus-value, and thus profits. So the total of the combined capital from both machine-production and human labor-power must always increase more rapidly than the total of profits, which originate in human labor-power alone. In a gradual cycle that is built into the DNA of industrial capitalism, there is an inherent tendency for the overall rate of profit to fall as profits are gradually outpaced by the faster growth of capital from always increasing mechanized production. The rate of profit is squeezed by the sheer mass of capital that has accumulated. According to this theory, when the mass of capital has grown so disproportionately large compared to the sum of profits, business activity cannot find adequate profit rewards and falls off. Stores and factories slow down, layoffs spread, the value of stocks and other investments go down, the system is plunged into crisis and a period of stagnation.

In Marx's theoretical analysis, no matter how modern our capitalism becomes, the eventual cycles of economic crash rooted in the very fact of that technological modernization only deepen. Foretelling the future end point of this capitalist mode of production and the coming of an entirely new mode of production & distribution, a new type of society.

But Marx's vision of capitalist crisis and the fall of the system itself never happened ... or is it gradually taking place right now?

Up to now we've been laying out this very stripped-down version of the core of Marx's theory. But is any of it true? More to the point, is it useful? It seems to me that Marx's theories on political economy can't be proven in any usual sense of the word. Being that they are more like a brilliantly arcane cultural criticism. i have only read the thick volumes of *Capital* once in my life, and it wasn't an experience i would urge on the innocent (only on the guilty). Parts threw light on capitalism, but on many pages my eyes glazed over with non-comprehension. i tend to agree with the anarchist Michael Bakunin's unhappy thoughts as he was trying to earn rubles translating "Capital Vol. 1" into Russian for a publisher: *Capital* was a "frightful work," he confided to a friend, although he also said that it was "extremely important, learned and profound, if very abstract."

As an experiment, we can take this one theoretical insight and see if applying it helps us to better understand the path of this crisis. After all, even clues at a crime scene don't have to explain everything or be some "final truth," in order to help an investigation advance. How does the landscape change when we look at it this way?

It is easy to pick up things in the present crisis that fit the jigsaw puzzle shape of what Marx was theorizing. Last year a business journalist said that in a global perspective, this crisis could be seen as "a crowd of Asian capital chasing each other around the world in search of profit." In other words, this crisis that has suddenly paralyzed country after country into Depression is a crisis of profitability, not primarily a crisis of insufficient demand. Last year statist economies such as the Arab Emirates or China had many hundreds of billions of dollars piled up as investment capital with shrinking choices of where to profitably land it. As we know, there has been an overflowing of investment capital for skyscraper office towers and luxury condominium complexes and multi-billion dollar hedge funds without end. But few of these had any real profitability in the end.

The most glaring feature of this landscape is that Keynesian state deficit remedies won't function very well here. Public works projects and improved jobless benefits will ameliorate some of the distress, but will not of themselves revive the capitalist economy. Since this crisis is not simply about stimulating demand at the shopping mall. As a theoretical tool, the concept of profitability crisis explains why the sainted liberal Keynesian regime of Franklin Roosevelt and its all-pervasive public works programs in every neighborhood went on year after year but didn't restore full employment and economic vitality. State spending can give society new highways and even a thin social "safety net" for the working classes, but does not change the system's basic overall profitability until they reach the level of a state capitalism (which has its own contradictions).

Wall Street speculators have become the "Jews" of this Crash, convenient one-stop shopping propaganda targets to take the blame. But speculation was not so much a furtive excess of the few as an entire stage of world capitalist activity. Lock-stepped into by the largest banks and openly encouraged by all the governments, because the dwindling of profit margins in ordinary production & distribution forced them into a zone of artificial profits by financial manipulation. We could say that speculation didn't cause the Crash since it was the other way around. The underlying crisis in profitability forced capitalists to jump towards speculation as their desperate solution.

Of course, nothing is free, as the capitalist saying goes. Speculation always undergoes a Dr. Jekyll-to-Mr. Hyde transformation, from being the capitalists' savior to being the capitalist nightmare. When the speculative bubble finally bursts, economic collapse is triggered and the artificial profits of speculation evaporate into thin air. Like the bankrupt Wall Street corporations whose vaults were stuffed with worthless paper billions in sub-prime mortgage bonds, real estate loans, and devalued stocks. This all turns out to be the normal progression of crises of the falling rate of profit.

"Financialization" is the term for the shift of capital from ordinary production into the fantasy of a purely financial civilization. And this "financialization" took over the center of the u.s. economy, which was the central economy in the capitalist world system. By the start of the 21st century, financial institutions accounted for nearly 30% of total u.s. corporate profits, a near-doubling in one generation. Although they produced nothing of human need in the real world. Financial employees earned nearly one out of every ten dollars in all u.s.

wages & salaries. In the financial center of New York, Wall Street employed but 5% of the city's workforce but accounted for 23% of all personal income in 2008. "Financialization" grew past these road markers, infecting and replicating itself within all other business activity. Without the artificial profits from speculation, today's capitalist economy would have crashed long before this. It has been held aloft by successive waves of speculation, such as the dot.com bubble, the housing bubble, the oil & commodities bubble, and the underlying credit card debt bubble.

The point is that far from being a "mistake" which must be prevented, speculation is capitalism's life raft to artificially extend their boom beyond its natural sinking. It will never not be used. Time after time, no matter that each shipload of capitalists pledge like boy scouts to never touch it again. But life rafts of themselves seldom reach shore.

Later in life Marx and Engels came to believe that the tendency towards the falling rate of profit was working very differently than they had originally predicted. The economic depressions that were so devastating and regular in the early decades of industrial capitalism, had leveled out near the end of the 19th century, becoming much further apart. Marx and Engels' analysis was that like any living organism, capitalism had developed defense mechanisms to cope with this potentially fatal cycle. The two most important of these "immune system responses" were the forming of giant national industrial trusts or cartels to fix prices and limit production, and the expansion abroad into world-spanning colonial empires. The far-flung occupied territories both absorbed "excess" investment capital, while returning homeward the superprofits wrung from involuntary colonial labor (a small part of which could be used to raise domestic living standards and bribe an important strata of the domestic imperial working class). Thus, the imbalance between the accumulation of capital and the rate of profit had been partially rebalanced at one shot of the gun. But it was not, obviously, from any peacefully productive, voluntary, or even civilian process.

If we follow Marx and Engels' thinking on this: paradoxically, a new level of contradiction was created out of capitalism's successful adaptation. Without frequent "burn offs" to destroy industrial capital, the long-term accumulations of capital started piling up in unprecedented mountains, threatening slides that blocked economic progress and could turn into avalanches. As Engels wrote underlining this observation in 1892, the violent holding back of economic depressions only laid the groundwork for far greater cataclysms: "So, each element that works against the repetition of the old crisis conceals within itself the seeds of a much more widespread and powerful crisis in the future."

And now we get to the heart of the matter. In a crisis primarily of the over-accumulation of capital relative to profits, if there is no magic wand to give capitalists instant tons of profits (such as the u.s. capitalists were given with military-economic hegemony over most of Europe and Asia in 1945), the only way to restore a working balance within capitalism is on the over-accumulation side of the equation. By destroying or "burning off" capital until an underlying balance is restored.

But there is no control room at a mythical Capitalist Headquarters with a big dial that lets someone measure how much capital has been destroyed and how much is yet to go. Nor is there a big joystick attached to a capital-destroying robot that lets the capitalists guide the violent pulverization. Even Wall Street or Washington is far less powerful than that. Practically speaking, falling into this situation capitalism neither knows what to do nor how to do it. The steering wheel disappears at the driver's seat temporarily.

The destruction of the over-accumulation of capital on such a world scale cannot be done in any even, harmonious, or controlled way. There is no mythical "burn off" tax where each corporation must blow up exactly two factories and each capitalist must put exactly $5 million in cash into a public bonfire in front of their home. Anyway, even if all that happened it would hardly cause a ripple today—we have already seen many established corporations and banks go under, whole industrial regions are being beggared, and the storm has not even hit its full stride, when entire classes and nations will rise or fall.

In fact, maybe the way we are supposed to think about severe economic crisis is off-center? Remember how Marx keeps insisting that the "real" capitalist business world of commodities flashing all over the globe is on a deeper level an illusion? Why should the destruction of capital solely be an "economic" activity? We are led to assume that manipulating capital and profits must be something safely confined to a civilian zone called "business" or "economics." Certainly, this does happen there. Capital pulled over to the side of the road is capital evaporating: factories and houses become empty derelict buildings, machinery becomes rusty scrap, famous brand names and companies vanish from the material world into the history books. But as of New Years Day 2009, the capitalist crisis had already "burned up" well over $2 trillion in business capital; in suddenly worthless bonds and devalued stocks, in shut factories and bankrupt companies—and the economic plunge hasn't found bottom yet. If Marx's theory about value is a guide, no one knows how much capital must be destroyed for capitalism to come out of a real depression. Perhaps a qualitative level more than anyone usually thinks about.

As an example: Europe and Japan in the 1920s already had walking wounded economies, already were in economic crisis, and were easily pulled into the abyss of the 1930s Great Depression. Clawing at each other for survival, the major capitalist classes saw the imperative of survival in winning each other's colonies and markets, which directly led to World War 2. The conventional capitalist wisdom today is that this was a political problem, which could have been avoided if the competing capitalist classes had shared instead of excluded each other from markets and raw materials; instead of arms races and clashes, compromising and working together to stabilize the entire world system of corporate dominance bit by bit into a general revival. In other words, a forerunner to today's Globalization. Probably that capitalist dream was unrealistic, since the amount of capital that needed to be "burned off" was so huge that it required social processes that could not be neatly controlled, and that would spill over in systemic conflict. Overrunning and blotting out the shape of what is "normal." **The general crisis and the world war were not two separate events, then, but different stages in one event.**

This hypothesis has interesting implications for our own future, not that the massive "burn off" of capital overaccumulation requires a formal world war, since things like the protracted downsizing of a population and society or other such events could do just as well.

After all, in most of the world the depression of the 1930s didn't start in 1929, but years before. Nor did it end in 1940. The process played itself out into World War 2, when over 100 million people were killed, many large industrial cities became miles of burnt-out rubble, four major imperialist powers were bled and reduced to secondary status—and had to lose their colonial empires one by one. But, as many

Western economists have said, this "creative destruction" of capitalism was enough to clear the ground for a vigorous revival of the world capitalist system in the 1950s. It worked. Was that unnecessary "overkill," too much destruction of capital, more than what was needed? Possibly. But as we said before, there is no joystick guiding these unleashed destructive social processes that go far beyond the boundaries of "economy."

This analysis is only an exploration, a test run. We don't know whether this particular theoretical tool actually works well. The broad outlines of the situation that it projects for us are thought-provoking. But no one theory can explain all of the dense unfolding of contradictions in any general capitalist crisis. Let me end with some quick, general thoughts on this crisis:

★ *Each general crisis in production & distribution historically has its own specific character and conditions, in which the sheer size of the changes can accelerate the falling away of an old order and the rise of a new one. This goes far beyond the insight that in the actual inner workings of the system in a general crisis, Keynesian state "recovery" plans simply will not work. This is even beyond the control of capitalists in their boardrooms or radical protesters in the streets, save those that are part of what is coming into being, the future-as-now. In the last such great crisis of the 1920s–40s, progressive classes as world-important as the German industrial working class were stripped of their identity and became sleep-walkers. Just as the even larger u.s. white working class ended up retiring politically to the apartheid suburbs. While untold millions of "backward" people of color in the colonial periphery experienced the crisis and world war as an unprecedented learning experience, their angry anti-colonial rising of many millions in the 1930s–70s shifting the center of the radical world outwards beyond us.*

★ *What is obviously specific to this crisis is the "creative destruction" of Globalization, as the capitalist system's metropolitan center and post-colonial periphery collide and merge into each other. Like Mexico disintegrating as a whole nation and merging into Amerikkka. This is the center of the crisis—not speculation or financialization or housing sales.*

It's like the IBM building or some corporate skyscraper awkwardly doing brisk business as usual, only with one side blown off and in shreds. Whole sections of classes in the metropolis are being torn off and disintegrated, only to rematerialize abroad. If u.s. capitalism must on pain of death transport large chunks of its production and its production roles to Mumbai or Shanghai, then the roles for managers, supervisors, engineers, designers, white collar workers, must eventually be transported there as well. The explosive growth of middle and upper classes in the former periphery is the explosive decompression of middle and upper classes in New York and Cleveland. As Budweiser becomes a Brazilian business and the venerable New York Times *must ask Mexican capitalist Carlos Slim to rescue it and become a major shareholder. So the national class system here is partially collapsing into itself, and then re-forming again to a seemingly discordant world rhythm.*

★ *The long-term evolution of capitalist civilization, as seen in other of Marx's theories, is pushing in this direction: the continuing concentration of capital into larger and larger and fewer and fewer companies. Which has reached a critical point of contradiction now, with the entire gigantic u.s. finance industry as mostly only different "storefronts" for one government-backed enterprise. The contradiction about the increasingly evident need for social control and ownership of the means of production & distribution, paired with the ruling class death-grip on the rotting form of private ownership—even to the point of having mercenary gunmen corporations help the u.s.a. invade other countries, as though now is still Dodge City. One after another, key u.s. industries leave Amerikkkan control, as multi-national corporations become too large for any national framework and drift out over the continents. The critical global growth of the urban working class, which is finally surpassing the peasantry worldwide, is taking place completely outside and around the old u.s.a.*

★ *Many of those who formerly were allowed to be in privileged demi-classes, allowed a little addict's taste of the parasitic life, are now being thrown overboard. Not only in the u.s., because every major metropolitan nation today has growing numbers of "useless" citizens, who it no longer has any need for in production or in running their tattered empires. Who are privileged "surplus" except as consumers or soldiers. Like the privileged lower class of permanently jobless "proletarii" of the decaying Roman empire, free citizens without an economic role in a master-slave society; who were given meager "bread and circuses" welfare and told to breed more sons for Rome's imperial armies.*

Endgame? "Some say the world will end in fire, some say in ice ..."

At the start we noted how "twilight capitalism" has become an expression common on the Left now. i think that this phrase resonates with us at least in part because we here are living through the sudden end of day of the u.s. empire. It is twilight here in North America. Only a few years ago anti-imperialists were like Chicken Little, warning everyone of what they said was the unprecedented danger from the "lone superpower" superduper u.s.a. Now, after military bankruptcy in Iraq, after financial bankruptcy on Wall Street, that seems almost embarrassing. There are many capitalist powers still—but no longer any capitalist "superpowers." It is reasonable to think that this general crisis is a turning point, an important stage in the protracted decline and fall of capitalism as a world system.

It is hard to seriously discuss "endgame" without a theory (or generalized conceptual frameworks) about how societies die and are born. To start with, radical theory, both about how human society evolves and specifically about the endgame of world capitalism, already exists, although much of it is old. Lenin, in his major work, *Imperialism: The Highest Stage of Capitalism*, written around 1916, believed that capitalism for the first time had become one single world-covering system, but that it had peaked and was starting to decline.

Without bothering to enumerate all his conclusions (or Marx's on his theory of historical materialism and the evolution of societies from one to another), Lenin's capitalism was a system where class worked through the outward form of nations. Of oppressor and oppressed nations, or a handful of imperialist powers each owning and parasitic over a number of colonies and neo-colonies. To Lenin, this stage of capitalism, however powerful industrially and militarily, was already decadent and "overripe," starting to decay as a civilization. Because in this stage entire large nations had become parasitic, no longer self-supporting, with parasitic working classes, even. That this kind of society could resolve its systemic economic crisis only through unprecedented world wars with itself—wars that were destructive beyond any previous limits to the point of being suicidal—was widely believed to be one important symptom of such systemic decline. While Lenin is often criticized for his bold use of state dictatorship that paved the way to stalinism, he was an unusually creative and innovative political theorist and strategist in action. It is important to understand his theories on imperialism as a distinct stage of capitalism, because without them we don't have a theoretical foundation to explore the post-imperialist capitalism that we are rocketing towards.

From a neo-Leninist vantage point, then, the decline of world industrial capitalism began roughly one hundred years ago. It's peak was also the moment it started to decline. So, in that moment of history, imperialism was both still furiously industrializing, energetically integrating all other local economies in the world into itself, and at the same time tipping over into a decay and decline that most could only see in retrospect. (Major societies often take a long time in human lifetimes to decline—famously, both slave-based Imperial Rome and the mercantilist Turkish Ottoman empire took centuries to decline and fall).

For example, at the height of its military-industrial power in 1945 the u.s. empire landed 10,000 Marines on the China coast in an attempt to start another Western neo-colonial enclave. But the much larger Peoples Liberation Army evicted the home invaders within months. Then the attempted invasion of North Korea in 1951 failed, ending in a grinding stalemate along the original North-South boundary. Then the Cuban Revolution smashed the Bay of Pigs invasion by the CIA. Followed by the eleven-year debacle in Vietnam during the liberal Democratic adminstrations of Kennedy and Johnson. The disasters in Iraq and Afghanistan are nothing new. So for generations now the u.s. empire has mostly been losing its frontier wars.

World capitalism as a civilization is visibly decomposing before our eyes. It isn't just anachronistic phenomena such as pirates as a major illegal industry off a Thailand or a Somalia. We see the growing number of "failed states," where there is a crude capitalist economy but the supposed national governments simply don't exist practically speaking. Even long-established nations such as Mexico and Russia are sliding closer to the edge of that dead zone. The most important u.s. military "surge" taking place right now by the u.s. isn't in Iraq or Afghanistan, but on the mutating moving u.s.-Mexican border. Where u.s. homeland security and the u.s. defense department have prepared for a major federal police and active-duty military troop shift to try and stop the Mexican narco-gangs from establishing informal but complete zones of state power over the border itself and much of the lower Southwestern u.s.a. Which they have already done in Northern Mexico, of course. In growing areas of Mexico there no longer is any central government. It is almost as though world capitalism is de-evolving.

Warlordism, which is when the strongest armed organizations of whatever kind simply informally assume the powers of government in the absence of any civil order, has arisen to become a major form of capitalist government. While the treaties and commercial integration of Globalization prohibit wars between major capitalist states, more and more of the "post-colonial" world seems beset by constant civil wars. These are as far away as many areas of the former USSR or as near as the South Side of Chicago. Being security guards or soldiers for some capitalist outfit are major occupations, in some Brazilian cities accounting for as much as one-third of all regularly employed men.

Much of the discussion we've heard around this world economic crisis assumes that the capitalism that is being remade is going to be just a poorer version of today's society. That the struggle will obediently follow the familiar painted lines on the street of civilian society. In other words, "business as usual," only a bit less of it. Nero and Tupac Shakur will sing together at the Met before that happens.

So radicals like the words, "Twilight capitalism." But are we ready to admit that since "twilight" is a different situation, a different period of world capitalism, we need theory to help us organize and adjust? There is a lot of theory that has dealt with transitional periods, which is what this "twilight" is. One characteristic of this time is that the capitalist ruling class cannot automatically hold the power anymore, but we cannot hold onto it, either. We've just seen the revolution in Nepal, where a democratic front led by Maoist guerrillas seized power and abolished the former monarchy and its feudal-capitalist regime. But only to create a more India-like capitalism. In the u.s. during the 1960s, revolutionary forces here learned how to take over neighborhoods, schools, and factories from capitalist domination. But we couldn't hold any of it; not only because of repression or for military reasons, but because we failed at building a new anti-capitalist culture for people to live in. Just like anti-colonial revolutions in Africa, Asia, the Middle East and Latin America forced

Western colonialism out of the capitol, but completely failed to build liberated societies yet. The battleline keeps shifting from one side to the other.

As you can either sharpen or dull a knife against a stone, this crisis makes certain we will either sharpen anti-capitalist theory or blunt it. One or the other will take place.

Postscript

Some radicals are saying that this crisis is an emergency situation, and therefore we must help lead massive new working-class movements to force economic concessions from the ruling class. Or a big united front to fight back against the imminent threat of a major white fascist offensive backed by the capitalists. Or some such talk. There are a number of problems with such perspectives, but the first one and smallest one is that it encourages corrupt thinking about ourselves. In the actually-existing Amerikkka, when the newspapers or television say "left" everyone knows that they mean Nancy Pelosi. Or maybe Howard Dean. Revolutionaries here do not yet have anything like the political strength or numbers to be leading any such imaginary movements. Even if we knew what we were doing. This is like the king has no clothes time, guys. We have to stop wasting our limited attention span on such talk.

We know that the general crisis affects everything that is happening politically, but too many people have stopped thinking about other things. This is like a record storm. It covers everything, changes everything to some degree, but it isn't necessarily the most important thing that is happening. If while you were trudging through the bad weather at night, several guys jumped you with knives and you were fighting for your life, you wouldn't appreciate a passerby yelling, "Keep your mind on preventing flooding, neighbor!" For you right then, the very most important thing is surviving the knife fight by any means necessary.

i use that parable deliberately, because to many people under immediate attack by capitalism, the idea that economic crisis is the most crucial problem isn't true. Not in Darfur for sure, not in the neo-fascist turf in the former East Germany, not in Gaza, definitely not in divorce court, not in so many places.

Take an event so ordinary that it never gets talked about on national television news or in politicians' press conferences. There are no t-shirts about it, no NGOs play at solving it, and no celebrities adopt it:

In the early 2000s, famous Cook County Hospital was in unsustainable financial crisis. This is the hospital model for television's "E.R." show, and the hospital of last resort for Chicago's lower working class. With shrinking government funding, the large public hospital for the Chicago ghetto could no longer keep going on as usual. The background is that like all government here, the hospital is not only a token reform to relieve class discontent, but also an important site of profitable corruption for the local Democratic Party's legendary Daley Machine. Cook County Hospital was not only free for patients, but also free for insurance companies and Medicare. No bills for patient care were ever paid because none were ever sent out. There was no functioning billing department at all. It was riddled with "no show, no work" patronage employees whose real jobs were elsewhere carrying out duties for the Democratic Party.

Mayor Daley's solution was to pass the hospital over to public control of the Stroger family, one of the three great Black political clans enforcing imperial rule in neo-colonial Chicago. Then Cook County Board president John Stroger pushed through a puzzling new plan, in which the old County Hospital would be replaced by a brand-new one next door.

How could throwing up a dazzling new building be an answer to a financial shortfall?

Needless to say, the construction of an expensive new hospital provided the Daley Machine with a festival of rewards & contracts & bribes & corruption. Most important of all, although the shining new hospital looked as large as the old one, it was a "Potemkin village." Like a Hollywood stage set, the new building was impressively wide and tall but behind that big facade physically very shallow. Ten years ago the old Cook County Hospital held some 3,000 patients, with beds crammed into crowded rooms and some patients sleeping on gurneys lining hallways. But getting needed care of some kind. Today, John H. Stroger County Hospital (yes, before he died and passed his County neo-colonial chiefdom on to his young son, Stroger modestly named the new hospital after himself) accommodates only slightly more than 300 patients. A wonderful 90% reduction in in-patient care for Chicago's primarily Black and Latino lower working class without health insurance. Disposable people who don't need to be given hospital care at all, since their assigned role is to die when they can no longer usefully labor for capitalism. And since new buildings are costly, some specialty clinics were closed, breast cancer biopsies postponed for months, ob-gyn care cut way back, voluntary surgeries indefinitely postponed. The large general medicine clinic in the old Fantas building nearby was essentially closed to most new admissions.

Crisis successfully dealt with in the liberal neo-colonial way. "Change We Can Believe In." The Stroger clan awards itself and its friends high-paying jobs in new offices. Thousands and thousands of working-class women and men denied life or death health care. Through it all, one important man who was right there carefully did nothing and said nothing. But what family man can blame him? For Mayor Richard Daley and the Stroger clan are among this man's nearest true kinfolks—his criminal co-conspirators. This guy is Barack Obama, of course.

It isn't about Obama as just another corrupt and indifferent politician. It's about how the neo-colonial destruction of one local hospital—and the wall of lies covering it all up—is a small window into a much larger ruling class strategy.

We mean the systematic forced depopulation and razing of the Black inner cities, one after another. While Obama was their "representative" in the state legislature, the Lawndale neighborhood had 57% of its adult male population under the crushing thumb of the neo-colonial slave system—in federal or state prison, local jail, on parole or probation. A community as an "open-air prison" with no economy except the police-regulated drug trade and the auto-homicide of Black youth. With Obama as one of the well-paid deputy wardens. All so that the dangerous Black lower classes can be killed off or dispersed away from the cities to the unwanted places, the margins of society. Always being moved on. Like what is being done to Palestinians today. And the large, complex, and fertile urban Black communities themselves are destroyed, like the original Indian Nations before them.*

While in capitalism's eye the u.s. empire's old center cities can become profitable white-majority real estate of the future again. All of which couldn't be done without the raising of a whole new "post–civil rights" African-American bourgeoisie to cover up and mislead the way. The class that Obama is now the poster child for, passing out the kool-aid with a warm smile on his face. In the past, even the Booker T. Washingtons had a connection to and a need for the survival of their Black Nation. Now, for the first time, there is an African-American leadership class (whom some call the "mis-leadership class") who have no common class interest with the Black Nation. Whether other Black people live or die is only a tactical matter to them. They are out of there. This is a leadership that is being specially trained and chosen by advanced capitalism, of course. The lies & misdirection are far more than just "Ponzi bonds" and stolen pensions.

What is an "emergency" is our need to orient ourselves in the crisis first of all. To seriously step up our political understand-

* This story true in 2009 and in essence true today. Although the Affordable Care Act and the expansion of Medicaid led to the more profitable rearrangement of the local health system.

ing, and thus our ability in the real world to help others make sense for themselves of a dramatically changing situation. A crisis for the capitalists is only great weather for us, because revolutionaries were made for crisis. This is our perfect environment, to move in the storm. It's exciting to see in the deepening crisis the things that radical theory has long analyzed. To use theory to trace the landscape that is coming into being. Because new groups of people are going to create unexpected movements with strategies and tactics that will surprise everyone. Count on it. And if this general crisis is going to last for many years, revolutionaries need to spend some time at the start to orient ourselves in the right direction. ★

Right-wing protest against McDonalds in Belgium

Aryan Politics & Fighting the W.T.O. (2001)*

> *"Don't watch the light, watch the cars.*
> *Light ain't going to hit you."*
> *Moms Mabley*

There's been an illusion that opposing the World Trade Organization is by its very nature a left issue. That it's all really *our* party, naively thrown for us by those establishment types, those innocent social-democratic officials of the AFL-CIO and all the nice global liberals and lobbyists. In this view, while some stuffed shirts may have disapproved of the ruckus—and a Pat Buchanan or two may have awkwardly crashed our party—in downtown Seattle we *were* the action in an anti-corporation festival. As the poet said at another revolution: "*Bliss it was in that dawn to be alive / But to be young was very heaven.*" Nice, but no cigar.

The anti-WTO protests in Seattle were a radicalizing experience for many, on a tactical level. But on a larger scale, the Left has unacknowledged strategic problems with this issue. **To sum it up simply, we have the problem**

Written for the book *My Enemy's Enemy*, first published by Anti-Fascist Forum in 2001 (and subsequently by Kersplebedeb in 2003). The political context at the time was one in which the militant protests against the World Trade Organization in Seattle in 1999 had kicked off a new cycle of struggle in North America, known somewhat problematically as the "anti-globalization" movement.

that we may be helping to fuel the explosive growth of the Right and neo-fascism. And we have to think of refocusing to fight the Far Right in the anti-WTO struggle—just as we need to on every other contested terrain.

There are three political currents opposing the WTO here, not just one. In basic terms: Center, Left, and Right. The Right-Wing wasn't partying down in Seattle that week only because they didn't want to be. Believe it, if Pat Buchanan or a David Duke had really wanted to bring thousands they would have. But why would they want their followers to unite with Jews and anarchists, mix with topless Lesbian Avengers by Trotskyist banners? And they definitely didn't want them clashing with the same cops they're busy educating and recruiting. No, they've got a different game plan.

Remember, we're not the only players. It wasn't the Right that got wiped out during the 1980s–90s, after all. That was the Left, and today the revolutionary Left has small groups of activists but no real social base in the u.s. While the Right has a major social base out of the traditional settler culture (and is rapidly growing). And it's within that blood-warm environment that neo-fascist currents have clearly developed.

Sometimes we unthinkingly misjudge the Far Right. Seeing only the most visible, what infringes on our own world. Mentally ill shooters or small groups of headline freaks in drag. Those are only tiny flashes, glimpses of what might be coming. The first important fact about the Right-Wing is that it is *still not coalesced*, but it *is* huge. Often they dominate the social dialogue in rural areas and small towns. They are a major political presence not only within the ranks of the police and military, but in school boards, talk radio, churches, even some unions and local governments. Again, they cannot be easily counted or measured because they are still uncoalesced. Kept diffused by various imperialist strategies in order to prevent their disruptive potential.

How much potential can be seen by the fact that in the 1986 Louisiana election, 55% of the total white vote for u.s. senator went to David Duke of klan and neo-nazi fame. Or the quiet use of steady, low-level, anonymous settler violence in aryan regions to both eliminate sources of abortion and to end u.s. policing of public lands (i.e. the faint beginnings of a shadow government).

That means even when the Far Right is not immediately present in person—as they weren't in downtown Seattle at the ruckus and the tear gas—they have the massified subcultures to take advantage of and even symbolically appropriate *our* struggle as their propaganda to build *their* following. That's not a hypothesis, that's a fact, what they're now busy at. **Even more easily because the establishment social democrats and liberals who run the anti-WTO campaign publicly welcomed highly visible Right-Wing participation in their coalition.** Trashing Niketown is always fine, any day of the year, but to think of only that while letting the racists in the front door, unopposed, says something.

There is no question that "the Battle in Seattle" touched a popular nerve. At times the protest unity on the streets hit the surrealistic mark on the meter. Not just hard-hat steelworkers, longshoremen, and teamsters marching with gay & lesbian groups, environmentalists and radical students, but AFL-CIO porkchoppers loyal to President Clinton sounding like they'd hired Karl Marx as their speechwriter. Notably AFSCME boss Gerry McEntree, who in Seattle's best-known quote shouted:

> "The system turns everything into a commodity! A rain forest in Brazil, a library in Philadelphia, a hospital in Alberta! We have to name that system: it is corporate capitalism!"

In such a rad atmosphere, it was only natural for Pat Buchanan's Aryan supporters to applaud as Amparo Reyes, a Mexican maquiladora sweatshop worker who has a 74-hour workweek, shouted into the microphone: "Long live the Zapatistas!" As Far Right, Center, and Left converged politically in Seattle.

And what are the class forces clashing here deep below in tectonic plate?

So this anti-WTO movement is, in strategic terms, very different from what we're used to. After all, if you march on city hall to protest racist police brutality, you don't expect the ku klux klan to be marching alongside you chanting "No justice, no peace!" But that is the exact situation here.

The anti-WTO movement is extraordinarily broad, ranging from the revolutionary left to the centrist liberals and social-democrats who manage it all the way over to the neo-fascists and Far Right.

The anti-WTO movement is also deceptively asymmetrical on a world scale. On paper it is a global unity, of grass-roots anti-corporate forces of North and South together. But the official anti-WTO *campaign* is as centered in the white metropolis as the trans-national corporations they oppose, both sides heavily European and North American. While the actual anti-WTO *struggle* (as opposed to the official campaign) is at its highest tide, and is most furious, in the Third World periphery. Where it is a matter of life or death to those involved. **That is, the class politics of opposing the WTO are asymmetrical.** With the Centrist anti-WTO forces in the metropolis being largely pro-capitalist, while much of the struggle in the periphery is anti-capitalist. As radical journalist Jaggi Singh observes of the ongoing battles in India, here first quoting a union and women's rights activist in Madras:

> "In Geetha's view, 'I think the American working class is worried about American capital going to the Third World to exploit conditions there.' She adds, 'That's an indirect fight.' ... One group directly connected to the international anti globalization movement is the KRRS, the Karnataka State Farmer's Movement, representing thousands of peasant farmers in the southern state of Karnataka. In recent years, the KRRS has physically dismantled—with iron bars—a

> Cargill seed unit, trashed another office of the same multinational agribusiness, burned Monsanto's field trials of biotech cotton, and trashed a Kentucky Fried Chicken outlet in Bangalore. Their actions put in some perspective the recent debate about so-called 'violence against property' in Seattle."

This is one important aspect of the anti-WTO struggle, that it is a common front that allows activists in the metropolis to support the struggles of the militant peasants in India, the Zapatistas in Chiapas, or the Ogoni fighting both Shell petroleum and the Nigeria military dictatorship. But we have to make certain that we're really doing that, and not just helping to rip-off these struggles for pro-capitalist agendas here.

While the official campaign against the WTO and the new global corporation economy has spread here, it arose earlier and is much stronger in Europe. In the London June 18th Protest, after all, ten thousand protesters literally took over "the City" financial district: burning cars, violently forcing banks to close, and in general making Seattle look timid & respectable. And it was in France where the indignant farmer José Bové became a national hero for "daylighting" a McDonalds with his tractor. Far from icing him in prison, a French "socialist" government paid his airfare to march in Seattle as a celebrity ambassador of French economic nationalism. By contrast, you can try trashing an AT&T office in Manhattan in protest, and you can be sure that instead of a free deluxe trip to Geneva you'll be sitting in a cell in Rikers. In Europe symbolic attacks on corporate property, farmers or truckers blocking highways, mass protest marches, and a sprinkle of black-clad anarchists clashing with riot police have been a normal part of the political landscape for years.

And yet, the whole political landscape in Europe has at the same time throughout those years been shifting steadily to the Right, with openly neo-fascist parties gaining a mass base in the millions unprecedented since WWII. Their violent emergence has monkey-wrenched the whole European political spectrum far to the Right.

How do we understand this new emulsion, of mass protest movements against u.s. imperialism & the trans-national corporations being part of the same historical wave as the eclipse of the Left and the reemergence of neo-fascism as an alternative power? There is no issue that radicals have to unpuzzle more than this, because, like NAFTA & the WTO, it is coming to our neighborhood.

We can see how part of this plays out in real class politics by zooming in for a moment on the trade unions, which played such a large role in Seattle N30. While the unionized major industry labor of the imperialist center is **a** working class, it is not on a world scale **the** working class. That is, it is a special labor aristocracy that is a class above the oppressed proletariat of the world. And has politics to match. A labor aristocracy that today is shrinking in importance in the metropolis. And, as an old middle class, is maneuvering with desperation against classes above and below it.

For example, the West Coast longshoremen (who are now both women and men) of the ILWU, AFL-CIO are in the thick of the fight against NAFTA & the WTO. Not only did they march by the many hundreds in Seattle, but they demonstrated "on the job" that day by closing down ports up and down the Coast. These ILWU members are for real about halting the WTO and all this global neo-liberal reorganization because they have so much personally to lose.

The average West Coast longshoreman **earns about $60,000–80,000 a year.** It's not unusual for highly-skilled longshoremen or clerks who push overtime to hit $125,000–150,000 per year. With income guarantees and a full benefits package. This is the kind of income that lawyers, accountants, corporate middle-managers, and successful small businessmen make. And union longshoremen have the vacation homes, boats, multiple cars, stock portfolios, and rental properties that are common for the u.s. middle classes.

How can capitalism pay blue-collar workers $75,000 and $100,000 per year? Because the Big Chalupa is only for a microscopic handful of strategically located workers in an increasingly mechanized and neo-liberalized transport industry. On the entire West Coast there are only 7,000 union longshoremen, with another 3,000 clerks and foremen (which is less than the number of airline pilots just at United Airlines). We are talking about the labor that handles the vast Pacific Rim trade in automobiles, electronics, grains, clothing, timber, ores, people, etc. for this continental u.s. empire of 250 millions.

There are less union longshoremen on the entire West Coast than waterfront truckers just in Los Angeles. But these truckers are forced to be "independent contractors" who must furnish their own trucks, have no benefits or income guarantees, and are hired only daily by the task. After job expenses, they often earn one-third or less of what the longshoremen make. And we're not even dealing with the much larger numbers of minimum-wage messengers, cargo handlers, and delivery men in major cities who are primarily Black and Latino and immigrant. Like the Afrikan immigrant men who deliver for the German-owned A&P, Waldbaum, and Food Emporium supermarket chains in Manhattan. According to the labor law violation suit just filed by the State Attorney General, these workers earn a nobel-prize-winning 87 cents to $1.74 *an hour* for 69-hour work weeks! Bet they didn't jet to Seattle.

The ILWU may *protest* the WTO now. But it has spent the past fifty years actually *fighting* the working class that is really below them. For decades it kept most Black and Latin longshoremen as casuals, who had to show up daily in hope of work, and out of the union itself. Only federal court civil rights rulings forced it to stop being a small white men's club. Ironically, while the union has changed a lot in race and gender—with many Latino and New Afrikan and women members—its class politics haven't changed at all. It still pushes American nationalism, "partnership" with the shipping companies, and fighting the workers below them.

ILWU leaders openly refer to the largely Latino waterfront truckers even in print by the racist slang term, "Gypos." And tacitly support the shipping companies in keeping them down. This isn't class conflict in the form of race anymore, but openly about class conflict. For *"Class is everything."*

Unlike managers or accountants, if union longshoremen lose their footing on the capitalist mountainside they can't simply transfer their highly-paid skills elsewhere. There's no waterfront at the 7-11. Just as u.s. merchant seamen are highly paid, but have mostly been replaced by miserably paid Third World seamen on "flags of convenience" ships, the state agencies and shippers want to reorganize labor in a more profitable way on the world's docks.

This is the onrushing wave of the capitalist future that these unions and others of the old middle classes are trying to hold off. And for some this may be something to resentfully protest about, but others are thinking that their countervailing leverage can only come from the power of their old nation state. This past February, some 2,000 union longshoremen on the East Coast packed a N.Y. government hearing to shout down and threaten their enemy—environmentalists protesting the ocean dumping of dredged-up sludge containing mercury and other toxic metals. Longshoremen were worried that halting the dredging might hamper seaport business expansion.

Working in the political hotspot of world trade, the ILWU bureaucracy has always used political camouflage. In what appeared to be a display of radical sympathies, last year the ILWU had a mass one-day work stoppage on the West Coast to support the radical death row prisoner Mumia Abu Jamal. What do you think the vote was like in the locals, particularly among white and Latin workers? Well, there wasn't any vote. Nor was there consultation or even much advance notice from what we heard. The grapevine has it that there even was a lot of resentment, especially from young Black longshoremen, that the union had dictatorially ordered them to give up hours over some guy on the East Coast who they didn't even know.

It's all part of the ILWU's historic strategy of looking very "progressive" and even radical as a propaganda cover, while they pursue business unionism. These public relations "political strikes" are privately worked out with the shipping corporations and the government in advance, of course (military cargoes, passenger ships, and freight designated as priority by the corporations were handled by union crews under the "work stoppage"). What was encouraging news in the stoppage was that the Mumia campaign had achieved such moral prestige and support that such opportunistic elements wanted to associate themselves with it, much as numerous bourgeois politicians already have.

These classes *in the metropolis* most bitterly up in arms against "McDomination" and the WTO are **not** the oppressed, **not** the proletariat. Who are quite capable of organizing themselves without any white help whatsoever. 250,000 Mexicans, Chicanos, and Central American immigrants

marched in Los Angeles against Prop. 187 on October 16, 1994. A year later a million New Afrikan men gathered on the Washington Mall. And after that some 400,000 Black women came to Philadelphia from all over the u.s. for the Million Women March. But not in Seattle—it wasn't their protest. Because those mass Latino and Black mobilizations were fighting the *same old nationalism* that is at the heart of the anti-WTO sentiment in the u.s.

It is the **old middle classes** of the imperialist center that are in motion here politically. Commercial family farmers; small retailers; the labor aristocracy of highly-paid craftsmen and unionized industrial workers; that stratum of intellectuals (more than a few of them liberal or "socialist") tied tit-to-mouth to the old welfare state. Plus the marginalized white lumpen-petitbourgeoisie, bitter at their social exile from paradise.

These are middle classes whose privileged but also precarious existence is bound up with successful national imperialism, and who look for security from their old national economy and the insular national culture of the "good old days." In a word, who deep down consider themselves rightfully part of the capitalist winners, not the oppressed "losers." (Don't forget that Oklahoma City bomber Tim McVeigh tried to be a career Army officer, while his comrade-in-arms Terry Nichols was a failed farm owner).

Instinctively, the liberal managers of anti-corporate protest have understood this. Which is why the WTO protest managers have catered to nationalism and accepted neo-fascists as their allies.

Just as the New Right has understood how much this WTO issue is on their ground, based in classes that are sympathetic to **their** world outlook.

This is not a matter of some intellectual "line," some slogans, as the Left dreamily thinks of as politics—*but of what you kill for.* And the Far Right *is* killing people. First a few, then more & more often, until they establish their unwritten Aryan law of what is to be "normal." Assassinating pro-Choice doctors or torching buildings full of immigrant laborers.

In Western Europe the foundation for the WTO fight was laid by years of anti-NATO, anti-u.s., and "Green" campaigns. Throughout the 1970s and 1980s mass protests regularly shook European cities, with the black-clad "masked ones" regularly darting out of the crowds to hurl their own missiles at the riot police. But the only result of all this by the 1990s was the Europe-wide reemergence of fascism into the daylight as a political force. In Britain, the neo-fascist British National Party for the first time crested 100,000 votes in last year's elections, gathering strength in smaller industrial cities. In Austria, the openly pro-nazi leader Jörg Haider has led his Freedom Party into a groundbreaking election victory. Like their French, British, German, Swiss, Italian, etc. counterparts, the Austrian neo-fascists make opposition to the WTO, globalization, and immigrant workers the main issues in their popular campaign to "save" their Aryan way of life.

And as they "tip" the social atmosphere, daily violent attacks on Afrikans, Asians, Turks, Arabs, and other non-Aryans become ordinary and normal. Not even news. Just as it was in the segregationist u.s. South. In Berlin, which officially celebrates its post-modern capitalist multi-culturalism, all Jewish synagogues and buidings are under constant 24-7 police guard. Because otherwise the resurgent fascist movement would torch them all. To say nothing of killing Jews. Which would be a big public relations embarrassment for post-modern imperialism's highly publicized German "Jew zoo" (the tacit understanding between the neo-fascist thugs and the police is that they concentrate on merely attacking people of color—less like a crime in Germany than a cultural activity—and the police let them proceed).

There was more than a coincidental connection between the reemergence of fascism and the politics of the earlier anti-NATO, anti-u.s., and environmental protest movements. In Germany, for example, this link was not unknown. **It**

had been sharply pointed out even then by the RZ (the underground anarchist guerrilla network of the autonomist Revolutionary Cells), which highlighted the way that these protest movements had pandered to a sentimentalized nationalism in order to gain wider public support.

This approach was, of course, just as popular in Germany then as it is today in "Born in the USA." What German radicals didn't want to face was that their popular brew of shallow anti-Americanism was really only another form of *German* nationalism. Left policies actually tilled the ground for Fascist regrowth. In 1982–83, a series of violent attacks on individual off-duty GIs was blamed on the RZ and other underground radical groups. Both the Left press and the security police talked about this as though it were obvious fact. Although it was finally revealed (as the police had known all along) that it was neo-nazis who had done the attacks.

The RZ pointed out in their Easter 1983 message "*Beethoven versus McDonalds*" that as internationalists they were neither "anti-American" nor "pro-German" (as the liberals, social democrats, conservatives, and neo-fascists were). While they had attacked u.s. military bases & officers, they had never been for attacking individual enlisted men or women off-duty. Further, that **the RZ condemned the "racist feeling" among Germans depicting GIs as "animals," "rapists," etc., and the exclusion of Black GIs from many restaurants and bars.** Correctly, they linked this type of anti-GI sentiment not to fighting oppression, but to the hatred of foreigners, immigrant workers, and other non-Aryans. The RZ were "even sadder" that the German Left press itself was also promoting this nationalistic racism, in an opportunist strategy which quite naturally the Far Right only fed on:

> "The political responsibility of the anti-American attempts does not fall on the armed left groups, but rather on a certain part of the peace movement which practices a diffuse nationalism. Which dis-

> seminates the absurd idea that the Federal Republic of Germany is an 'occupied country'. Which is awakening a German patriotism and is abandoning left politics while it equates the question of missile deployment with a question of national identity ... Those who make Coca-Cola a synonym of genocide and consider it a principal form of cultural imperialism, and place it on the same level as the American government support of all military dictators, remove from themselves the possibility of understanding the fascist origin of nationalist or anti-American actions.
>
> "... And this is the way in which the will of the peace movement alliances led in part consciously, in part with naivete, to nationalist or fascist positions. The occurrence of fascist groups, of anti-semitic actions, is not surprising. In the first place they operate on only one line: racism and hatred of foreigners."

The key understanding is that to gather mass support those anti-NATO and "Green" movements kept playing the chord of **Germans as victims** (while Germans are really among the oppressors and beneficiaries of global imperialism).

This resonated popularly in the racist-nationalist psyche, along with the ever pleasing nostalgia for the supposedly better "local" capitalism (like Old Dixie) and the nationalist culture of the "good old days." And this is more than a little like today's mass anti-WTO united front between progressives and the Far Right.

No one is saying that those protest movements were the cause of the regrowth of Fascism. They were but one element in a much larger reaction. However, those policies had a double importance: of keeping the Left entranced in a cinematic fantasy of mass popularity, while much of its energies were being bled off to feed the growing Far Right.

The issue of Right-Wing activity inside the anti-WTO issue has been raised already by the Dutch

group De Fabel Van De Illegaal (The Myth of Illegality). *De Fabel,* which had been active in organizing early anti-WTO forces in the Netherlands, protested the Seattle organizers reaching out to the Right-Wing in a grand white-on-white alliance.

Mike Dolan of Ralph Nader's Public Citizen lobby, who was the chief organizer of the Seattle mobilization, is quoted by *De Fabel* as not only accepting the participation of but enthusiastically endorsing Right-Wing politician Pat Buchanan: "Whatever else you say about Pat Buchanan, he will be the only candidate in the 2000 presidential sweepstakes who will passionately and unconditionally defend the legitimate expectations of working families in the global economy." *De Fabel* adds: "As long as they are conservative and obedient, and not unemployed, black, gay, woman, lesbian or Jewish."

In *De Fabel's* analysis, the problem is not so much the Buchanans as it is the international lobbyists and opinion-makers of the anti-WTO campaign. While student activists, grassroots environmentalists, and white radicals created the militant action downtown in Seattle, it was the NGO (non-governmental organizations—such as Nader's Public Citizen) leaders represented in the elite "think tank" of the International Forum on Globalization that built the alliance in the first place and set the overall politics. And **they** are largely conservative behind a thin humanitarian veneer, in *De Fabel's* view.

This WTO shoot-up has more going on than anyone can discuss at any one time. Everyone's got moves, everyone's got cover stories. The Left as well, we should see. On her way to Seattle, a prominent European feminist who works with Third World women's groups stopped off to give a speech. It was thoughtful, zeroing in on the WTO as both a special new menace to people everywhere and a rallying point for anti-capitalist unity against "the race to the bottom." She emphasized how workers in the affluent North now have real common cause with the oppressed of the South.

"We stand to lose everything we have gained since the War, World War II. The so-called 'family wage', where one person's salary can support the whole family, sick leave, medical benefits, subsidized child care, union protection, all our rights. Everything is in danger of being lost!" Our audience of almost entirely white middle class intellectuals nodded in a wave of agreement.

Afterwards, a woman comrade who at age sixty is a minimum-wage blue collar worker, remarked angrily to me: "What is she talking about, '*We* stand to lose everything ... '? I never had *any* of those things, and I don't have them now! Health benefits, child care ... we don't have those things. Doesn't she know that? My entire life as long as those white men with big union contracts got theirs, their big bucks, they never lifted a finger for the rest of us."

My comrade spoke the truth that the political strategy of the middle classes try to conceal. Their "We" does not mean us. The anti-WTO campaign *in the metropolis* primarily represents the needs and desires of certain middle classes. A fact that both Far Right and Left cover up with lots of populist talk ... and lots of nationalism.

It's paradoxical that a world-wide campaign that advertises internationalism is more like an alliance of little nationalisms.

The Aryan grassroots appeal of a Pat Buchanan is only that of the old settler nationalism, of code phrases which they all understand to mean "White people first." His program demands that Government, trade laws, and corporate policy all place—as his slogan says—"American workers and people first" (just as "Austrians First" is Jörg Haider's slogan). The AFL-CIO unions have this same program, and had it before Buchanan did (which is why they supported the Vietnam War down the line), but put liberal talk on top of it. So the unity in practice is not really around any kind of internationalism, but around the decaying old nationalism. How else could the Far Right and the establishment liberals work together?

But the Right's influence extends far beyond its own followers. There is an almost palpable distortion in the political field from the suddenly magnetic attraction of retro capitalist nationalism. Seattle's Town Hall debate on globalization that week, sponsored by the IFG and *The Nation*, featured pro-capitalist views on *both* sides. Figures like David Aaron, u.s. undersecretary of commerce for international trade, and Ralph Nader. But in his report on the debate, *Left Business Observer*'s editor Doug Henwood was clearly most surprised by the line of Indian physicist and well-known eco-feminist author Vandana Shiva:

> "Shiva, rightly denouncing the WTO as an agency of imperialism, urged a 'return to the national decision-making which we control,' apparently not noticing that the nation-state itself was an imperial inheritance, nor disclosing just when it was that 'we' (whoever that is) controlled its governance. Her India seems like one consisting almost entirely of displaced peasants; she spoke of it as a single thing, as if unriven by class, ethnic, and regional differences. She also claimed that business was once limited by ethical concerns, but with the WTO, the logic of profit maximization has taken over—a strange version of capitalist history indeed."

It wouldn't be unusual in a nation where Hindu Right-Wing nationalist gangs murder with impunity and the rural police are well-known for raping and torturing women, for an activist to seek some protection by sheltering her work under the umbrella of a vague anti-colonialism or a "loyal" nationalism. But we still have to say clearly how misleading this nostalgic talk about "our own" nationalism is. And you have to be in a delusional state of mind to believe that there ever was anything ethical about *anyone's* national capitalism. These two words don't even go together.

The reality is that the anti-WTO issue is in danger of being pulled onto the terrain of demagoguery

and nationalism. Just as earlier anti-u.s., anti-NATO, and "Green" movements were in Europe. This is a natural environment for the Far Right, one in which they are strengthened and will grow a hundred-fold. They are past masters on this ground.

Even in Vandana Shiva's India, where the grassroots anti-WTO movement of workers and peasants is radically anti-capitalist, Jaggi Singh has reported that the Hindu neo-fascists have mounted their own anti-WTO protests. They're not unaware, they're in tune with new neo-fascist strategy world-wide. When Hindu Right-Wing union, farmer, and student organizations angrily confronted WTO director Mike Moore during his January 2000 visit, they condemned Western corporate "biopiracy" and "a global system, which actually protects and supports the rich and the powerful ..." In other words, they are utilizing a certain kind of radicalism which stirs up popular anger at what is foreign, appropriating the language of anti-colonialism. In their case, of course, the "foreign" enemies to be killed or driven out include Indian Muslims, Christians, socialists, feminists, anarchists, lower castes, and indigenous tribal peoples. A program they have well underway, as we can tell by the bodycount in the thousands already.

By demagoguery we mean the depicting of the WTO as some vast foreign conspiracy which steals our supposed local or national capitalist "democracy." Was it the WTO which placed a major sewage treatment plant right in Harlem, knowingly pushing up air pollution levels just as an epidemic of Black and Latin childhood asthma was starting? No, that criminal act was committed by our very local capitalism. For N.Y. anti-WTO protesters, it might be that Seattle is much closer to them than Harlem, if you know what i mean. Was it the WTO that has killed and is killing thousands of Navajos by radioactive uranium ore waste poisoning? No, that was the "democratic" u.s. government.

Which is why Pat Buchanan attacks "the Jewish lobby" and immigrant labor, why neo-nazis have come out in public applauding the "angry white people" who "shut down the Jew World Order" at Seattle, and why the Right-Wing is pretending that the WTO is as alien as "The X-Files" (when it's really just Pat and Jörg's cousins).

Beyond the street scenes, the Far Right may be less visible now but they are investing heavily in this campaign. Part of their re-manufacturing of themselves not as defenders of corporate America but as "populists" fighting for their own nation & its workers against the sinister forces of the New World Order (sounds like the Left, doesn't it?). On the front page of the December 27th issue of *Spotlight*, newspaper of the Right-Wing Liberty Lobby, the headline reads **"POPULISM GAINS MOMENTUM AROUND THE GLOBE."** Under it is a big photo of an anti-WTO banner at Seattle, over smaller photos of four anti-WTO "populist" leaders that the Liberty Lobby specifically applauds as "nationalists": Pat Buchanan, Jörg Haider of Austria, Christoph Blocher of Switzerland, and Mahathir Mohammad of Malaysia.

The fact that the Right-Wing has a major social base is one reason that the anti-WTO campaign leaders are so eager to enter into an alliance with them. While the Left has preoccupied itself post-Seattle with a debate on trashing Niketown, the anti-WTO campaign itself is being used in propaganda to legitimize and popularize world neo-fascism. It's only a natural consequence of this that major anti-WTO campaign leaders are now calling for *more* u.s. police arrests & repression of radicals. Don't take it lightly. For this is one "anti-WTO" demand that imperialism is sure to take care of! **For us, fighting neo-fascism and its new friends seems to the immediate point in the anti-WTO campaign.**

It's telling that there have been many social-democratic criticisms of the "Black Bloc" etc. for trashing stores, for "undemocratic" violation of the N30 non-violent pro-capitalist official strategy. But who got to vote on the top-down legitimizing of Pat Buchanan and racism? Who should be accountable for this?

There are many important sides to the anti-WTO campaign which have not been discussed here. Not because they aren't urgent, but because we felt it necessary to focus on a strategic question that has not been brought into full consciousness yet. We know that we've raised more questions than were answered. But this is only one contribution among many.

One last thing. We have to deal with the truth that the revolutionary left has no social base of support in the metropolis right now. To say this is simply facing reality. Because we don't, there is a natural tendency to seize on "get rich quick" schemes. To look for "magic bullets" or some issue we can jump aboard that will magically gain us a mass following. This is like furiously mining "fool's gold." For reasons in the basic class structure, Left politics have been marginalized in the metropolis, certainly in the u.s. We exist on the far edges of society, politically speaking. This is not of our making, and is not even necessarily bad. In the world of Babylon, the oppressed are the ones who are marginalized, first and foremost. Undocumented workers, classes of disposable women, exiles, Third World workers fighting even to survive. The world's majority exists at the margins. And, like them, we are faced with our marginalization, and with the knowledge of how much we must transform ourselves and our own culture just to survive.

Frauen War
die einzige parteiamtliche Frauenzeitsch
HEFT 19 · 8. JAHR
1. APRILHE

The Green Nazi: An Investigation into Fascist Ecology (2007)

Did the fall of the Fuhrer Adolf Hitler and his Third Reich set back the cause of environmentalism by a hundred years? Does healing Mother Earth of man's crude ravages require the world rule of the white race? These sound like only the delusions of a few neo-fascist boneheads, but they are questions to take seriously. If only because this type of ecological politics is held not just by a few fanatics but very possibly by millions of people. Surprising though it may be, this represents one possible future for insurgent Green politics. Challenging usual assumptions that Green politics must be progressive, the nexus of the radical right and white environmentalism needs to be reexamined.

When we enter environmentalism from way on the other side, from the political far right, it gives us a view that is familiar but in a strange way. What comes into focus is just how blurred the line is between so-called Green fascism and mainstream Green politics and environmentalism.

Green is a New Fascist Color

Fascists are far from indifferent to environmentalism. In fact, they believe themselves to be the true forefathers of today's Green ecological concerns. For example, a letter to the editor published in the *North Carolina Times* in the year 2000:

> "Back a few weeks Steve Stults got all over a Mr. Darréll Beck for something he said about the Green Party and some possible Nazi connections ... Anyone who wishes to research Germany's so called Green connections can read "Blood and Soil: Walther Darré and Hitler's Green Party," written by Anna Bramwell and published by The Kensall Press. The big difference between American Greens and Nazi Greens is that the Nazi Greens were a real item and the American forgery is a collection of phony tree huggers that squeal for conservation but at the same time squeal for open borders and unrestricted immigration. You can't have both, Mr. Stults.
>
> TOM METZGER Fallbrook."

Tom Metzger is, of course, the former national Ku Klux Klan leader who now leads WAR (White Aryan Resistance). So did the fall of the Fuhrer Adolf Hitler and his Third Reich set back the cause of environmentalism a hundred years? Does healing Mother Earth of man's crude ravages require the world rule of the white race?

With such vocal fans from the klan and neo-nazis, it's no surprise that the book *Blood and Soil* has been ignored by the left of center on the political spectrum. Equally forgotten is the book's subject, Nazi Minister of Agriculture R. Walther Darré. Actually, this book is an important intellectual work that is full of surprises. The usual historians of the Nazi era criticize and condemn their subjects, but defiantly punching out to a different drummer, *Blood and Soil* plunges us into the biography of Darré as a peasant leader, whom the author passionately defends as a decent man—and even as a pioneer of today's environmentalism.

Nor is the author, Dr. Anna Bramwell, some fringe neofascist writer as her type of fans might lead you to suspect. She is the most prominent Western historian of ecological politics, and her subsequent study, *Ecology in the 20th Century. A History*, was published by Yale University Press and is widely assigned in college classes. At times Bramwell may sound like some neo-fascist in *Blood and Soil*, but her own very conservative politics are different. Like her Nazi hero, Dr. Anna Bramwell is now deeply involved in remaking the Eastern European frontier: she is currently the administrator overseeing environmental programs in Poland and the rest of Eastern Europe for the European Economic Development Fund. Not a fringe nutcase at all, but a mainstream capitalist environmental official—yet one who traces her ecological politics back to the Third Reich!

The trail is getting warm ...

Re-manufactured Aryan

R. Walther Darré got into environmentalism through his dual interest in both agriculture and ideology, since he was the most powerful peasant political leader in Germany in the 1930s. It really struck me that the persona reflects the ideology here. While Darré and other fascists were proclaiming how the tribal unity of the Aryan race was only "natural," it was in fact so politically compelling in part because it was so completely artificial, manufactured to up-to-date specifications. Like offering teenage boys the chance to play roles in a real life "Star Wars." That's what Darré did, in effect. He remade himself into a peasant leader

although he came from a quite prosperous merchant family. He asserted his German nationalism although he was educated at an English prep school, and was Latin American.

Just like Adolf Hitler or Nazi propaganda head Goebbels, Darré was not a native German. He barely knew where Germany was until he was sent to Europe at age ten. Coming from a prosperous German immigrant merchant family in Argentina, Ricardo Walther Darré is pictured by Dr. Anna Bramwell in her biography as an "accidental" Nazi. He had decided to become an agriculturalist, even obtaining his PhD in farm management during long unemployment in the turbulent 1920s Depression years of the Weimar Republic. Gradually drawn into politics, Darré became known as an independent "Nordic" racial theorist trying to lead North German farmers. He first popularized the memorable slogan "Blood and Soil" in his writings, putting it on everyone's lips for use by future Nazi propaganda.

When Adolf Hitler made his stretch drive towards control of the government in 1930, the fascists were a South German urban party with insufficient support in the countryside. Hitler decided to offer the long-unemployed Darré an important salaried position as the Party leader for the Aryan peasant class, what became known as the Imperial Peasant Leader ("Reichsbaurernfuhrer"). So at that relatively late date Darré first joined the Nazis. After the Nazi Party won state power in 1933, Darré also became Hitler's first Minister of Agriculture for the Third Reich. It was only then that he opportunistically dropped his inconvenient Latin first name and finally gave up the security of his native Argentine citizenship.

Like many other Nazi leaders Darré was a self- manufactured German Aryan. He chose it.

Green & the National Socialist Drive to Power

Imperial Peasant Leader Darré may be completely unknown today except among loyal fascists, but he was a key player in the National Socialist drive to power. Like many other Nazis he was a hardened soldier of capitalist race war. Like his Fuhrer, Darré, too, was a proud nationalistic veteran of the German imperial army. Both men had survived intense combat in the trench warfare of World War I, been wounded, and had been awarded the Iron Cross. Like Hitler, Darré always spoke of his army service in World War I as the happiest time of his life, and after being discharged Darré eagerly joined the Steel Helmets (the Rightist veterans organization). He was to speak bitterly of how he and other right-wing veterans were afraid to wear their uniforms, as any who did were being physically attacked by gangs of "Reds" on the streets (even among military veterans the fascists were far outnumbered then by those in Left veterans' associations).

Darré was never just a thug. His value to the fascist movement was that he had racialist class politics in Green populist clothing. And strong class vision. It wasn't an accident that he was the one who popularized the racist slogan "Blood and Soil," for Darré was a radical Right-Wing leader of the North German peasantry, those family farmers who worked their own small plots of land. As a middle property-owning class, these farmers can swing to either the right or left in times of economic crisis, often being successfuly mobilized by the right as a mass force for rearranging capitalism. As happened in 1920s fascist Italy, in settler White America against the Indian nations, in Canadian support for the Social Credit movement, or in Japan during the u.s. occupation. Just as significantly, in the Vietnamese, Chinese, and many other anti-colonial movements the peasantry became the main force for revolution to the left.

An Austrian urbanite and bohemian like Hitler knew nothing about peasant organizing, but Darré knew enough to lead the entire Party in the countryside. For it was in the

Northern countryside that the Nazi movement put on its most radical face—and became the strongest—as a revolutionary anti-bourgeois movement.

Conservative political parties, such as the Catholic German Center Party of the Weimar era or the Republican Party in today's u.s.a., are pro-bourgeois supporters of the existing capitalist order. Fascism is pro-capitalist but *anti-bourgeois*, and this is a critical difference. The Nazis called for violently purging Aryan society of everything they considered "bourgeois" (and Hitler explicitly used that word as identifying an enemy order). Bourgeois meant a culture preoccupied with the dirty quest for money; rule by decadent aristocrats and bankers; the swarms of "useless" intellectuals; the blurring of the primary biological differences and different missions of men & women; and, of course, the "unnatural" mixing of different races and peoples on sacred Aryan land. Keep in mind that fascism didn't promote capitalists as icons or role models, but called for society to be ruled by a hierarchical statist caste of male warriors.

What Darré's career exemplified was the Nazi populist backing of the Aryan peasantry—small farmers who owned their own little plots of land—against the big aristocratic landowners. Of all the old classes, the one that Hitler and his fellow National Socialists had the most contempt for was the landed gentry and aristocracy, most particularly the Prussian Junkers. Not only did that class personify the inherited privilege that Hitler so resented, but as a class they had staffed the old imperial state. Especially the failed military leadership. (Despite this most aristocrats went over to the Nazis once they saw where things were headed—eventually some 18% of the upper SS leadership were of the aristocracy.) We can see one side of fascism as a partial revolution within the body of capitalism. One that leaves the bourgeoisie in possession of production and distribution, but temporarily no longer in control of the state and nation.

All during the rise of the euro-fascist movements in the 1920s and 1930s, the left dissed & dismissed them as pawns of the capitalist class. Whether in the brilliant German Communist photomontage posters of Heartfield or the pronouncement from Moscow that "fascism is the terroristic dictatorship of the big bourgeoisie," there was a constant message that Italian fascism and German Nazism were only lifeless puppets for the big capitalist class. This was fatally off center and produced an actually disarming picture.

Today we think of fascism so much in terms of its repression, that we forget how much Nazism built its movement by campaigning against big capitalism. One famous National Socialist election poster shows a social-democratic winged "angel" walking hand in hand with a stereotyped banker, with the big slogan: *"Marxism is the Guardian Angel of Capitalism."* Hitler promised to preserve the "good" productive capitalism of ordinary hard working Germans, while wiping out the "bad" parasitic big capitalism of the hidden finance capitalist Jewish bosses. In fact, tens of millions of Americans (and not just white folks) would support such a program right here & now. Fascism blended together a radical resentment against the big bourgeoisie and their State, together with racist nationalist ideology, into a political uprising of the local small bourgeoisie, the lower middle classes, and the declassed (the declassed, or lumpen, are those who have fallen out of the working class or the middle classes and no longer have a relationship to economic production and distribution).

New Nazi leader Darré threw himself and his party followers into the political war for the countryside. There the Brownshirt tide came to run so strongly that Darré once even offered to use his peasant Stormtroopers to just seize the government for Hitler. A measure of Darré's importance to fascism was that his new Agricultural Organization overrode all previously established Nazi Party structures and hierarchies in the rural areas, cutting across provincial and specialized party departments. He even took control of the *Landpost*, the party's rural journal, away from Goebbels' powerful propaganda department. In those years, as Imperial Peasant Leader, Darré reported only to the Fuhrer himself.

The North German countryside was already up in class war, and both Darré's military experience and his new "bio-dynamic" enthusiasm for organic farming served the fascists well. He had quickly built a farm network of party members and sympathizers, tied together by special rural organizers that he had trained in farm issues. Always Darré stressed both the ideological and the practical together. Improved yields through organic intensive farming, plus cooperative associations plus the vision of a neo-tribal Greater Germany, finally able to "reclaim" its supposed historic lands in Eastern Europe and Russia.

The 1930s class war in the countryside had already reached the point of dynamiting government offices and rifle fire breaking up bank auctions of bankrupt farmsteads. Farm activists were receiving prison sentences, while half the farms were losing money. Even "red" Communist organizing was winning supporters. Darré's crash party-building program trained angry farmers to become Nazi public speakers for farmers' unions & cooperatives—but at the same time also experts on land settlement, fertilizers, insurance, debt management, livestock raising, and so on. Not just talk alone, but practical help and sympathetic class organization built the Nazi machine in the countryside.

In December 1931, Darré's rural Nazis captured the elected presidency of the *Landbund*, the large farmers' union. This was just a taste of things to come. As Bramwell notes:

> "In July 1932, Hitler's Party attracted the largest vote it was to have before gaining power, 37.4% of the vote. In a system of multiple minority parties, it was an overwhelming victory. The North German Protestant farmers and villages and small towns had voted for Hitler—averaging some 78.8%. In some areas of the Geest, Nazi votes were 80–100% of the total. The smaller the village, the larger the proportion ..."

Reichsbaurernfuhrer Darré had, essentially, in only a few years led in swinging an entire class to join the Nazi movement. A stunning feat. Not just votes, remember, but whole villages as fascist eyes and ears, and new thousands of Stormtroopers who could be trucked into the cities at critical moments—no wonder a proud Darré could offer to seize state power for the Fuhrer. This wasn't just declassed fascists being thugs for the big capitalists, as the Communists endlessly shouted to no effect. It was a different dissenting class politics, and for awhile, until the long awaited War began, the Aryan peasantry was seemingly rewarded with new preferential policies and laws.

Dr. Anna Bramwell claims that what Darré argued for in writings and promised through his Nazi peasant movement, he actually *did* once installed as Reichsminister. He was already under the influence of the naturalist, "bio-dynamic" agricultural theories of the white supremacist nature-romantic Rudolph Steiner. Organic farming, Nazi-sponsored marketing cooperatives, new inheritance laws preserving small farms, as well as forested green belts and other soil conservation measures were at first promoted. With difficulty, Darré attempted to get measures adopted by the new regime favoring small peasant family farms over the large aristocratic estates.

When Ecology is Really Ideology

i think that the subject here—for Darré as well as for us—is really more fascist ideology than ecology. A confession: i really like Bramwell's book. Instead of bland academic abstraction, she really was unafraid to challenge the whole tilt of existing historical work on this subject. Her work doesn't allow us to just nod along, but presses us from out of ambush to reexamine and defend our own views. This is simply a book from hell. And not for the politically faint of heart. There are always books that slip through the cracks, go out of print, but still have a fevered cult following, and *Blood and Soil* is right up there as one of those cult books. The kicker here is that for good reasons this book's loyal fans tend to be of the neo-nazi persuasion, as we will discuss later.

So this is a political biography of a Nazi leader, but it is definitely not what we're used to. The author defiantly praises and identifies with her subject. Bramwell tells us:

> "Darré was to write before his death that he had been a fool to think that the Nazis could have repaired the broken link between man and soil, nature and God ... It is the core of my argument that one should not let the existence of the uniforms and swastikas interfere with the evaluation of Darré's attempt to 'watch over the inviolability of the possible'. He was guardian of a radical, centrist, republican critique which pre-dated National Socialism, and which still lives on."

Bramwell definitely uses every ideological trick her steely mind can think of to defend Reichsminister Darré's honor and politics. That is, she gives us a cram course in white racist and capitalist evasions, justifications, and half-truths ("Oh, please don't be so narrow-minded as to let the SS uniforms and swastikas influence your opinion!"). i mean, she's really "bombs away" on this, and her mad reactionary diva performance alone would be worth the price of admission. But there's much more, including serious political discussion of a reactionary class point of view.

Far from being deferential to her former Cambridge University colleagues, the author is open in her hatred of socialist intellectuals (on this point her opinion is much too timid and conformist for me). Bramwell, noting the death toll of Stalinist crimes, suggests that being a fascist while a mistake is not nearly as bad as being a socialist. So at the very least, *Blood and Soil* gives us a workout, exercising us against the skewed worldview of half-truths used to justify the Nazi experiment at ending humanity. And this book gives us much more than that, for it carries the understanding that fascism is not conservative but anti-bourgeois, violently radical. This is the radioactive element at the heart of fascism's continuing danger to us in the mutating world.

In author Anna Bramwell's eyes, Reichsminister Darré was no racist criminal but a true popular leader and ecological visionary. Bramwell convincingly details how awkward he was at inner party intrigue and politicking, how he never understood the power games of his Party rivals, refusing to make friends while indifferent to his growing intra-Party enemies. Of course, being a bad fit as a party animal didn't make Reichsminister Darré any less of a fascist, and this is typical of Bramwell's sly uses of half truths to advance bigger lies. Trying to reposition Darré as a "centrist" not a member of the far right, as a "republican" although he was a leader for ten years in a fascist movement that openly despised democracy and promised dictatorship, war, and terror.

Reichsminister Darré's Oxford biographer uses his agricultural career, his interest in defending German family farmers, even his non-conforming racial theories (some of Darré's early racist comrades ended up as Gestapo suspects for being enemies of Hitler to the ultraracist Right). All to push forward a picture of Darré as a peaceful radical idealist trying to help the poor and forgotten of the countryside. *"Like a more nationalist Che Guevara, he opposed capitalism and the town,"* is how she clumsily tries to reposition him. This is a bit over the top. **Speaking for himself, Darré made it clear that his big problem with urbanism wasn't capitalism but Black people and Jews.**

Darré's fascist idealization of pastoral living, small family farms, and rural life wasn't a plan for peace. Under his guidance the SS developed a concept of Master Race forward settlements, whereby German peasants would be soldier-farmers who would grow their own food, rule their own households of women and children, and band together in armed Aryan militias under the SS to gradually cleanse the frontier of the inferior natives. This was modeled on the experience of white American settlers on the Western frontier, only for him the white frontier was the East, and the natives useless to civilization weren't Indians but Poles, Latvians, Czechs, Romany, Ukrainians, and Russians. As Darré said:

> "The German people cannot help coming to terms [with the Eastern problem]. The Slavs know what they want—we don't! We look on with dumb resignation while formerly purely German cities—Reval, Riga, Warsaw and so forth, are lost to our people ... The German people cannot avoid a life or death struggle with the advancing East. Our people must prepare for the struggle ... only one solution for us, absolute victory! Furthermore, the concept of Blood and Soil gives us the right to take back as much Eastern land as is necessary to achieve harmony between the body of our people and geo-political space."

As is so often the case in fascist politics, bloody plans for genocidal aggression are justified as only self-defense, as only restoring what is "natural," and by the maudlin self-pity of oppressors. Invading and conquering other nations is justified as "taking back" land. Unlike Hitler, Darré's kind of expansionism would have been more gradual, incremental, always talking of the right of ethnic regroupment on the sacred tribal land—much like Sharon's genocidal policies in Israel. And like Israel's steady, violent squeezing of the Palestinians back further and further off of their lands, Darré for all his "natural" talk would have used the machine gun and the tank as his main agricultural tools.

The conquest and genocidal absorption of Poland, Czechoslavakia, Latvia, Estonia, and the rest of the East was a major tenet in Nazi doctrine. Reichsminister Darré was right on the same page as Adolf Hitler in depicting the other peoples of Eastern Europe as somehow "advancing" on poor innocent Germany, while demanding that cities like Warsaw be ethnically cleansed into German cities in the name of restoring what was natural. Darré also always insisted on Germans' "right" to seize as much territory as they wanted from other peoples.

So there was no real difference between Darré and other SS strategists such as SS Oberfuhrer Konrad Meyer, the author of the infamous "General Plan East" (which was approved by both Hitler and Himmler). Under "General Plan East" at least 31 million of the then 45 million inhabitants of Eastern Europe would have been eliminated—they used the word "deported." Jews were not included in these numbers, of course, since it was assumed that they would already have been exterminated. Then the annexed lands would have been thoroughly "Germanized." Bernt Englemann, in his account of being in the anti-fascist underground during WWII, quotes from a conversation then with his Nazi cousin Gudrun. She had married an SS Gruppenfuhrer and police lieutenant general serving in the fascist Government General of Poland:

> "The Government General, as it's called now, is just sort of a colony. The Poles are being trained to work for us. Horst-Eberhard told me the Fuhrer wants to give the whole country to the SS as a present. Then they'll build fortresses, and every deserving SS soldier will get his own estate and a few thousand Poles as workers. It sounds boring to me—I'd rather be in Berlin."

Naturally, in this violent "solution" (a favorite word of Darré and his Nazi comrades, since it implies a prior problem where none existed) there was no "geo-political space" for the millions of Jews in the East. Darré the agriculturalist referred to Jews as "weeds" and "essentially parasitic." We certainly don't have to guess what that meant. Yet his biographer claims that Darré was not a real anti-semite, and wasn't involved in the Holocaust. Of course, in researching her book she couldn't find one word or act by Darré opposing the attacks against the Jews of Europe. The very idea that someone who was a top Nazi leader wasn't *for* racist crimes and genocide stretches belief way beyond reason. That Darré may have been more wisely discreet on this subject doesn't mean that he had any significant differences with Hitler (about whom Darré wrote privately that he was in "awe" of) or with his party ally and one-time friend Heinrich Himmler of the SS.

We've arrived at a point here. Reichminister Darré's kind of "love" of nature could not simply be, was not just itself, but was a romanticized part of his ideological racism-nationalism. Just as his idealized vision of the peasantry and uncomplicated village life had its roots in his fear of "contamination" by inferior races (who must be physically removed). He denounced the cosmopolitan cities with their "... danger of uncontrolled introduction of inferior blood with natural children. One thinks of the large towns, where the dark-skinned student, the colored artist, the jazz trumpter, etc. ... feel perfectly at home ..."

If there was a foredoomed quality to Darré's white pastoral fantasies, it was not only because a resurgent fascist-capitalist Germany would demand air fleets, panzer divisions, and a heavy petro-chemical industrial base for oppressor civilization. Even Darré's simple frontier settlements would have required an ever-present modern military—since the conquest of other nations, the enslavement and elimination of tens of millions was not going to happen without heavy resistance (too heavy for our macho Nazis to handle, as it turned out).

Even beyond that, the very idea of Imperial Peasant Leader Darré as an "ecologist" strikes a false note. We're running into a good case of deceptive advertising for Aryan politics. It is telling that in this political biography—despite the subtitle—racism occupies a much larger place than ecology. For the simple reason that Reichsminister Darré's record on racist-nationalist ideology was far greater than his record on ecology. Even leaving aside the reality that someone who wanted the military invasion of all Eastern Europe and the wholesale ethnic cleansing of cities like Warsaw, has a strange relationship to the word "ecology." Darré advocated smaller, more carefully farmed family agriculture, using organic methods not chemical fertilizers and pesticides, because it improved yields and peasant income, and decreased the relative power in the countryside of the "upper class" landed gentry. Needless to say, it was also a policy thrifty with expensive imported petro-chemical stocks (Germany had to import all of its oil). Hitler was delighted with this program—as he said, a good grain harvest was *"worth twenty-two divisions"* to him.

Ricardo Walther Darré's supposed "Green" politics were more in the category of *husbandry*, the careful & thrifty exploitation of Man's resources, rather than any true environmentalism. Which shouldn't be any big news, since the same better living through more commercial management philosophy soaks through contemporary capitalist environmentalism here ... as species disappear and the earth is sterilized.

Not Going Down With Adolf

An important point in Bramwell's defense of Reichsminister Darré is his break with Hitler, which she uses to disassociate him from Nazism's moral trajectory. Again, this is an inspired use of a half-truth to promote a larger lie. While she tries to picture Darré as naively principled, he ends up coming across as narrow-minded but shrewdly opportunistic, self-centered beyond loyalties to any movement or party. A number of early fascist leaders fell out with Hitler, but unlike Darré most of them ended up being executed or else fleeing into exile. Reichsminister Darré ended up out-surviving not only many of them but the Fuhrer himself, deftly stepping out of the way as his Nazi movement and their tank divisions motored off into the abyss.

Reichsminister Darré quietly opposed Hitler's 1939 decision to go to war, making his views known within the top levels of the Party, but only there. He was even more opposed to

Darré speaking at a Reich Food Society (Reichsnährstand) assembly under the slogan Blut und Boden, Blood and soil, in Goslar, 1937.

Hitler's later decision to invade the USSR—though of course not on moral or humanitarian grounds. Darré judged that the earlier "Hitler-Stalin Pact" of 1937, trading Russian oil and minerals for German military technology while agreeing to divide Finland between them, had allowed the Red Army to grow too strong. This part of his opposition to the war was really just tactical, although his pessimistic judgement proved to be accurate.

Reichsminister Darré's broader objection was from the ideological imperative of racism. That such new conquests changed Germany from an ethnic empire into a colonial empire, diluting the foremost goal of a racially "pure" Germany. An immediately expanding empire and world war was forcing Germany to incorporate more and more non-Germans into its institutions. As an example of what he meant, by 1945 the majority of the elite SS soldiers were non-

German, while 60–80% of the workers in various defense industries were non-German as well. Biographer Bramwell suggests that Darré was a reasonable racist-nationalist (which she implies was good) while "real" Nazis like SS chief Himmler were greater empire expansionists (which she implies was bad). i say, shoot them both and worry about the slight differences later!

Just before he joined the Nazi Party, Darré wrote a pamphlet *"Why Colonies?"* which positioned him as one of the Inner Colony nationalists. They advocated redeveloping Greater Germany (including the Eastern frontier, of course) racially as the alternative to unsuccessful Third World conquests. Even a large continental empire would inevitably mean that Germany's borders would include an "unhealthy" polyglot mix of different peoples (here in the u.s. Pat Buchanan has the same point of view). While to Darré, Germany's future strength as a nation depended upon the "purity" of the possession of her territory by only those of the Master Race. As Bramwell puts it:

> "The basic difference between Darré and Himmler was that Darré was a racial-tribalist, and Himmler an imperialist with romantic racial overtones."

It's hard not to laugh when reading about a "basic difference" like that. Bramwell breaks a sweat finding ways to describe Darré's fascist racism in a positive spin, with neutral-sounding labels. Just as she repeatedly interprets Darré's racism as "only defensive." She writes: *"Darré's position seems to have been that he was a political anti-semite, and felt no personal animus towards particular Jews ... Many of Darré's attacks on Jews were because he associated them with democracy."* It's nice to know that he didn't mean anything "personal" in helping to create the Holocaust.

In the early 1930s, Darré was a powerful ideological force within the developing Party. Both in public writings & in inner party struggles, Darré fought for ever more racist thinking as the determinant of all policy. That he considered the 1930 Nazi Party as not dedicated *enough* to Master Race politics gives you an idea of exactly how racist Darré was. While Hitler was a fantasy Aryan, Darré was a hard-core "Nordicist," a believer in an imaginary Nordic superior race of tall blond-haired men that inhabited Scandinavia and North Germany. In their view, the short dark-haired South Germans and Austrians (such as one Corporal Adolf Hitler) were at best of mixed blood and not true members of the Master Race. Darré never abandoned these views but did soft-pedal them once he joined the South German–based Nazis.

Reichsminister Darré dismissed his hated rival Goebbels, the party propaganda czar, as not being up to *"scientific racial thinking."* Darré's main personal friend and ally in the party hierarchy was none other than SS chief Heinrich Himmler. In those early years the Brownshirts of the SA (*Sturmabteilung* or Stormtroopers) were the mass paramilitary arm of the Party, the street fighters, while the black-clad SS (*Schutszstaffel* or Security Squad) were growing from being Hitler's small elite bodyguard into a future ideological military caste, the very heart of the Nazi subculture.

Imperial Peasant Leader Darré was also simultaneously a top SS officer, the first chief of the SS Race and Settlement Office. He was one of the ideological godfathers of the SS, having helped mold the young organization. It was Darré who introduced the idea of regular SS classes on racist theory, and, in 1931, he convinced SS chief Himmler to make racial examination of all prospective brides of SS men a mandatory requirement. The idea of mass "racial examinations" of women is hard to explain as Green politics, but this fetish about women's biology was an obsession of Darré's (and many other Nazi pervs as well).

It was not as an environmentalist that Darré was best known then, but as one of the most extreme and controversial racial theorists. The 1920s & 1930s was a time when eugenics, that racist pseudo-science, was riding high in Western capitalism. Darré added his voice to those arguing that the white master race had to be "rescued" genetically by culling out not only the "contamination" of other races but inferior whites as well. Parents should leave defective children to die, as wild beasts do. Even his own children if necessary, Darré said. All German women should be subjected to racial heredity examinations, and graded into different categories regulating marriage and child-bearing. Men, he believed, could prove their racial soundness by their achievements, but since he believed that women could have no achievements to judge, their child-bearing value to the Master Race could only be determined by physical examination and tracing their family background. This, too, was preserving the natural environment according to Darré.

Privately, Darré had asserted that even his own children were not "100%" Master Race enough in their heredity. But, he added, if his wife (whom he had abandoned to marry someone younger and much wealthier) worked hard enough at their children's racist upbringing, they could at least grow up to be satisfactory German citizens. No wonder that some other Rightist nationalists sneered at what they called Darré's "chicken-breeding mentality," while he was hated by more than a few nationalist women. **Contrary to what his faithful biographer claims, there is a direct connection between the vanguard racist-sexist ideology spread by Darré and others, and the gas chambers at Auschwitz.**

By 1939 Darré was only a figurehead minister in a tailored black SS uniform (Hitler hated to change his cabinet ministers in public, so let Darré stay on as a figurehead sitting in an isolated office, while his deputy became the real minister). Even the Allied War Crimes Tribunal after the war decided that he'd been out of the loop, and Darré ended up escaping the hangman's noose, serving only five years in prison (in his cell he still received mail from German farmers requesting advice or help addressed to "Minister Darré"). For his biographer this triumphantly confirms that he did nothing wrong. A more searching interpretation might be that the Allied Powers were indifferent to genocidal fascist politics per se. (Remember that British prime minister Winston Churchill had even publicly expressed his regret that Mussolini had sided with Germany instead of allying fascist Italy with Britain and the u.s.)

Charged initially with many crimes, Reichsminister Darré ended up being convicted on only one charge, that of expropriating "hundreds of thousands of Polish and Jewish farmers." Kind of like being part of the group that attacked the World Trade Center but getting sentenced only for illegally double-parking at the airport. Turns out—not too surprisingly—that being a Nazi cabinet minister was less criminal to world capitalism than "Driving While Black" on highway I-95.

Survival of the fittest?

Paradoxically, the Nazi movement believed itself to be in harmony with Nature—even with all its intoxicating shouting clanking hierarchical-mechanical subculture and snappy film set costumes. Of course, by "Nature" fascists didn't recognize an ecology with complex interaction & interdependency of all the myriad life forms. Fascists tried to own nature as their own capitalist ideological property, and Nazism in particular projected its own ruthlessly mechanistic class agenda onto the "natural." Ernest Lehmann, a Nazi professor of botany, declared that fascism was only "politically applied biology." They saw a hierarchical food chain, a ceaseless conflict of stronger predators upon weaker prey, as the perfect metaphor for their own terroristic political economy.

It was only "Nature's law" to Hitler and Darré for one biological group—a species or a race—to totally unite under its strongest males to compete with other species or races for territory and resources. For crows to war with wrens, wolves to dominate elk, and master race civilization to rise up on the conquest and slave labor of the inferior races. Some Nazi leaders even mused about a fantastic science-fiction re-population of Afrika by millions of Aryans, supported by vast labor armies of slave Black workers. Peter Staudenmaier perceptively remarks:

> "Such arguments have a chilling currency within contemporary ecological discourse: the key to social-ecological harmony is ascertaining 'the eternal laws of nature's processes' (Hitler) and organizing society to correspond to them. The Fuhrer was particularly fond of stressing the 'helplessness of humankind in the face of nature's everlasting law.' Echoing Haeckel and the Monists, *Mein Kampf* announces: 'When people attempt to rebel against the iron logic of nature, they come into conflict with the very same principles to which they owe their existence as human beings. Their actions against nature must lead to their own downfall.'
>
> "The authoritarian implications of this view of humanity and nature become even clearer in the context of the Nazis' emphasis on holism and organicism. In 1934 the director of the Reich Agency for Nature Protection, Walther Schoenichen, established the following objectives for biology curricula: 'Very early, the youth must develop an understanding of the civic importance of the "organism," i.e. the co-ordination of all parts and organs for the benefit of the one and superior task of life.'"

In the Nazi worldview the superior being was a predator. This supposed recognition of "Nature's laws" is just capitalist culture with a biological wrapper. In life it isn't true. The lofty eagle isn't any more successful than mom sparrow. If anything, less so. If survival and dominance were everything, cockroaches might get olympic gold. Ecology is endless diversity, unending change, and development and interdependency of life forms that is complex beyond Man the Manager.

Again, there are class issues hidden in these man-made pronouncements about "Nature." Although the Nazis always claimed to be a "Workers Party" (and at their electoral peak in 1932 received about 25% of their votes from workers, primarily the long-term unemployed), this ideology of "nature's iron laws" was profoundly anti–working class. The so-called German National Socialist Workers Party had intractable problems with the German proletariat. Which is why both Hitler and Darré wanted to do radical surgery and actually eliminate the German proletariat as a class. Which was done.

For even political conquest hadn't eliminated National Socialism's constant clashing with its own industrial working class. As the Party's German Labor Front reported in 1937 over mass resistance to speed-ups and Taylorism: *"Workers, whether of National Socialist persuasion or not, still hold on to the Marxist and union position of rejecting critera of production ... Controls over individual achievement are rejected. Therefore they resist all attempts to time them."* Remember that until well after 1933 the Nazis could venture into hard-core proletarian neighborhoods only in large groups.

As we've discussed, Imperial Peasant Leader Darré wanted to de-urbanize German society, limiting industrialization. Which would have automatically shrunk the proletariat. They would have become a useful niche class, in a society dominated by militias of racist militarized peasants, just like the mythic u.s. frontier that Darré admired so much. Instead, the Nazis pursued Adolf Hitler's evolving strategy, which was to simultaneously promote both techno-industrial development and the Aryan re-organization of classes spilling over frontiers. After all, if it is the superior race man's destiny to be both a fierce soldier and ruler over others—as the Nazis held as a core belief—then how can he at the same time be shelving groceries for women at the supermarket or bucking production on the assembly line?

Fascism de-proletarianized Aryan society. Or to put it more precisely: it created an Aryan society that had never existed before by de-proletarianizing the former German society. By the millions, Aryan men were shifted into military service and into being labor aristocrats, supervisors, straw bosses, and minor bureaucrats of every sort. In 1940 Nazi Labor Front leader Robert Ley said in a speech: *"In ten years Germany will be transformed beyond recognition. A nation of proletarians will have become a nation of rulers. In ten years a German worker will look better than an English lord does today."* The new proletariat that started emerging was heavily made up of involuntary foreign & slave laborers, and—despite Nazi ideology about women's "natural" place in the kitchen and nursery—was largely becoming a proletariat of women.

Nazi slave labor is seldom dealt with in its class reality. Usually it is mentioned as a side-effect of the Holocaust, or as a short-lived desperate measure of a tottering regime facing military defeat on all fronts. The truth is that it was much more than that: slave and semi-slave labor was a necessary feature of mature Nazi society. If Hitler had been successful, slave labor would have gone on for his entire lifetime and beyond. Even conquered Eastern Europe and Russia, in official Nazi plans, would gradually have given way to the spread of vast Aryan-owned agricultural estates, whose rural proletariat would have been involuntarily furnished by the inferior races.

By 1941 there were three million foreign & slave proletarians at work in National Socialist factories, farms, and mines. Coincidentally, the SS—which had only 116 men at its first public display at the July 4, 1926, Party Rally at Weimar (the u.s.a. and the Nazis celebrate the same founding holiday)—had also grown to three million. Soon the overrun territories of Europe and the East provided over four million more slave laborers for Nazi industry & the war machine (the majority of whom were used up, consumed, that is to say killed, in accelerated capitalist production). The fascist class structure that had cloaked itself in Nature was revealed to be bizarrely artificial. Nazism's peculiar class structure was parasitic as a mode of life. One history sums this up:

> "The regime's increasing use of concentration camp and foreign forced labour made the working class more or less passive accomplices in Nazi racial policy ... The first 'recruits' were unemployed Polish agricultural labourers, who were soon accompanied by prisoners of war and people abducted en masse from cinemas and churches. These were then followed by the French. By the summer of 1941 there were some three million foreign workers in Germany, a figure which mushroomed to 7.7 million in the autumn of 1944 ... A high proportion of these workers were either young or female. By 1944, a quarter of those working in the German economy were foreigners. Virtually every German worker was thus confronted by the fact and practice of Nazi racism. In some branches of industry, German workers merely constituted a thin, supervisory layer above a workforce of which between 80 and 90 percent were foreigners. This tends to be passed over by historians of the labour movement.
>
> "Treatment of these foreign workers was largely determined by their 'racial' origins. Broadly speaking, the usual hierarchy consisted of 'German workers' at the top, 'west workers' a stage below them, and Poles and 'eastern workers' at the lowest level. This racial hierarchy determined both living conditions and the degree of coercion to which foreign workers were subjected both at the workplace and in society at large."

Darré's early friend & collaborator, SS leader Heinrich Himmler, knowing the distance they were pushing their own cadre to mutate, urged them on in unmistakable terms:

> *"The SS man is to be guided by one principle alone: honesty, decency, loyalty, and friendship towards those of our blood, and to no one else ... Whether other peoples live in plenty or starve to death interests me only insofar as we need them as slaves for our culture; for the rest it does not interest me. Whether 10,000 Russian women keel over from exhaustion in the construction of an anti-tank ditch interests me only insofar as the ditch for Germany gets finished. We will never be savage or heartless where we don't have to be; that is obvious. Germans are after all the only people in the world who treat animals decently ... If someone comes to me and tells me, 'I cannot dig these anti-tank ditches with children or with women, it is inhuman, they will die on the job,' I must say to him, 'You are a murderer of your own blood' ..."*

This is like a criminal investigation, where digging up the basement of a suburban home suddenly unearths a jumble of bodies. We started with "Green Nazi" R. Walther Darré and the claims for his ecological pioneering. Yet, step by step, we've followed a corridor until finally we turn a corner ... into the "ecology" of a slaughterhouse, and a capitalism temporarily given seeming paranormal strength by the radical resection and fusion of race, class, and gender.

Green Nazi Tip of the Capitalist Iceberg

R. Walther Darré and other Rightist Green politicians could be significant to new generations of neo-fascists, and not only because they give fascism a plausible claim to being the forefather of today's ecology movement. Far from being a political innocent, Darré was if anything even more developed about his racial supremacy than Hitler, and was certainly more practical and strategic. Who knows, if his views had prevailed maybe the Nazi Party might still be ruling Western Europe today? His rural settler strategy is in tune with much of the white racist Far Right in the u.s. (no small coincidence, since like Adolf Hitler himself Darré used the u.s. white settler Western frontier as his genocidal model). It all pushes us to check out what words like "Green," "Nature," "ecology," and "peasant" mean in our politics.

First of all, capitalist culture has always exemplified Social Darwinism, using a manipulated model of nature to justify its hierarchical class civilization as merely "natural." Hitler, Darré, and the other Nazi ideologists were just the most glaring tip of the iceberg. John D. Rockefeller built the Standard Oil petro-monopoly not only by business guile but by fraud, bombings, arson, and the violent repression of both Indian land rights and workers' unionism. Yet, he always justified his success as Hitler did his genocide, by stressing how it came about in accordance to "Nature's laws": *"The growth of a large business is merely survival of the fittest,"* Rockefeller once said. *"The American Beauty Rose can be produced in the splendor and fragrance which brings cheer to its beholder only by sacrificing the early buds which grow around it. This is not an evil tendency in business. It is merely the working out of a law of nature and a law of God."*

Peter Staudenmaier and Janet Diehl, in their valuable study *Ecofascism: Lessons From the German Experience**, use phrases like "untrustworthy" and "grave error" on the rare occasions they discuss Bramwell's book. They gently say that her "grave error in judgement indicates the powerfully disorienting pull of an 'ecological' aura."

This is an interesting kind of polite misstatement, this claim that Bramwell's defense of Darré's politics comes from her sympathy with his environmental vision. No, it's the attraction of his racist class politics that has so magnetized her to the big white supremacist refrigerator. People's moral disorientation doesn't come from anything ecological—how

---

* Not only available in print as a book, but the entire first edition is posted online at www.spunk.org/library/places/germany/sp001630/ecofasc.html

can it? that's just the cover story—but from the continuing attraction of capitalist racism. That's true whether we're talking about Reichsminister Darré or Ralph Nader.

The London Telegraph of September 3, 2000, reported:

> "BRITISH neo-nazi groups are attempting to hijack the animal rights campaign by infiltrating protest groups ... The neo-nazi groups are frequenting animal rights demonstrations in an attempt to capitalise upon the tensions and controversy generated by the issue. Many of them subscribe to Adolf Hitler's orignal doctrine of a vegetarian, chemically untainted agrarian society in which vivisection is outlawed.
>
> "Their template is the so-called 'Blood and Soil' doctrine drawn up by Hitler's agricultural minister Walther Darré. Their adherence to racist doctrine is, however, only thinly veiled ..."

As useful as it is to blow away illusions about Green Nazis, it is even more useful to understand how these lessons apply. It's not about the past, it's about the future. The Darré type of "Green" policy with its air-brushed romanticizing of nature and similar stage props is very popular right now. As we know, labels are so important in capitalist mass civilization. Every shoddy product seems to say "new" or "natural" on the box. Same with Green politics.

Trying to shrink down environmentalism so it could fit inside Reichsminister Darré's steel helmet, Dr. Anna Bramwell basically defines it as organic family farming, conservation, and better technology: *"On the whole, ecologists do not call for a return to pre-industrial ways of life as such. They tend rather to stress research into new forms of technology which are more suitable to small communities, and which would avoid damaging the balance of nature to the extent observable today ... It is not widely known that similar ecological ideas were being put forward by Darré in National Socialist Germany, often using the same phrases and arguments as are used today.."*

She is correct, but only when we turn her meaning upside down.

There is no question that if anything she understates her case. Led by Darré and Hitler, the Third Reich was the first European nation to make cruelty to animals a crime, to set up forested green belts and other anti-erosion measures, to push organic small farming as the main form of agriculture. Side by side with a high-tech military of millions of soldiers. This is the pattern that u.s. Green politics are only following. The Nazi Party certainly had a much better record on ecology than u.s. president George W. Bush and his administration have. Certainly the Darré wing of the Nazi movement were pioneers. The question is ... pioneers of what?

We're running head on into that popular illogical notion that being for something healthy somehow means that you are a good person. Adolf Hitler himself was a veritable Olympian of all the "healthy" and "natural," not only a vegetarian but one who used alternative health care, who ordered cigarettes stripped from his soldiers' ration packs, and who passed the first laws banning experimentation on animals. (Kind of like, "Don't experiment on animals, use Jews and Romany. And don't smoke while you do it.")

The Nazi policies were the very model for the modern capitalist industrial commercial "environmentalism" that's the mainstream of today's Green politics. Which is why Germany's Green Party voted for approval of the u.s. invasion of Afghanistan, and why America's Green Party has been working with far-right white supremacists. And their environmentalism isn't much better.

Theirs is the kind of boutique environmentalism that trims around the edges of the huge global capitalist machinery. Well intentioned though it might be for some, it is essentially a fraud. Small organic farming is good in itself but only a sand grain lost in the global landslide of ecological destruction that capitalism has unleashed. The mass dying of coral reefs and frogs and certain marine and bird species, the suburban cementing over of the landscape, disappearance of mature forests and marshlands to say nothing of wilderness, spreading desertification in Africa and Eurasia, new epidemics claiming millions of lives, bio-genetic industrial agriculture with compulsory ingestion of hormones and antibiotics, huge skyscraper cities being expanded without any natural water resources, global warming, loss of the ozone layer—these are capitalist ecological disasters on a scale difficult to grasp. But they are now just ordinary things we know and live with.

Today in America everyone is "for" the environment. It's just that no one wants to give up their white-collar job in some air-conditioned officeplex, their right to travel the concrete highways in their air-conditioned SUV on the way back to their air-conditioned suburban home, which is filled with "consumer electronics" and closets packed with clothing imported on container ships across oceans. Does everyone on planet Earth have the right to such a distorted lifestyle? What happens as the billions of Asia, Latin America, Africa, and the Middle East start to reach for this advanced capitalist life (they are being aimed there, that's for sure)? Now that researchers have discovered that jet airplane exhausts are the principal cause of the thinning of the ozone layer, what country will be the first to give up air travel? Would Americans vote for abandoning JFK and LAX? To realize that industrial capitalism is the deepening negation of all healthy ecology is not just to criticize corporations, but to see the real price of actual capitalist civilization as a whole.

Those who do see this great threat and act on it suddenly find themselves labeled as enemies of civilization. The late Judy Bari of Earth First!, who not only organized against destroying first growth forests but also defended timber workers and mountain communities, was car-bombed with obvious f.b.i. complicity and then was herself arrested as a "terrorist."

Meanwhile some white defenders of the environment have decided that reducing the busload on planet Earth through genocide is both necessary and "natural" (another supposed eco-thought that the Nazis had anticipated). These are small but dangerous trends in a world where genocide has become an unspoken social tool. Because it represents a reflexive response within contemporary capitalism to crisis of the social environment, the publicized quest for "natural" purity is the visible symbol of a deeper hunger for a certain kind of repressive "social purity" (just as the German nationalists yearned for). Many people in Tokyo or Aspen or Vienna support these kinds of ideas, but they don't have anything to do with Nature. Just as some of the wealthy backers of today's Anti-Globalization movement want an advanced capitalist metropolis that is like a green parkland—with all the dirty basic industry and agro production pushed out to the slums of the Third World periphery. The Big House and the Field, only to global scale.

The eco-writer Edward Abbey, author of *The Monkey Wrench Gang* and the literary saint of the white radical ecology movement, was well known for his opposition to big corporations and their government. Less publicized was his dislike of Blacks, Latinos, and Indians (though he did put a Tonto figure or two in his stories), whom he thought had to be limited and controlled by whites in order to protect the holy wilderness. Like his fellow Aryan eco-writer, Reichsminister Darré, Edward Abbey wanted the militarization of the national borders to prevent the lesser races from immigrating. He was sincere in his subjective love of the wilderness, but politically it was a facet in his overall racist-nationalism. Just as those suburbanites worried about the fate of mountain gorillas in Africa push for Western-style military controls over the local populations there.

Fortress America's foremost Green politician is Ralph Nader, Washington "consumer advocate" and the Green Party's presidential candidate in the 2000 elections. Nader has for years been in a tight alliance with various white supremacist figures, notably far rightist Pat Buchanan (who like Darré and Abbey also calls for militarization of the border to keep out the inferior races) and racist textile billionaire Ralph Milliken. One fruit of that well-paid alliance was the election of George W. Bush, where Nader's 6% of the Florida vote skimmed off enough liberal votes to help hand the right wing of the Republican Party the presidential election. Because of his Green image, Nader could win support for a covert right-wing agenda of nationalism, economic protectionism, and white supremacy from environmentalists and even old left groups.

This is being written in part for generations that have no experience with fascism as a mass happening (or with violent government repression, for that matter). We should be thoughtful about who we work with, whose campaigns we are supporting. Whether it's the environment or Anti-Globalization or anti-racism, criticizing some obvious evil is easy for anyone to do. And sometimes masks disturbing agendas that orbit around the most reactionary aspects of capitalism.

When we remember that Dr. Bramwell, an admirer of "Hitler's Green Party," is one of the foremost environmental administrators in Europe, we can see a trend. Supposed Green concerns that are really romanticized symbols growing out of a variety of regressive capitalist politics. The ongoing class struggles between oppressor and oppressed are the deep structures of politics, and even the ecological concerns which seem at first so simple can only be acted on in this context. Human self-liberation from oppression is the prerequisite for saving the Earth.

White riot against busing, South Boston, 1975.

When Race Burns Class: Settlers Revisited (2000)

Solidarity: *In the early eighties you wrote* Settlers: Mythology of the White Proletariat, *a book which had a major impact on many North American anti-imperialists. How did this book come about, and what was so new about its way of looking at things?*

J. Sakai: *Settlers* completely came about by accident, not design. And what was so "new" about it was that it wasn't "inspiring" propaganda, but took up the experience of colonial workers to question how class really worked. It wasn't about race, but about class. Although people still have a hard time getting used to that—it isn't race or sex that's the taboo subject in this culture, but class.

Like many radicals who struggle as organizers, i had wondered why our very logical "class unity" theories always seemed to get smashed up around the exit ramp of race? At the time i'd quit my fairly isolated job on the night shift as a mechanic on the railroad, and was running a cut-off lathe in an auto parts plant. The young white guys in our department were pretty good. In fact, rebellious counter-culture dope smoking Nam vets. After months of hanging & talking, one night one of them came up to me and said that all the guys were driving down to the Kentucky Derby together, to spend the weekend getting drunk and partying. They were inviting me, an Asian, as a way of my joining the crew. Only, he said, "You got to stop talking to those Blacks. You got to choose. White or Black."

Every lunch hour i dropped in on a scene on the loading dock, where a dozen brothers munched sandwiches and had an ongoing discussion. About everything from the latest sex scandal to whether it was good or not for Third World nations to be getting A-bombs (some said it was good ending the white monopoly on nuclear weapons, while others said not at the price of endangering our asses!). Plus the guy from the League of Black Revolutionary Workers in our plant area had recruited me to help out, since he was facing heavy going from the older, more established Black political tendencies (various nationalists, the CPUSA—which had great veterans, good shop floor militants—etc.). And why would i go along with some apartheid agenda anyway? Needless to say, the white young guys cut me dead after that (though they later came out for me as shop steward, which shows you how much b.s. they thought the union was).

That kind of stuff, familiar to us all, kept piling up in my mind and got me started trying to figure out how this had come about in the u.s. working class. So for years after this i read labor history and asked older trade union radicals questions whenever i could. Finally, an anarchist veteran of the autoworkers' historic 1937 Flint Sit-Down strike told me that the strike had been Jim Crow, that one of the unpublicized demands had been to keep Black workers down as only janitors ... or out of the plants altogether. This blew my mind. That's when it hit me that the wonderful working-class history that the movement had taught us was a lie.

So i decided to write an article (famous writer's delusion) on how this white supremacy started in the u.s. working class. i didn't know—maybe it was in the 1920s?, i thought. So *Settlers* was researched backwards. i knew what the conclusion was in the mid-1970s, that white supremacy ruled the white working class except in the self-delusions of the Left. "No politician can ever be too racist to be popular in white amerikkka," is an amazingly true saying. *Settlers* was researched going back in time, trying to find that event, that turning point when working-class unity by whites had dissolved into racial supremacy—1930s, 1920s, pre-World War I, Black Reconstruction, Civil War, 1700s, 1600s, i kept going back and back, treading water, trying to touch non-white supremacist ground. Only, there wasn't any!

By then it was years later in our lives, and i'd been recruited into doing national liberation movement support work. And was reading Black nationalist writings. One day i caught a speech in which u.s. whites were referred to as "settlers," meaning invaders or interlopers, as in South Afrika and Rhodesia. Of course, white history always talks about settlers with the non-political connotations of pioneers or explorers or the first people to live in an area. (Native peoples didn't count as real people to eurocapitalism. They were part of the flora and fauna.) *This was a moment of the proverbial light bulb turning on in my mind!*

First chance i got, i asked the UN representative of an Afrikan liberation movement if he thought u.s. whites as a society, including workers, were settler oppressors in the same way as Rhodesians, Boers, or Zionists in Israel? He just said, *"Of course."* Upset, i demanded to know why he didn't tell North Americans this. He only smiled ironically at me, and i won't even bother telling you what certain Indian comrades said. So *Settlers* didn't involve any great genius on my part, just finally listening to the oppressed and what the actual historical experience said about class. Finally.

From there it was hard research work, but no conceptual leap at all to see that **in general in u.s. history the colonized peoples have been the proletariat**, while the white working class has been a labor aristocracy. This has been camouflaged in capitalist history by retroactively assigning white racial membership to various european immigrant peoples who weren't "white" at the time. For instance, when leading u.s. capitalists started the "Interracial Council" to promote patriotic nationalist integration during World War I, the "races" they wanted to bring together were the Irish race, the Welsh race, the Polish race, the Lithuanian race, the Hungarian race, the Sicilian race, the Rumanian race, and other Europeans that we now think of as only nationalities within the white race. Shows you how race is another capitalist manufactured product.

So groups who we think of as "white" today, were definitely not considered "white" in the past. Like in the Midwest steel mills just before World War I, when native-born American WASP men were all foremen and skilled workers—what was called "white man's work"—while the backbreaking laboring gangs were made up of "Hunkys," Eastern Europeans. Like immigrant Finnish workers, who weren't citizens, didn't speak English, weren't considered white but "Mongolian," who were oppressed like draft animals in small-town mines and mills in the Northern Midwest, and who made up something like 60% of the total membership of the early Communist Party. They wanted armed revolution right then, just like against the Czar, and most of them were actually imprisoned or deported. Wiped out as an oppressed class and national group. It's a long distance in real class from those oppressed revolutionary women and men to the middle-class pedants and would-be commissars of today's Left. *Settlers* goes through this real class history.

Solidarity: How is settlerism different from racism?

J. Sakai: This is a useful question, because people are confused about the two. Some people think that "settler" is just a fancy way of saying "white people," and that it's all just about racism anyway. Racism as we know it and settlerism both had their origins in capitalist colonialism, and are related but quite distinct. Settler-colonial societies started as invasion and occupation forces for Western capitalism, social garrisons usually in the Third World, as Western capitalism expanded out of Europe into the Americas, Afrika, and Asia.

Racism **as we experience it today** didn't exist before capitalism, which is why many revolutionaries see rooting out the one as requiring rooting out the other. To Europeans before modern capitalism the most important "races" were what we would call nations. Indeed, until well into the 20th century it was widely assumed by Europeans that even different European nationalities were biologically different, and had different mental abilities and propensities. Slavs were thought to be biologically different from Nordics, and Jews were thought to be an exotic race all by themselves.

Pre-capitalist and even early capitalist Europe was a lot different from our racial stereotypes. It wasn't that oppression and bigotry didn't exist. Obviously, for example, there was a long tradition of anti-semitic and anti-Romany persecution in "Christendom." But the whole context of "race" was unlike what we usually think of. i was astonished to learn that in early 18th-century Germany, a leading philosopher, Anton-Wilhelm Amo who lectured at the University of Halle and the University of Jena, was a Black German (born in Africa, he also signed his name in Latin as "Amo Guinea-Africanus" or Amo the African). Or that Russia's greatest poet, the 19th-century aristocratic Pushkin, was Black by American standards. And nobody cared. And in the time of Marx and Bakunin, the major leader of early German radical unionism was also very visibly Black, and his part-Afrikan heritage accepted.

Well, what we've been saying all along is that "race" in modern capitalism was originally changed from an undefined difference into a disguise for "class." Capitalism, after all, always prefers to restructure class differences in drag of some kind (all the better for their manipulations). Like Northern Ireland, where there is supposedly a "religious" or "ethnic" bloody conflict between Catholic Irish Republicans and Protestant Loyalists.

Actually, this has been an up-front *class* conflict between British capitalism's historic settler garrison population (the Prots) and the historic colonial subjects (the "Catholics"). Both sides European, both "white." The Northern Ireland Protestant settler working class has always had relative privilege, including the best jobs (sound familiar?). Belfast's traditional blue-collar "big employer," the Harland & Wolff shipyard, had always been so dominated by Protestant settler workers that the shipyard union called a pro-imperialist political strike in the 1970s, closing down the yards, to oppose granting any democratic rights at all to Irish Catholics. (Now, of course, the obsolete shipyards are going out of business, and a globalized British imperialism has much less need for their loyal Unionist servants).

The"Orangemen" settlers in Northern Ireland have hated the Irish with just as much crazed viciousness as white u.s. workers hate the oppressed. Irish revolutionary Bernadette Devlin McAliskey picked up on this same comparison in real class when visiting the u.s. in the 1970s. She said afterwards:

> "I was not very long there until, like water, I found my own level. 'My people'—the people who knew about oppression, discrimination, prejudice, poverty and the frustration and despair that they produce—were not Irish Americans. They were black, Puerto Ricans, Chicanos. And those who were supposed to be 'my people', the Irish Americans who knew about English misrule and the Famine and supported the civil rights movement at home, and knew that Partition and England were the cause of the problem, looked and sounded to me like Orangemen. They said exactly the same things about blacks that the loyalists said about us at home. In New York I was given the key to the city by the mayor, an honor not to be sneezed at. I gave it to the Black Panthers."

So settler-colonialism usually has taken racial form, but it doesn't have to. In fact, one of the newest examples—the Chinese capitalist empire's Han settler occupation of Tibet—is all Asian.

What we never should lose sight of is that these may be socially constructed differences—but they are *real*. There's a certain trend of fashionable white thought that claims that race (or nation) is nothing more than a trick, an imaginary construct that folks are fooled into believing in. So we even find some middle-class white men claiming that they've "given up being white" (i can hear my grandmother saying, "More white foolishness!" with a dismissing headshake). Needless to say, they haven't given up anything.

Race as a form of class is very tangible, solid, material, as real as a tank division running over you ... tank divisions, after all, are also socially constructed! About another form of this same white racist game—white New Age women deciding to play at "becoming Indian"—Women of All Red Nations used to wearily suggest that if they really really wanted to "become Indian" they should live on the rez—the u.s. colony—without running water or jobs, without heat in the winter or education for their children, with real poverty, alcoholism, and violent oppression.

So both racism as we know it and settlerism each had their origins in capitalist colonialism and are related, but are also quite distinct. Settler-colonial societies have a specialized history, because they started as invasion and occupation forces for Western capitalism. Usually as social garrisons in the Third World, as Western capitalism expanded out of Europe into the Americas, Afrika, Asia.

Solidarity: Some critics have argued that your book suggests that "racial issues" should take precedence over "class issues" ...

J. Sakai: This liberal intellectual polarity that "race issues" and "class issues" are opposites, are completely separate from each other, and that one or the other must be the main thing, is utterly useless! We have to really get it that race issues aren't the opposite of class issues. That race is always so electrically charged, so filled with mass power, precisely because it's about raw class. That's why revolutionaries and demagogues can both potentially tap into so much power using it. Or get burned.

You can't steer yourself in real politics, not in amerikkka and not in this global imperialism, without understanding

FREE THE LAND!!

AND THE

RNA 11

WILL FOLLOW

race. "Class" without race in North America is an abstraction. And vice-versa. Those who do not get this are always just led around by the nose, the manipulated without a clue—and it is true that many don't want any more from life than this. But wising up on race only means seeing all the class issues that define race and charge it with meaning. **Why should it be so hard to understand that capitalism, which practically wants to barcode our assholes, has always found it convenient to color-code its classes?**

When i started high school way back in the daze, it was up North and in theory there was no segregation. But our city school system had five intellectual levels or "tracks"—from the highest college-prep track to the lowest remedial vocational ed track. In a high school that was 85% Black, the top college-prep track never had more than one or two New Afrikans. In fact, those classes would literally close for Jewish holidays. When we started high school all of us non-white types were automatically assigned to the bottom two tracks, which we could only rise out of by "achievement." Those two "colored" tracks (although there were a few hillbillies in them, too) were non-academic, which meant that after four years of attendance you "graduated" high school—but instead of a diploma you only got a paper "certificate of satisfactory attendance." This was real good for getting you your slave job as a porter or at the garment factory—my first fulltime job, the summer i was 14—but in fact you couldn't qualify for college with it even if you had somehow managed to get literate.

So college education and middle-class careers just "accidentally" happened to be legally forbidden to most New Afrikans in our city. Everyone knew this who wanted to, it was just a fact of life. So much so that when i started working for the neighborhood gang council (some small gangs not the later big vice-lords and cobras and D's) as a nerdy ten-year-old, the leader said that they wanted me to go on to graduate from high school since none of the rest of them would (obviously, even then Asians were designated to finish school). Of course, now neo-colonial capitalism has had to get much slicker and share some loot, create neo-colonial bourgy classes.

Starting a new movement, a new radicalism, we need a better map of class. Which means we need to see what's really happening with race just for starters. *Settlers* did that for u.s history, particularly for the Black-Indian-white main structure of colonial capitalism here, but that's only a beginning. An outline not a full map. It might be good to come at this from a different angle than the customary Black/white situation. Let me use an obscure example from my own life in which race and even anti-racism played out a different kind of subtle class politics.

A number of years ago, i was trying to help a group of young Chinese-American activists on an anti-racist campaign. This was an interesting case of how a pure "race" issue only fronted for class politics. Now, these folks were "paper Maoists" in every worst way you could think of—and all my friends know that i'm someone who has warm feelings for the old Chairman. Not only did they have what Mao once called "invincible ignorance," but were also arrogantly full of Han nationalism. They did have physical courage, at least. Their project was to protest the sports racism in the famous industrial town of Pekin, Illinois—which was originally named in the 19th century after Beijing, and whose high school sports teams were colorfully named "the Chinks"! (Capitalism, what an ever-amazing civilization—what next? *"Auschwitz! The Perfume!"*)

Every week a few carloads of young Asian protesters would arrive in Pekin to picket the high school and city hall, hold television news conferences, and keep the issue simmering in the news. You see, the small flaw in the campaign was that all the protesters had to be imported from New York and Chicago. There were only eight Chinese families in town, and all were refusing to have anything to do with the anti-"Chinks" campaign (not wanting to lose their livelihoods, homes, and be driven out of town by the controversy).

By accident, not in any political way, i had casually met two vaguely liberal young white guys there. One was a teacher in that very high school. The second was a UAW (United Auto Workers union) shop steward at the nearby giant Caterpillar tractor assembly plant, which was Pekin's main industry. So i thought maybe they could be persuaded to get some local people to take a moderate wishy-washy public stand, anything just to give the Chinese families some local community cover if they wanted to speak out (there was zero local support of any kind, including all the unions and churches of course).

When i suggested it to this Maoist group, there was a moment's startled stony silence. Then the leader barked, "We do not work with white people!" Discussion over. So, is this a good example of that error of "racial issues taking precedence over class issues"? i know some radicals might think that, but they'd just be getting faked out.

First off, to those activists running it, "race" was *not* what was central to their thinking. After all, if those Asian American dudes had really been into either "race" or anti-racism they might have started by organizing and working with the local Asian families. They might have tried to help find some survival strategy for these families, who couldn't just drive off into the sunset after each press conference (being an isolated Asian family in a heavy white racist scene is no joke, obviously). This is just a normal problem in anti-racist work, which folks had to deal with all the time in small towns in 1960s Mississippi, for instance.

It also wasn't true that those Chinese-American leftists "didn't work with white people." They did that all the time, when they wanted, and these Han nationalists even argued for the "revolutionary" nature of the white working class. What i came to realize was in that situation they didn't want any broad community support for the Chinese families there, or to let others into "their" issue. Because they had a really different agenda. Which was to get sole public credit for this and other anti-racist issues, so that their little Maoist "party" could vault into political dominance over the Chinese-American communities. Later, when they thought it necessary, they even used physical violence and death threats to drive other Asian groups away. They intended to be the people in ethnic power, in effect like replacing the tongs. These "paper Maoists" had a pure class agenda, alright, only it was a bourgeois agenda. Although they themselves might have honestly believed what they did was "revolutionary," they had anti–working class politics hidden by "anti-racism" and left people of color talk.

And this Maoist group really did get their Andy Warhol–like "15 minutes of fame," becoming large in part because the *more* dishonest and destructive their "anti-racist" maneuvers became, the *more* support they got from white middle-class liberals and "progressives" (coincidentally?). i mean, from many white social-democrats, those white anti-repression "experts," academic leftists, etc. Those types that subject us to those endless droning lectures about "the working class" (which they aren't in and don't get, of course). As a sage comrade of mine always says, *"Like is drawn to like"* even if their outward appearance is very different.

This is a more difficult, easy to slip and fall on, even dangerous way of seeing things than radicals here are used to. But either we learn it well or we're lost in this post-modern decaying civilization. **That dead left way of thinking about "race" and "class" not only isn't radical, it's corrupt and anti–working class.**

Why the giant United Auto Workers local down there near Pekin never saw anything wrong with Asian children being forced to go to school in a white supremacist haze, surrounded by constant references to "the Chinks," was just business as usual for the labor aristocracy in America. In the 1960s and 1970s all those government regulated American unions fought even elementary Civil Rights tooth and nail. Including the most liberal, including those run by white "socialists" like the East Coast garment workers and West Coast longshoremen.

Many dissenting Black longshoremen in the 1960s and 1970s were literally barred from the industry for life by the dictatorship of the settler "socialist" labor bosses of the ILWU. As outrageous as it may be, those "socialist" union dictators could just issue orders that this New Afrikan or that Chicano was not to be allowed to work on the docks again ever. Oh, they *loved* Martin orating and marching non-violently far off in Washington, but they fought Civil Rights inside their industries & unions every bitter step of the way (it's also true that in places, in Detroit, San Francisco, Flint, New York City, there were small handfuls of maverick white socialists and anarchists who sided with the Black and Latino workers even against their own white Left).

The funny thing is that for all the constant "Marxist" blah-blah about government unions as "main roads of the class struggle," in our lifetime the AFL-CIO unions have been on the wrong side of just about every major mass movement. That's why they have been back-slapping with Pat Buchanan and helping to legitimize white racism in the current anti-WTO campaign. i guess because that's their job.

Many people conveniently forget that these business unions were rebuilt to conform to tight capitalist laws, are constantly u.s. government regulated and monitored, have involuntary "membership," and are about as democratic as the USSR (which had elections, reforms and repairs, too, before it broke down under the mismanagement of primitive capitalist empire). Once workers' "unions" were free associations, were wild, were outside bourgeois law and part of a counter-culture of the oppressed, but these genetically modified creations only use the same name.

Solidarity: Speaking of white workers, another criticism I have heard is that you are denying that there even is a white working class in the United States. Would you say this is an accurate reading of your work, or are people missing the point?

J. Sakai: Now, there obviously is a white working class in the u.s. A large one, of many, many millions. From offshore oil derricks to the construction trades to auto plants. But it isn't a proletariat. It isn't the most exploited class from which capitalism derives its super profits. Far fucking from it. As a shorthand i call it the "whitetariat." These aren't insights unique to *Settlers*, by any means.

Unfortunately, whenever Western radicals hear words like "unions" and "working class" a rosy glow glazes over their vision, and the "Internationale" seems to play in the background. Even many anarchists seem to fall into a daze and to magically transport themselves back to seeing the militant socialist workers of Marx and Engels' day. Forgetting that there have been many different kinds of working classes in history. Forgetting that Fred Engels himself criticized the English industrial working class of the late 19th century as a *"bourgeois proletariat,"* an aristocracy of labor. He pointed out how you could tell the non-proletarian, "bourgeois" strata of the English working class—they were **the sectors that were dominated by adult men**, not women or children. Engels also wrote that the "bourgeois" sectors were those that were *unionized*. Sounds like a raving ultra-leftist, doesn't he? (which he sure wasn't)

So that this is a strategic and not a tactical problem, that it has a material basis in imperialized class privilege, has long been understood by those willing to see reality. (The fact that we have radical movements here addicted to not seeing reality is a much larger crisis than any one issue.)

Solidarity: Don't some of the benefits of living in an imperialist metropole trickle down even into some of the internal colonies, causing some of the distorting effects of settlerism to be replicated within, for instance, the non-white working classes within the United States?

J. Sakai: Yes, absolutely. Radical workers themselves have often understood this, although the official "Marxist" Left has always worked to silence them.

Way back in the 1970s two Detroit auto workers wrote a short pamphlet about politics, addressed to *"fellow workers who have begun to wonder whether they are going to spend the rest of their lives just hustling for more money ..."* What was so striking about this was the authors, James Boggs and James Hocker, who between them had over fifty years experience in the plants. Strikes, militant factory caucuses, revolutionary organizations, Black nationalism, mass ghetto rebellions, they had taken part in it all. One of them, James Boggs, had been a close comrade and co-author of the Pan-Afrikan revolutionary historian C.L.R. James. Boggs was one of the leading working-class theoreticians of the 1960s Black Revolution.

The role of the white racist construction trades unions back then, who were used by the u.s. government as their unofficial goon squads to beat up Anti–Vietnam War protesters, was infamous. But Boggs and Hocker don't let their fellow factory workers escape responsibility, either. They remind them (and the rest of us) that all the AFL-CIO unions, even the liberal ones, *completely backed* u.s. military aggression in Asia, the Caribbean, and Latin America.

Nor did it stop there, since Boggs and Hocker saw a direct relationship between the opportunism of all the unions and the opportunism of a bribed u.s. working class. What was so refreshing was that Boggs and Hocker expressly rejected the time-worn and worn-out "radical" argument that u.s. workers are free from all sin (sort of like the ultimate condom of immaculate conception), since supposedly "it is only sell-out by the union bureaucracy which has kept the workers in check."

> "Workers coming into the auto plants today receive economic benefits undreamed of by their predecessors. These benefits tie workers to the company, par-

> ticularly the high senority workers. It also creates in them a vested interest in the system which exerts a growing influence on how they view the social reality around them. More and more they think only about their own interests. They worry only about how to 'get mine' or, at best, 'get ours'."

The two pointed out how auto workers in Detroit refused to fight for better mass transit, because, although they know how much poor people need this, *"they also think that adequate public transportation might mean fewer jobs for them."*

> "This opportunism is clearly demonstrated in dealing with the most important issues of our time, such as the war in Indochina and the inflation caused by the war.
>
> "The war in Indochina took the lives of thousands of youth in this country, many of them sons of working class families. But it was the workers and their organizations who demonstrated enthusiastic support for the clearly illegal war perpetrated by the United States government, even when other groups in the society, especially students, were showing by their actions increasing distaste for the war.
>
> "Many workers, when challenged individually, would deny that they supported the war. But at the same time they refused to take any actions to exhibit opposition to the war and clearly were hostile to the students who opposed the war. The attitude of most workers was 'The President knows best' and in any case what mattered was their jobs—even if their job was making bombs or napalm to burn up the Vietnamese ..."

These guys were seriously pissed off at their own class, at their brothers and sisters, and not afraid to lay it all out. But saying that u.s. industrial workers are not as a whole revolutionary or "class conscious"—and check out that Boggs and Hocker, who worked in the Detroit auto factories that were Black-majority, are definitely not just exposing the "whitetariat" alone but Black workers as well—isn't the end of the road. i'm not saying that we should forget about working-class organizing. **What i am suggesting is that radical working-class politics here needs different strategies than the traditional Left has understood.** Everything that we've discussed just clears away all the middle-class left underbrush, so people can see the actual path before us and get down to work. *Settlers* didn't directly deal with all this, naturally, since it's historical analysis of the oppressor class structure and history.

Solidarity: Would you say that organizing within the present-day white working class is hopeless?

J. Sakai: We need to talk about how people unthinkingly objectify the working classes. It never occurs to anyone to believe that the metropolitan middle classes are going to overthrow the system that privileges them. No one says, "The white doctors and professors and managers are the revolutionary class." Yet, without any big fuss or posturing, middle-class radicals just organize in those classes when and where they can, all around themselves. Students just form issue groups in even the most elite universities. Teachers try to open minds to social justice, while even some doctors volunteer to serve in refugee camps or argue with the majority of their criminal profession about being healers not rip-offs or stock market addicts. For better or worse, success or defeat. No big political deal, it's just living the life, the meal that's set before us.

But when it comes to the working classes, whoa, then it's all this ideological ca-ca. To believe what we're told, no one should want to organize or educate workers unless they can be sure that the entire class is "bound for glory" as the main force for revolution! (which you won't see here in this lifetime, trust me). So the white workers as a whole are either the revolutionary answer—which they aren't unless your cause is snowmobiles and lawn tractors—or they're like ignorant scum you wouldn't waste your time on. Small wonder rebellious poor whites almost always seek out the Right rather than the Left.

There's an underlying assumption that revolutionary movements worldwide share, that's always there for us, that we are part of the working classes. That we live our lives in these communities, hold those jobs, try to live productive lives not just do capitalist bullshit, struggle within these class situations. We're talking in a wide arc here, maybe, but to a point: to how we need to build movements that have the learned skill of the recognition of reality. That understand revolutionary politics as more than abstract ideology, in more than an academic or reform movement way.

If radicalism can build small counter-currents of liberation in the overwhelmingly corrupt middle classes, why should similar work be questioned in the white working-class communities? What i am fighting is the slick "Marxist" or "anarchist" opportunism, which sees aligning with the white settler majority and reform politics as the absolute necessity.

Malcolm X and Women's Liberation, ACT-UP and Wounded Knee II, Anti–Vietnam War draft card burning and radical ecology, were all shocking to the majority of North Americans. Radical threats to "the American Way of Life"—and loudly condemned not only by the majority but more specifically by the white working class—these political offensives by the few turned everything upside down. Because in the metropolis, radical and democratic change can only come *against* the wishes of the bribed majority. That may be tough to swallow for white folks, but reality is just reality.

This obsession with needing a social majority has nothing to do with being "practical." What it has to do with is bourgeois and defeatist thinking.This is like the left thinking that could not build a *practical* anti-fascist movement in Weimar Republic Germany during the 1920s and 1930s, although millions hated Nazism and wanted to do something, because that German Left was too preoccupied with fantasies of either seizing or getting elected into state power for itself.

That Left was too lost in delusions of success almost within their hands, delusions of maneuvering together a majority, to bother even really understanding fascism coming up fast in their rear-view mirror. The urgent need was to organize a working minority to counter fascism in a much more radical way. Not by trying to defend liberal bourgeois rule. All the real things that had to be done by scattered German anti-fascists later after the Nazis were put into power—such as to survive politically, to significantly sabotage the war effort, to rescue Jews and Romany and gays, to build an underground against the madness of the Third Reich—all these things were attempted bravely but largely unsuccessfully, because they had to be done too late from scratch. This is a much larger subject, too large to dive into now, but it is on the horizon, like the smoke of a distant forest fire.

Solidarity: Are the settler societies of North America different from the racist and imperialist countries in Europe in any kind of fundamental way which should be important to anti-fascists?

J. Sakai: Which takes us into somewhat different ground. i'm not knowledgeable enough on European politics—or on Canada—so that i could do a list of point by point comparisons. What i'd like to do instead is to talk about u.s. society, and readers themselves can see if the comparisons make any sense. And, yes, i've run into young fascists of the "stormtrooper" variety, with their gray semi-waffen SS uniforms, open veneration of Hitler, open talk of "mud races," etc. i still think that fascism here has been very influenced by its birth within a settler society, instead of being just some lame copy of the German experience. Just as Israeli settler neo-fascism has a very different language and public look from that of their Nazi tutors (taking a religious fundamentalist form).

The most conspicuous difference between Europe and North America was class in the outward form of race. In the centuries before World War II, the overwhelming mass of the European populations were poor and in misery. They were the proletarian classes, the laborers, poor peasants, and oppressed industrial workers. But in the settler colonies and nations, the lowest classes, the proletarians, were the natives, the conquered, or the imported colonial laborers. While white settler workers were automatically, from birth, no matter how poor, a whole level up. As W.E.B. DuBois remarked about poor white workers in the post–Civil War South. Thanks to imperialism. Which is why the mass of French *colons* in Algeria solidly supported imperialism against the Algerian people. Why millions of working class and poor whites in the segregationist u.s. South were more than willing to help police and kill and terrorize Black people. And even today, a century and more later, if we left it up to the white majority, the u.s. would secede from NAFTA and the WTO all right—and fly the Confederate flag!

In many settler societies, historically the white population not only supported the police, in part they were the police. **Unlike in Old Europe, where in general the masses of people were kept disarmed and landless, in settler colonies often the entire euro-male culture revolved around common and cheap access to land and rifles and the bodies of the oppressed.** Posses or militias or "Committees of Correspondence" or lynch mobs of armed men enforced the local settler dictatorship over Indians, Latinos, Afrikans, Asians, New Afrikans, women, etc. And white men of all classes joined in, to affirm their membership in the most important "class" of all. **Settlerism filled the space that fascism normally occupies.**

So in the 1920s and 1930s large fascist movements arose in Old Europe out of the bitter class deadlock in war-torn societies. But in the u.s. then, while there were little-noticed fascist groups and certainly real currents of sympathizers (enough to fill Madison Square Garden in Manhattan on one occasion), there was **no mass movement for fascist seizure of power itself.** Nor was the ruling class close to implementing fascism. The sputtering flareups of attempted fascist coups by ruling class elements against the reformist Roosevelt New Deal (Colonel McCormick's *Chicago Tribune* newspaper calling for the assassination of the President, or the DuPont-Winchester half-baked plan for the seizure of Washington using suborned u.s Marines) were easily shrugged off. There was major u.s. imperialist support for Italian, Spanish, and German fascism before and even during World War II, as opposed to support for fascism at home. Fascism was distinct from racism or white supremacy, which were only "As American as apple pie."

Neither the ruling class nor the white masses had any real need for fascism. *What for?* There was no class deadlock paralyzing society. There already was a longstanding, thinly disguised settler dictatorship over the colonial proletariat in North America. In the u.s., settlerism made fascism unnecessary. However good or bad the economic situation was, white settlers were getting the best of what was available. Which was why both the white Left and white Far Right alike back then in the 1930s were patriotic and pro-American. *Now only the white Left is.*

The white Left here is behind in understanding fascism. When they're not using the word loosely and rhetorically to mean any repression at all (like the frequent assertions that cutting welfare is "fascism"! i mean, give us a break!), they're still reciting their favorite formula that the fascists are only the "pawns of the ruling class." No, that was Nazism in Germany, maybe, though even there that's not a useful way of looking at it. But definitely not here, not in that old way.

The main problem hasn't been fascism in the old sense—it's been neo-colonialism and bourgeois democracy! The bourgeoisie didn't need any fascism at all to put Leonard Peltier away in maximum security for life or Mumia on death row. They hunted down the Black Panthers and the American Indian Movement like it was deer hunting season, while white America went shopping at the mall—all without needing fascism. And the steady waterfall of patriarchal violence against women, of rapes and torture and killings and very effective terrorism on a mass scale, should remind us that the multitude of reactionary men have "equal opportunity " under "democracy," too. They don't need fascism—yet.

Right now under neo-colonial "democracy," the system of patrolling and confining the Black Nation is at a fever pitch. Every known narcotic is being shoved and shoveled onto the streets of the Nation like it was confetti at parade time—coke, heroin, malt liquor, Bud, crack, commodified sex, you name it. The huge 2-million-inmate u.s. prison system contains the largest single Black community of all. One out of every four Black men in Washington, D.C. is in jail, prison, on parole or probation, or awaiting trial—i.e. under direct supervision by the law enforcement system. Even Ronald K. Noble, the new Secretary General-designate of INTERPOL, has written that he regularly gets stopped, questioned, and sometimes even searched by u.s. police (in Europe, too, of course). And if the top law enforcement official in the capitalist world gets routinely stopped as a Black man for u.s. racial police checks, guess what happens to the unemployed, to young working-class Black men.

The old Black industrial working class has been largely wiped out, and warlord armies and gangs given informal state permission to rule over much of the inner city at gunpoint. A few years ago i went home with a comrade. When we got off the bus, all the passengers started walking home down the middle of the street. My friend explained that all the sidewalks were "owned" by one or another dope gang or dealer, reserved for their crew and customers. You walked in the street or you got taken down by a 9mm. While the new Black middle class takes itself out of the game, flees the old communities and disperses itself into the suburbs. Why would capitalists need fascism? "Democracy" is doing the job for them full gale force—and let's not forget that North America has at the same time become the conscience of the world lecturing everyone else on human rights. "How sweet it is!" (Guess Leonard Peltier must be a prisoner in China).

But i am not saying that the situation is static, or that past history isn't being razed and rebuilt. All variants of capitalist metropolitan societies are becoming slowly but surely more alike, Quebec and Raleigh, Tokyo and Frankfurt, as capital expands, develops, and merges. While Western European farmers complain about McDonalds and agrobusiness, they willingly accept the most significant "Americanization"—the replacement of Western European labor with Algerians, Turks, Albanians, etc. Throughout Europe the proletariat has been pushed outside of national boundaries socially—just as euro-settlerism once did in the Third World—and is being redefined as Arab, Filipino, Algerian, Turkish, Albanian, Afrikan, and so on.

And, as Arghiri Emmanuel has noted, imperialism is gradually abandoning its own kith and kin, its settler societies. We first saw this in Kenya in 1960, where the British settler colony was unceremoniously dumped after the Mau Mau Rebellion in favor of an Afrikan neo-colonial regime. Then in Algeria, where French imperialism gave up on what had by their laws been an actual province of France—and left a million French Algerian settlers to lose their farms and homes and possessions, to flee in a frenzied mass evacuation. Capitalism has no loyalties, after all, only interests (to paraphrase a famous statesman). It was only then that the *colons* and their military sympathizers sought an end to French bourgeois democracy, to start a new fascist interlude. Even in North America settlers are being told by imperialism to move over and make room for new immigrants from Asia, Latin America, the Middle East and Afrika. To pay the bill as the state gives back some land and reparations and tax concessions to Native nations. And they certainly hate it!

So there is a certain convergence, of settler and non-settler metropolitan societies becoming more alike. In the u.s. the increasingly global ruling class has no need of domestic fascism—so far. But white mass politics is not confined to taking phone calls from the ruling class. Far from it.

Solidarity: How do you view the rise of the Far Right, specifically the American Far Right?

J. Sakai: We can see that neo-fascism is a growing factor in u.s. politics. Still marginal, but already more significant than,say, white Marxism. The Far Right is politically strong enough, represents so much mass sentiment, that its momentary electoral champion—Pat Buchanan—has become the hero of some trade unions and the closet ally of white socialists and anarchists in the anti-WTO campaign. And again, to understand this dynamic we have to lay aside 1930s political formulas and take the social reality in a fresh way. Were Timmy McVeigh and his comrades "tools of the ruling class" when they dusted the federal building in Oklahoma City? Does finance capital & the big bourgeoisie pull the strings behind the Militia Movement as it spreads doctrines of tax resistance, seizing federal land, and targeting the imperialist

state as white man's main enemy? You'd have to be nuttier than they are to believe that! The old "pawns of the ruling class" 1930s analysis of European fascism does not apply right here in the old way.

This is too big a subject for me to go into fully here, but the broad outline is obvious. The Far Right is growing steadily, moving on the offensive, as white settler society itself is fragmenting and being forced to gradually give up its old national form under immense pressures from the new global imperialism. In this fragmentation, some sectors and classes of the old settler society are now more open to neo-fascism in their desperate search for a new civilization for themselves in which they will still be masters of the land.

While in Europe the much larger fascist current has manifested itself by violent attacks on immigrant labor and on defending the concept of the old nations, in the u.s. the New Right is primarily concerned with attacking the u.s. state itself, using both armed struggle and mass political organizing, and founding new self-governing cults and societies. That is to say, it is an emerging revolutionary movement, albeit still a small one. The Left has little daily contact with the fascists, because they are in different classes and live in different geographic areas and are in *diverging* societies.

In the best guerrilla fashion, this New Right is bypassing the major cities, with their massive Third World populations, corporate economies, and large state machinery. Rather, their focus is on winning de facto power inside the marginalized white male populations. Romeoville, Illinois rather than Chicago. Prisons rather than Ivy League colleges. *Theirs is a re-statement of the early settler vision*, of setting up independent outposts of a racially-cleansed culture, on re-pioneered white land. With heavily armed bands of once-again-masculine white men pushing out the mercenary u.s. authorities. For a period of time we could see both white fascist Right and the white Left—working in geographically separate cultures on this vast continent—grow without impinging on or really clashing with each other. Both mostly white "Free Mumia" campaigns in the old major cities and the quiet ouster of federal agents from Western lands.

The old Right of the 1920s Klan or 1960s White Citizens Councils or Minutemen or Jewish Defense League were patriotic & pro-u.s.a. They saw themselves as "saving" the traditional America, and often cooperated closely with and were led by local business, police, the f.b.i., and government officials.

In a major reversal, the new Far Right is radically anti-American. It sees their white male settler empire of *"America from sea to shining sea"* as really lost. Its cities taken over by the sub-human millions of the "mud races," its economy drained by the "Jew banks" and the alien corporate economy, its culture polluted by hostile genetic contaminants, its once-proud citizens increasingly without rights and dictated to by the shell of the former "u.s. government" which is now the "Zionist Occupation Government." And while the masses of conservative euro-amerikans are not yet fascist, neither are they anti-fascists.

And the hard-core of the new Far Right is very fascist, since neo-fascism represents the basic ideology that the aspiring white "lumpenbourgeoisie" need to restart and reorganize a part of settler society as their own private fiefdom. The u.s. constitution just doesn't work for them. Just as Tudjman and Milosevic, who once were Yugoslavian patriots and "socialists" when that met their class interests, turned to neo-fascism and genocidal ethnic nationalism to be "born again" as the local "lumpenbourgeoisie" under global imperialism.

Take the David Duke phenomenon. As we all know, in 1990 Louisiana state representative David Duke ran for the u.s. senate. **In losing Duke still won a large majority of the statewide white vote, some 55–57%. His highest percentage of votes came from white workers with incomes under $15,000 a year.** This despite the fact that Duke was and is notorious not "merely" as a racist, but as someone who has spent his entire adult life as a very public neo-nazi organizer, propagandist, and leader. He was opposed by both Republican and Democratic Parties, and the churches, civic and business organizations. The entire media machine kept exposing and criticizing him, repeatedly running old photos of him in his American Nazi Party uniform. Yet, if it wasn't for the Black voters, David Duke—naked fascist agenda and all—would have emerged as one of the most powerful politicians in the u.s. senate. You can see why granting Black people the vote was so important to u.s. imperialism—and why the white masses were carefully never given a chance to directly vote on it!

For sure, the growth of fascism here has many class contradictions of its own, and their Aryan future is far from certain. But it is significant that while the masses of euro-amerikans are not fascists, *being neo-fascist* is quietly acceptable to many of them. Today the radical future is dividing into those who—whatever their strategies and ideologies—recognize that fact, and those who still wish to avoid facing it.

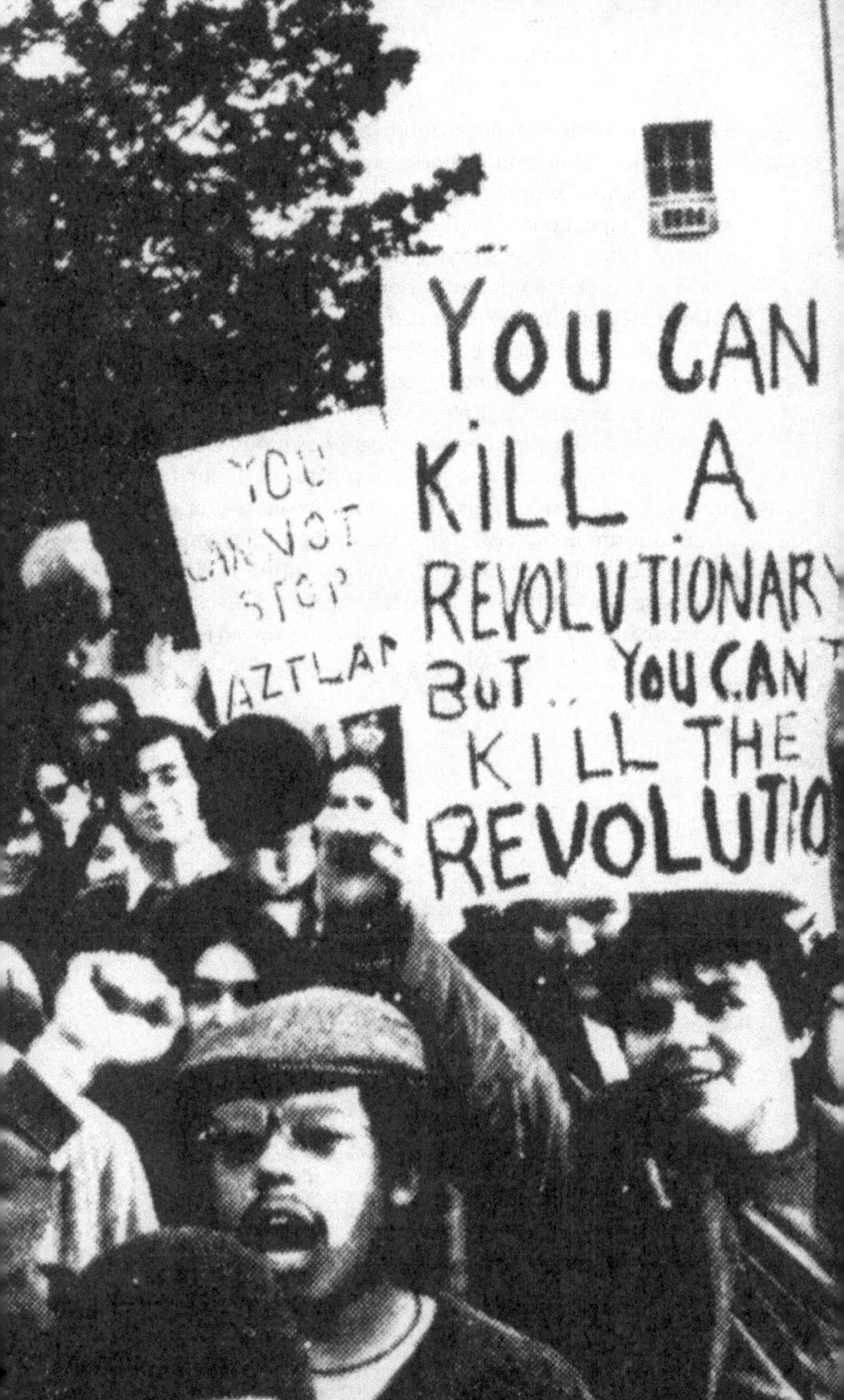
YOU
CAN NOT
STOP
AZTLAN
YOU CAN
KILL A
REVOLUTIONARY
BUT.. YOU CANT
KILL THE
REVOLUTIO

Stolen at Gunpoint (2003)

This interview was conducted on June 17, 2003, by Ernesto Aguilar and was originally aired on the Latino-culture program Sexto Sol on KPFT radio in Houston, Texas.

Ernesto Aguilar: In the early 1980s you wrote *Settlers: Mythology of the White Proletariat*, a book that took a deep historical look at the role of white workers in the lives and histories of oppressed people. Can you break down for listeners what inspired you to write *Settlers* and the most important ideas that you put forward in it?

J. Sakai: Well, I wrote it because at that time—and we're talking about the mid-70s when I started working on it—it seemed to me that every time there was a struggle or an outbreak of something, or an act of injustice happened, racism, there were always more and more calls to study people of color. More books piling up about us, we're getting funded to do things, but actually, we're not the problem. The problem is white people. So I said "What about them?"

The other thing, of course, is, at the time, I was working in an auto parts plant. As a revolutionary, I had been taught all this stuff about class unity and how white workers and workers of color were going to unite. Except in real life I didn't actually see that. What I saw was there were some good guys who were white, to be sure, but basically the white guys were pretty reactionary and they were always selling us out. So I was trying to figure out where did racism in the white working class actually begin? Was there a point where they started selling out or got misled or something?

Ernesto Aguilar: And where did that lead you?

J. Sakai: That led me all the way back to Plymouth Rock! I'm not a historian, or wasn't then. I started reading and figured "Maybe it happened in the 1930s, before we were born." Or "Maybe it was the 1920s," going back and back. It was like treading water. I never found ground.

I figured out that actually there wasn't any time when the white working class wasn't white supremacist and racist and essentially pro-Empire. Yet I couldn't figure, "How did this happen?"

That's when this whole idea came to me, which isn't my idea. But at the time I knew a lot of African revolutionaries in exile from Zimbabwe and South Africa, whose people were waging guerrilla wars against the colonial powers. They were always talking about white people, but they didn't really mean race. They kept using the term "settlers" and they kept talking about "settler colonialism." Then I ran into some Palestinians and they talked about the Israelis that way. It was "settler colonialism," i.e., that European populations had been imported into these countries to act as the agents for capitalism and for the ruling classes. And at that point, of course, the light bulb went on over my head and I said, "My god, that describes Amerika." That's the central idea in *Settlers*—that the U.S. really isn't a society in which there's different races and we're trying to get along. That may be true on the surface, but, in its actual history, it's an Empire of imported European settlers who always were given special privileges to be the occupation army over all the rest of us.

I can't say that made my book popular, but it certainly raised a lot of controversy at the time.

Ernesto Aguilar: Do you think some of the historical points you brought out were the most important points of the book? Especially when you look at revolutionary literature, particularly anti-imperialist literature over the past 30 years, 40 years, 50 years even, you don't see that point brought out as clearly as it was in *Settlers*, which put it in a way that really crystallized it for a lot of people.

J. Sakai: In part because it was written at a juncture in history where we were going through all these intense struggles, in the '60s and '70s, and my feeling and I think a lot of people's feeling was, we've waited 400 years for the unity, so if it can't come in 400 years, then how long are we supposed to wait for this stuff? How real is it? Why don't we take a look at this idea instead of just taking it as a given?

And I've gotta tell you that, even in integrated stuff, the difference between different peoples really meant a lot back then. One of the things I tell young people I know who are starting to learn about stuff, is not to believe what's in the history books and television because a lot of it is not true.

Ernesto Aguilar: Indeed it isn't. To put this in a context for the gente, what was Mexican land was settled in the early 1800s and resulted in the U.S. seizing over half of Mexico's land in 1848 with the Treaty of Guadalupe Hidalgo. The places we know as Texas, Califas, Arizona, and many of the other States in the Southwest were ancestrally held by Mexicans, and became part of the United States as part of a forcible campaign to take the land. It isn't taught that way in history books. How was the Amerikan West settled, and how does that differ from popular conceptions you were just mentioning? I can think of, off the top of my head, cowboys and rugged individualism, people coming and settling the land that was just here with buffalo just dancing around and ready for the taking ...

J. Sakai: The mythology of the West and Southwest is that all this land was empty, and the Europeans came and filled the land because there was hardly anyone there before. And, if they were there, they weren't important because it was a few people, they didn't know what they were doing, or were just wandering around in the sun and so on. No idea is given

The American Indian Movement

Comes to Chicago

Hear AIM Speaker, Ellen Moves Camp, talk on:

The Continuing Struggle at Wounded Knee

Ellen Moves Camp is a resident of Pine Ridge Reservation. She took part in the occupation of Wounded Knee and is presently the Chairperson of the Wounded Knee Defense/Offense Committee.

Sunday
Dec. 15
7:30 PM

Church of the Holy Covenant

2747 N. Wilton

(The Corner of Diversey and Wilton)

Sponsored by:

- Haymarket New American Movement
- Rising Up Angry
- Chicago Women's Liberation Union
- Puerto Rican Socialist Party

$1.00 Donation Requested

Refreshments will be served.

to the fact that these are whole other nations, whole other societies. The settler invasion, powered by immigration from Europe, and the development of capitalist armies, mechanization and industrialization, over the course of centuries, completely overwhelmed all these other societies on the continent.

The United States is a unique nation because it's always been an Empire. It's never been just a nation of ordinary people. From its very beginnings, it has been an illegitimate nation in the sense that, in order to become a nation, it had to conquer other people, take their land, and enslave them. There literally has been no point in Amerikan history where that wasn't true, because that's the basis of what being Amerikan is—which is, of course, the whole problem in the social character of the question of justice here.

Ernesto Aguilar: Certainly.

J. Sakai: So you see these struggles going on. I remember in the '60s when Reies Tijerina and the Alliance were fighting on the Spanish land grant question in the Southwest. A lot of people had no idea that these grants had ever even existed, or that legal title to much of the land in the Southwest was held, and still is held, by Mexican families and Chicano families. Or that this land was never, ever legally part of the United States in terms of being owned by white business interests. This land was all stolen at gunpoint. Time after time, Reies and his people would hold meetings and produce documents, records from Mexico City, proving all these things. So this whole illusion that the Southwest, for example, was not populated and they just expanded into it, filling the empty space with shopping malls, factories, and whatever they did, is just nonsense. This is just conquest. It's no different than Japan invading China in the 1930s, or any other conquest of Empire. That produces a peculiar dynamic inside Amerika because this is a country where the various citizens, the various parts of the population, their fundamental relationship was formed by war, not by peace. And that still echoes into our lives today.

Ernesto Aguilar: One of the important things about Reies Tijerina's work around land grants, was that it exposed to a lot of Mexicanos that a lot of the grants and treaties were violated. Not that it's much of a revolutionary concept to a student of history to see that the United States violates land grants and treaties. But it exposed to a lot of young Chicanos and Chicanas that the U.S. doesn't have a good track record at all. I know we're getting into topics of settler colonialism and its implications. Just so we're clear, how does settlerism differ from racism and white supremacy?

J. Sakai: That's a good question. Certainly racism is a phenomenon that's worldwide; you have it in Japan and France and Russia and so forth. But what's different here, and in countries like Canada, Israel, South Africa, and other places, is that the European population is not indigenous. The European population actually was imported as part of the process of colonization, to be an army of occupation over the conquered territories and peoples. And that's formed the essential character of the United States as a settler country, so that the question isn't just racism. The question is national divisions between people. For example, the question of self-determination for all colonized peoples always is at the heart of political matters.

During the '60s, there was a lot of revolutionary nationalism. People talked about liberating Aztlán, the whole Southwest. Black revolutionary nationalists talked about liberating a Black nation in the historically Black-majority South, the five States of the Black Belt. And, of course, Indian activists talked about their Native lands.

A lot of people didn't understand what this was about, and viewed this almost as legal questions of "Are you entitled to this territory or that territory." But this isn't a legal question, it's a question of self-determination.

The essence of decolonization is really simple: the oppressor can't decide for the oppressed. In Amerika, that means the white majority has no right to decide for the oppressed. How could that ever be just? It's true they could have the majority of votes—under their system—but I think only Mexican people, indigenous people, Chicanos, various Native American peoples have the right to decide the destiny of the Southwest, because that's theirs. I don't think white people have any vote in it at all. Not because I think there is something wrong with them as a race, but frankly the oppressors have no vote in deciding what the oppressed do with their society and their lives. That's the simplest kind of understanding of decolonization one can have, but it's essential. The revolutionary nationalism that a lot of people in the '60s talked about gets confused when people look at it today, but it's really all about self-determination for oppressed people.

Ernesto Aguilar: I think it is critical what you were saying about the growth of the Chicano movement in the '60s, and the growth of consciousness about Aztlán and nationalism itself. Particularly as it relates to Raza, one of the criticisms I have heard from white theorists is this: although Chicanos identify as opposing the miseducation and genocide unleashed by the colonizing society, our identification—as Latinos, Chicanos—with historical or cultural icons such as the Aztec warriors is no better. Of course, this is from academic theorists or whatever else. You've analyzed a lot of these counterinsurgencies directed at oppressed people. How should young Chicanos, in your view, look at this criticism?

J. Sakai: Well, all I can say is, as an Asian guy, Bruce Lee was an enormous cultural divide to us, because, before Bruce Lee, we had no role models. I guess it sounds funny to people today. We had no images. We weren't on TV or movies. We just weren't there. Although we were the cooks in the Westerns, where there were almost no Mexicans because

I guess they'd been killed. And the Indians were being killed, but there'd always be one Chinese guy who'd be cooking because the goddamned cowboys couldn't cook for themselves, I guess. We had no image of ourselves that was strong.

Bruce Lee was fantastic, in terms of that. It just made an incredible difference, even though there was nothing radical about his ideas, per se, but culturally it doesn't work like that. A lot of the political correctness theory about who you should identify with or not is pretty artificial, and a lot of it is worse than artificial.

This is a long explanation, but if you read *Occupied America* by Rodolfo Acuña—

Ernesto Aguilar: Great book!

J. Sakai: Great book. It's heavy. Incredibly detailed. Rich. Fantastic. He talks about Reies Tijerina, and he mentions in a line, "In May and June 1968, Tijerina participated in the Poor People's Campaign. There he proved to be an independent leader, threatening to pull the Chicano contingent out unless Black organizers did not treat them better." That's only one sentence. But to somebody who was there, for a lot of us who were there, Reies Tijerina was like a stroke of lightning falling on us. It was just tremendous; meeting him and watching him and the other people from the Alliance, although I think at that time they were calling themselves the Confederation of Free City States.

Ernesto Aguilar: José Angel Gutiérrez, one of the founders of La Raza Unida Party, calls Reies "the Chicano Malcolm X" for the way he approached his politics and the way he was out front about it.

J. Sakai: He was an incredibly strong guy. I heard there's been criticism of him later because he got more conservative or tactical, but back then, it wasn't just that he'd led his men and women to occupy Kit Carson National Park, took over land, and arrested sheriff's deputies and things like that. Their illegal acts are tremendously just. It's just wonderful! And this is the kind of thing you don't get out of these history books.

We're talking around 1968, and those of us who had been through the Civil Rights movement that had brought us into politics, a lot of us were pretty cynical and pretty disillusioned. Things had changed. There was a lot of money to be made in the Civil Rights movement if you wanted to sell out, cater to various interests—political interests and businesses and such. A lot of corruption was starting to take place at the top. Lots of bureaucracy. The Poor People's Campaign is what got Martin Luther King killed because he got out of the straight Civil Rights thing and said "We need to unite all the poor people in Amerika, and I'm calling on everyone to come to Washington, DC and we're just going to take over the DC Mall. We're going to pitch tents and live there until our demands are met. We want an end to the Vietnam War, we want all these things."

King had always very consciously had a policy, which he was public about. He fought local white Southern racists. He did not fight the Federal government. He kept saying he wouldn't fight the Federal government. This is when he decided he had to fight the Federal government, and he was proposing that all poor people unite in one movement against the government. In my opinion, that's why they killed him. That was too much. He was supposed to be the safe alternative to Malcolm X, but he was turning radical himself.

So even though he'd been assassinated during the preparations, his group went ahead and held a Poor People's Convention. Just imagine a sea of tents taking over the Mall in Washington, which, with the rain and everything else in the middle of the summer, was a sea of mud. Thousands of people were living there and trampling there. And, frankly, conditions were miserable—there was no food. I remember a lot of mornings for adults, there was no food, because the inside Civil Rights bureaucracy had stolen all the money that had been donated for food. Some of the kids would get little boxes of dry cereal, no milk and no fruit. So when we met Reies and he heard about this, he just invited us all, "Bring your kids, come to our place for lunch." He had taken his people out, totally out, he took the Alliance out of the mud. He said we don't have to live like this to make our point. He demanded that they find some place better, and, in fact, they found a private school that was unoccupied during the summer, and got permission for the Chicanos to use it. So hundreds of Chicanos moved in, fired up the kitchen, it was just a tremendous place. It was like a carnival and school. Reies invited us and our kids to come eat lunch. He was an incredible guy.

We were used to these top-down leaders. I don't want to mention any names, but the big leader would appear. He wasn't staying with us, of course. He was staying at a luxury hotel in DC, and literally, I'm not fooling you, a limousine would pull up, and this guy would get out. This guy would get out and have his overalls, but they were brand-new, starched, just taken out of the bag. Brand-new starched white t-shirt. Lead us in a few chants, pop back into his limousine and drive off.

Ernesto Aguilar: That's messed up!

J. Sakai: Y'know, and Tijerina was a one-man leadership type guy, but he interpreted that as meaning, if he wanted everybody to get up for a demonstration at 8, he'd be up at 7. If there wasn't enough food, he'd eat less. And it was just really impressive. Actually one of the things that impressed me about him most is he had this phenomenal memory. You'd talk to him for two minutes. And a week later, you'd meet him. He'd remember your name; he'd remember every word you said, because he was really listening to you. The Crusade for Justice people from Denver, Corky Gonzáles's people?

Ernesto Aguilar: Yeah?

J. Sakai: They were really impressive. There were about 400 of them. They were about half-Chicano, half-Black. I could be wrong, but it seemed to me very much Black, and very shoulder-to-shoulder, very tough group of people.

Ernesto Aguilar: I've spoken with Jesús Salvador Treviño, a writer who documented a lot of Corky's work, and the Raza Youth Liberation conferences in Denver, and I think one thing he mentioned as he came to consciousness is key to that. He said as he grew up that it was a given that there were Chicanos and oppressed people who were working lawns, going to jail and such, but something he learned from people involved in movements and who talked about history was that they put these things in context. They made sure people understood there is a systemic reason why oppressed people are at lower economic rungs in this society. The reason they're there is not because they're lazy or shiftless or whatever else the education system puts on you. Jesús said Corky brought a lot of these ideas out to so many young people to understand that oppression does not occur in a vacuum, but is deep and historical, and there's a reason for it.

J. Sakai: The other thing is—and I really remember this about the Chicano movement of the 1960s and '70s—people really practiced Solidarity: between oppressed peoples that you hear some people talk about, but sometimes it is more lip service than real. When AIM did the takeover at Wounded Knee, and got surrounded by the U.S. Army and had the siege and got shot up and everything? The largest demonstration in the U.S. was in Denver supporting them. The only large one, and it was the Crusade for Justice, it was mostly Chicano.

When Affirmative Action first started getting attacked in California in the early '80s—the law school I think it was at Berkeley ended the quota for Asian Americans, and the Chicanos offered to give part of their slots to Asians to fight for the principle of representation. And a lot of that spirit has been lost.

There's this thing that's happening; what used to be militant politics against systemic injustice, against capitalism as a system, has turned into ethnic politics for a lot of people, with the veneer of seeming to be militant, protesting about this and that, but underneath it is an attitude of "we should just look out for ourselves. We really shouldn't care about anybody but ourselves. And as for everyone else, we should say nice things, but potentially they could be an enemy, so we really should only think of us." I know that Asians are told that by conservative forces in our communities, and certainly Black people are told this, because it's the Amerikan way to subvert militant consciousness in people's movements by trying to make them more capitalist.

Jefferson tried to do that with the Indians in the Iroquois Confederacy. He sent them messages saying, "You should join the United States. You're good people, we want to get together with you, but your laws aren't any good. That's why we need to bring you into our country instead of just leaving you in your country, because your laws don't protect private property. You share everything in common." And although he didn't say it, of course, he knew in the Iroquois Confederacy that women had tremendous legal powers under their laws and government. You couldn't have a war unless three-quarters of the mothers, women who had borne children, voted for the war, for example, under their laws. No men could vote for war. This was the indigenous way of having a society that Jefferson thought was really crazy. "You really need to join us, have our laws, which protect private property, you can get rich, and you'll like it much better." Of course, what he really meant was, "we want to take you over and, if you don't have private property, you can't sell us everything you have, which we want you to do. So we're going to get you to do this or we're going to shoot you, one or the other." Which is their standard approach to these things, as we can see in Afghanistan and Iraq.

Ernesto Aguilar: I was about to mention that!

J. Sakai: They're bringing democracy to Iraq, only they don't seem to be doing a good job of it right now.

Ernesto Aguilar: You see a lot of mounting resistance.

J. Sakai: The thing is, they're invading the whole world essentially, and it's true they can conquer any part of it they want to, but that doesn't mean people are going to like them, or put up with it, or not resist. Of course people are going to resist, from all kinds of points of view. I don't think this is ever going to end until they leave. That's actually what I think. And I think the same thing is true for Amerika. I don't think there is any solution to any of these problems until Amerika is desettlerized.

Ernesto Aguilar: One question from a listener is: How do we "desettlerize" a country like the U.S. or Israel? Especially in a place like the U.S. where many righteous national liberation movements, such as the Black/New Afrikan and the Chicano movements especially, overlap and may contradict Native land claims and national liberation?

J. Sakai: I don't think any of us are going to have problems solving our relations with each other as long as we get the U.S. Empire and capitalist rip-offs out of the way. There is plenty of land in Amerika. Everyone could live here who lives here, quite well, with a lot of autonomy, a lot of justice, a lot of room for expression and development. But the obstacle isn't each other, in that sense.

As for desettlerization, it's already happening, because settlerism is a phenomenon of the past, really. All over the world, settler societies, as we saw in Africa, are going out of business. In Algeria, which was officially a province of France until the 1950s revolution, you had a million French settlers living there, and virtually the whole of the French army occupying it. Finally they all had to leave. Yeah, Algeria has a lot of problems, but it *is* Algerian.

I don't think that's going to happen here, obviously, because there's no place for that kind of migration to happen. But desettlerization isn't happening that way. Like in Israel, the problem is not that Jewish people live in Palestine. The problem is there are special laws, unjust laws, that deny land to Palestinians who live there while, of course, giving land to Zionists, even though they may have no connection whatsoever to Palestine that anybody can prove, except they say they follow the Jewish religion. They come from Russia, they come from Brooklyn, they come from wherever.

People look at Amerika and they don't see how Amerika could be desettlerized, but it's being desettlerized right now.

It's funny. The place where I work, the other guys who work there are Mexican. They're not Chicano, they're Mexican. First-generation. This is not their home—their home is back in Mexico. Very conservative family people in a social way. More conservative than I am, for sure. They're exactly the kind of Mexicans that the Republican Party and Bush are aiming at as the ideal minority. In fact, some of the guys voted for Bush, because he sounded like a better leader or something. So they're not radical in any political sense whatsoever.

But it's interesting when you talk to them about Amerika. They don't believe in the United States. At all. What they think is that the United States and Mexico are really just one country. To them it isn't just Aztlán. It isn't just the Southwest. It's that, there's Mexico, which is, to them, a special place, a really good place. Too poor, but a good place. As they say, "It has everything but money." And then there's Amerika. Lots of different people live here. They think that's great, and just how it should be. But, they've noticed this funny thing. And I don't want to insult anybody, but the way they look at it,

Amerikans don't like to work. We're in the wealthy suburbs, and there are Mexicans all over the place, of course. All the landscaping, porters, guys unloading trucks, people laying masonry for the patios, all the workers are Mexican. So their view is they don't quite understand Amerika, but they've figured out one thing: real Amerikans aren't into working. They don't understand it, but okay, fine by them. To them, there's this huge land, which frankly needs them, because they're the people who are going to do the work. They actually don't believe in a separate United States in any real sense of the word—immigration laws, borders. They think that's nonsense. It isn't just because of the legal history, but really, to them, it's their country as much as it is anyone else's. And they're not nationalistic in any narrow sense about it. They talk about the fact that, "Yeah, Mexican guys live here." One guy knows a guy who married a Polish woman, who immigrated from Poland, and he thinks that's great. But to them, Amerika doesn't belong to the people who call themselves Amerikans. That's where they differ from the Republicans and George Bush. They're part of the actual reversal of the Treaty of Guadalupe Hidalgo that's going on, only it's happening in a very postmodern way. It isn't simply reversal in terms of the Southwest. Clearly the whole character of the Southwest is changing year by year.

I'm in the Midwest, and when the Mexican Consulate said it was going to issue ID cards so that people could get bank accounts and everything else, we literally had a traffic jam. There were 10,000 people lined up on the main business street. Completely bizarre. And all the right-wingers are having fits! They're writing letters to the newspaper saying, "This Mexican ID card is as good as an Amerikan birth certificate. How can we let this happen?" But the logic of modern globalized life is that they have to. The banks want bank accounts with this money in it, so they want these people to have consular IDs, which aren't Amerikan in any way whatsoever. You can just see, year by year, the whole shift starting to happen socially, culturally. It has to happen in a political sense, of course, and it hasn't yet. But you certainly can see the underlying migration that is a migration not just geographically, but is changing politics just as surely as when Black people left the South and immigrated to the Northern industrial cities, or when we Asians came to Hawaii and the West Coast in the nineteenth century.

Ernesto Aguilar: Is that how you see desettlerization working, where you see this migration of peoples? It sounds like that is how it is working in practice in the Midwest, and historically how it has worked in the South as well as the Northeast—would you say that is how desettlerization will happen in the United States over the next few years?

J. Sakai: That's the underlying historical thing that will happen, but it isn't going to deal with the whole political struggle, which we're now engaged in, because, of course, the white settler population has essentially had a historic 400-year pact with capitalism, which is that they will get the best of everything. Maybe that won't be a lot, but it will be the best of the little. They will get the best of everything that is available in return for supporting capitalism and the U.S. Empire and its conquest over other people, as well as its exploitation. Well, frankly, globalization and the desettlerization of North America is threatening that. How long can you have a population in which more and more people don't actually work? I mean, you say the word "welfare" in Amerika and everybody's supposed to picture a Black woman in a housing project. But the real welfare is for white middle-class people. You have entire office buildings and cities full of people who don't actually produce anything. They move paper around, they bill people, they do things, but they don't actually produce anything. Everything that is produced is produced somewhere else by somebody else. And the question is how long can that be maintained?

I would say it's breaking down even now. It certainly is in Europe, and that's why there are fascist movements and all this right-wing stuff happening in Europe. Because the social compact is breaking down, and it's going to happen here too. And the political struggle is not going to happen peacefully, in the sense that it's not going to be some gradual social process. The underlying economics are one thing. The political struggle over who gets what out of that and whether there will be a just society or not is a whole other question.

Ernesto Aguilar: Another question from the audience: What are some of the biggest misconceptions about your writing, and how do you respond to some of the critics who have written about your writing?

J. Sakai: Actually, although I've heard a lot of criticism, there hasn't been a lot of writing criticizing it. I always tell people I don't have a problem with criticism, just write down factually where the mistakes are and we can argue about that. At that point, people disappear, because they can't seem to locate those things.

I'd say the biggest misconception, though, is that people think I'm talking about race alone, that everything in Amerika is determined by race, and that's not really what I'm saying. What I'm saying is that race in Amerika has been used as an identifier for capitalism to form and control classes, that race is not just a metaphor for class, but an identifier of class in real terms. So that everything is upside-down—things that are racial are really about class. Like Affirmative Action. The real Affirmative Action is the enormous built-in advantages that white middle-class people, particularly from the suburban school systems have, that get them into universities, and getting corporate jobs and networking. Everybody knows this. It's not a big deal. It's just a fact, right? So that's the actual Affirmative Action. These other programs are really to compensate for that, and are just the warped forms that the Civil Rights victories of the 1960s forced upon the society. I mean, I don't personally view them as significant. The fight over them really is, in a funny way, a fight within settler society, within imperialism itself, over how it's going to manage itself.

In the University of Michigan case, where Bush—supposedly on the advice of Condoleezza Rice, his African American advisor—weighed in on the side opposing the university's Affirmative Action policy. All of a sudden, the three former Joint Chiefs of Staff, former heads of West Point and the Naval Academy, as well as General Motors, Microsoft, and dozens of other major corporations all filed briefs supporting Affirmative Action. So we're not in this fight actually. This is a pure ruling class fight, having it out with each other. That's what's interesting about it—it's their problem.

Since it originally arose over law school—not something I would ever myself want to do, nor would I urge any sane person to do—I really couldn't care less.

Ernesto Aguilar: Another question from the audience: To what extent does this analysis depart from traditional Marxism that reduces everything to class? Where does your analysis relate to or differ from anti-racist feminism as presented by people like Gloria Anzaldúa, who argue that all systems of oppression are connected in some way?

J. Sakai: To the last, I really agree. All systems of oppression are connected. The difficulty is in figuring out what these connections are. Part of the problem I have with anti-racist feminism is that a lot of it is very middle class, and it's used to actually muddy the question of oppression, i.e., suddenly everybody's oppression is equal. Well, actually, everybody's oppression isn't equal, and I tend to be very concrete about those things myself.

Ernesto Aguilar: Thank you!

J. Sakai: Growing up in a Japanese American family, you've been to camp. When I was a little kid, people talked about camp, "going to camp," "this happened at camp." When I was a kid, I didn't know that—and this happened in everyone's family—it was a way of talking about being in the concentration camps without being blunt and saying it, so if you were overheard by the kids, then they won't know what you were talking about. I didn't actually find out about concentration camps until white people started stopping me on the street and giving me various explanations of why I shouldn't blame them for it. When I was a young kid. I can't count the number of people who told me, "That wasn't a real concentration camp you and your family were in. That was the Jews in Germany. They got killed. That was the real concentration camp. You weren't really in a concentration camp." Oh, thanks.

Actually, I would never say—I've never met a Japanese American who said—what we went through was anything like what the Jews in Europe went through under Nazism. Literally never heard anybody even hint that that could be true, because that would be crazy. You'd have to be a nut to think that. But it doesn't mean what we went through wasn't real. It doesn't mean that there weren't terrible human losses out of it. It doesn't mean that the reparations program that Ronald Reagan and Bill Clinton did isn't just a piece of junk, in my opinion, compared to what happened. And is not any actual reparations or justice.

There's this funny thing where middle-class people are always inventing trendy ways to be oppressed, in which their oppression is somehow just as real as yours. I don't think so, but it's not my appointed task in life to argue with them.

I do think, and this is true, that because the interconnection of oppressions is something we still don't understand real well. Like a lot of people were having this political fight over Oliver Stone's movie *JFK*? It was supposed to be so radical because it says he was killed by a conspiracy? Well, it's this complete piece of junk. Who were the conspirators? I was sitting in this movie and couldn't believe what I was seeing. The conspirators were this group of gay, stereotyped, mincing kind of queens, who, at one point, even wore dresses. So, gay people were the conspiracy that killed JFK?! This is the progressive, radical, threatening movie? Gimme a break. It's nothing but homophobic junk. If you really wanted to have a movie in which you really showed the people who killed JFK, they'd be white guys wearing three-piece suits, sitting in corporate boardrooms and hanging out at the Pentagon. They wouldn't be gay people from Latin America. The fact that that could go over in Amerika without people burning down movie theaters shows how deeply ingrained the homophobia in this society is, for real.

Ernesto Aguilar: Can you give people an idea of some of the things you're up to?

J. Sakai: Well, along with some other comrades, I've been working on trying to better understand the whole new popular wave of far right-wing politics and fascism in the world, because, to us, that's the new threatening phenomenon happening. Not just in Europe, but here, in India, etc. You've always got to watch the new semi trailer coming up in your rearview mirror, threatening to drive you off the road.

Beyond McAntiwar: Notes on Finding Our Footing in the Collapsing Stage Set of the u.s. Empire (2005)

1. Conspiracy Theories Can Be Themselves The Question

Ever since World Trade came crashing down, conspiracy theories have been like the favorite beverage of men's protest politics. Wilder the better. Major problems exist with being obsessed about these possible conspiracies, however. We see grainy photos "proving" that the Pentagon was never hit at all (and guesses that the United Airlines passengers were probably flown to a remote desert base in Area 51 to be executed secretly by the c.i.a.). The whole of 9/11 was supposedly manufactured u.s. government propaganda, all the better for the falling real bodies. All prearranged behind the scenes by the f.b.i., c.i.a., Mossad, Jewish Wall Street, Saudi intelligence, and the Bush royal family working together with perhaps a dash or two of Arab dupes. Iraq itself was invaded by most of the u.s. army straining to pretend that it can still win wars only so that W. and Cheney could personally guzzle their oilfields. And so on and on. These dirty-sexy imaginary politics are, of course, only fitting for a crazed neo-colonial world. Where the supposed "liberator" men have become as deranged as the imperialist men.

Any of this could be true as far as it goes. After all, now even the *Washington Post* is asking why the head of Pakistani military intelligence once sent $100,000 to Mohammed Atta, the supposed leader of the 9/11 suicide hijackers?

And the *Wall Street Journal* revealed that Saddam requested in late 2002 that $30 million of the UN-administered "Oil For Food" funds be used for NATO-standard military gas-masks! Was that to be with or without pepperoni? An amazing request that was approved without any publicity by both the Bush regime and UN officials. Why would an invading u.s. empire shouting about the threat of Arab chemical-biological weapons want to help equip its supposed enemy to use them—unless they slyly wanted to encourage "Sad Damn" to use poison gas on GIs? Are you confused enough now? There is enough raw material in the daily machinations of global capitalism for a thousand conspiracy theories.

If you believe in any of these conspiracy theories you certainly aren't alone. A recent Zogby public opinion poll showed that 49% of New Yorkers believed that u.s. agencies "consciously" aided the 9/11 attack. Similar opinion poll figures pop up in Germany. And certainly in the Muslim world there's near 100% belief in 9/11 as a greater u.s.-Jewish conspiracy. Life in capitalist society makes a belief in conspiracies only rational, since we know that there are multiple layers of secret and illicit decision-making all around us reaching high up to the thrones of power. From the drug dealers paying off the police to the mafia garbage removal contracts to the Enronization of natural gas prices by the Bush clubhouse to those never-solved assassinations of so many trade unionists and journalists in the Southern Hemisphere to ... It runs on without end, since by its basic soiled nature capitalism = conspiracy.

But there are several big problems with being obsessed with these political fantasies. Or believing that conspiracy theories are the real politics.

2. Leftover Anti-Imperialism Doesn't Get System Breakdown

These conspiracy theories all conjure up and build towards a picture of a vast u.s. imperial power, omnipotent almost beyond imagining, a brilliantly evil empire like in Star Wars capable of reshaping and turning inside out the entire world. But what we (and our sisters and brothers in the rest of the world) live with every day instead is a so-called u.s. empire that is increasingly thugz with guns in hollywood sets and poses. A poser empire, whose elected emperor is not a gate-crasher but an accurate representation of a euro-settler people whose bullying frontier ways only cover for fear and confusion about their collapsing future.

An elected emperor who is a known coward but who loves to dress up in military uniforms and police jackets he never earned and make speeches at military bases and aircraft carriers surrounded by obedient buff white soldiers. Yes, still a nation that is very violent & very large but also terminally clumsy almost beyond belief; that once had great industrial resources but is so rapidly wasting away that even its mighty huffing-and-puffing techno-wars against tiny nations can only be done by maxing out on its Masterscard.

For example, we now know that the f.b.i. had agents and informers all over the "Oceans 19" Arab men who later made their mark as the Al-Qaeda teams that hijacked the airliners and crashed World Trade. Was this f.b.i. disinterest before 9/11 really a covert encouragement or even manipulation? Maybe, but the same f.b.i. also ignored obvious clues and let its wacko agent Robert Hanssen betray all its intelligence secrets and double-agents to Moscow for years. (On the known facts, you could even argue that if there is a gigantic shocking superduperconspiracy it is that the Russian KGB secretly took over the f.b.i. and c.i.a. years ago and everything American is really Russian—oh, but then the Russian empire has self-destructed, too.) Maybe historical obsolescence by the dinosaur imperialist State and that entire stage of capitalist civilization is a bigger factor than we want to believe.

Their superduperconspiracies real or imagined are not even the big deal anymore. What is overriding everything is the material rearrangement of the entire human world, and the class change that flows out of that being dominant over all. Step by step, we need to go into this new world disorder—to unfold the order emerging within it.

Destructive power now exists everywhere, after all, on all levels. That's why W. had to secretly fly into Baghdad on turkeys day 2003 with his jet's lights off and maintaining radio silence—for a handjob of a media visit that never got further than the airfield hanger itself—because the mr. mighty of this mighty empire has to zig-zag in fear of any 19-year-old unemployed former Iraqi army private with an old Russian missile. You can catch the wave, but not by standing on the shore.

While the u.s. empire has since its birth sent arrogant military expeditions into other lands & continents, the "natives" have seldom been able to retaliate before. To be sure, Cherokee warriors angry at the sell-out treaty signed by

bogus "chiefs" slipped into u.s. president Andrew Jackson's inaugural party at the Whitest House—and assassinated a pro-u.s. "chief" (thus starting the whole agency of Whitest House security, which hadn't existed among the white settlers before then). After World War I, Pancho Villa's Army of the North led cross-border raids into the Southwest, and in the 1950s Puerto Rican Nationalist Party activists shot up the u.s. congress and the VP's home to protest the murderous wave of u.s. political repression in Puerto Rico.

But while the anti-u.s. resistance of the oppressed has always spilled into Smallville, 9/11 marks a qualitatively changed level of war. So when those real "Oceans 19" with a budget of only thousands and some box-cutters brought down the World Trade, killing thousands of affluent euro-settler men (80% of those killed were upper-middle class white men), and blew out part of the Pentagon itself, it set off a worldwide shockwave. Fuck Bush, Cheney & Rummy, this was real shock & awe.

It was a smack so devastating that many couldn't really believe that it was the lowly "sand n—s" (as the GI guards at Guantanamo so charmingly refer to the Muslims there) that had stuck a cap up Captain America's ass. To this day millions of confused people of color are convinced that only the white man is sophisticated enough to have pulled off this fantastic scheme. Confused conspiracy theories "proving" that the c.i.a. or the International Jewish Conspiracy staged it all are mostly just pathetic, showing how a slave-like inner awe of White Power and feelings of inferiority still infects many nationalists of color (and "Socialists" for that matter). But that sure isn't what Osama and his boys are feeling, because they are the wave.

On the ocean's edge old refuse and different dead things drift closer and closer on the tide to be washed up together side-by-side on the shore. Similarly, dead white left propaganda and Black cultural nationalist propaganda on the u.s. empire are coming together now, washing up and decaying together in the backwash of world events. Theirs are only scare tactics, in which the overreaching dying u.s. empire is pictured as the world's boogey-man, as everyone's greatest threat. "American Empire, Not 'If' But 'What Kind?'" is a typical headline in the liberal *N.Y. Times*. Noam Chomsky, White America's favorite anarchist, titles his new book, *Hegemony or Survival: America's Quest For Global Domination.*

Or the same dead ideas recycled and dyed black in cultural nationalism, like the well-meaning *Frontline* hip-hop zine editorial which warns of Jewish domination of the media in 9/11, and says: "we must overstand the objectives and goals of those in power to control your mind, body and soul ... a so-called 'conscious Black man or woman' is not necessarily keyed in on the European objective—White Supremacy. This beast wants to control this planet and everything in it." (yawn—been there, done that).

These kind of stances are just flickering late-night movie reruns of faded 20th-century events and ideas. European capitalists actually took over title to the entire planet and its planetary population (including—as my comrade Butch always says—not only all humans but every animal and plant down to the last seal and tree and stalk of grain) in the Berlin imperialist conference around 1884 or so. But as rising Asian billionaires can happily testify, Whitey is definitely losing it double-time.

In this real new world order, militarily victorious Vietnamese "Communism" is begging for more Nike sweatshops. Post-colonial Ethiopians and Eritreans with their own tanks and artillery aplenty slaughtered their own people in Black-on-Black border shoving matches in numbers like the u.s. military in its Muslim wars. Remember that funny Black cultural nationalist line from the 1980s that Africans are the supposed "Sun people," genetically predisposed to be more humane and civilized than those admittedly nasty "Ice people" from Northern Europe? Clowns don't always make you laugh.

Speaking of which, right now the Hindu ethno-nationalist fascists of India's Bharatiya Janata Party (who openly styled themselves after the Nazis) should have become international pariahs for mass slaughters and pogroms attacking Indian Muslims, but have only found new allies like the u.s. empire and the Zionist Sharon regime of Israel, which loves anything anti-Muslim ... which has itself been applauded as Allah's chosen true owners of Palestine by none other than our own Minister Louis Farrakhan. Why aren't the superduperconspiracy addicts shouting about this?

It's all less like a c.i.a. conspiracy and more like a capitalist interracial circle jerk. So today's biggest u.s. Black Muslim politician is in reality going along with the slaughter of Muslims, while Zionism going on about the Holocaust in their dishonest way (they soon will accomplish the once-impossible, making even the Holocaust seem only like an ordinary capitalist commodity) are backing other peoples' fascist pogroms and schemes for genocide. Simple-minded politics can definitely get a person's ass killed in this world.

Compared to the rush of the real, those obsessive 9/11 conspiracy theories are timid entertainments at best. Even if one or another part of these theories are true—and patriarchal capitalism is a gigantic conspiracy by its very nature—they can be used in a misleading way because they aren't about the main thing coming down the road.

3. Yesterday's World Empire Not Expanding But Crashing

Televised pictures of u.s. soldiers repossessing bad boy Saddam's unused Scud missiles & empty palaces. Gloating white men in suits speaking publicly of ruling the first true world empire since the daze of imperial Rome. One that will nakedly command the known world by force, caring nothing for the wants or views or laws of others. Yet the slanting light that now shades Washington is not dawn but twilight. For we are living in the age of the decline and fall of the bubble empire. And the final ending of amerikkka as we've known it, beyond good or evil. This war may or may not be downstream by the time you read this, but it's useful to break down the inner development of how the world is changing for us all and by us all.

We can use imperialism's wars as our gauge of its historic decline. Two generations ago the u.s. empire fought a great world war 2 against other industrial capitalist powers. A brutal, bloody, fighting toe-to-toe war of near-equals in which millions of soldiers crisscrossed oceans and borders, leaving well over 60 million dead bodies as their rotting residue. In one single European battle alone, in one week in a forgotten Luxembourg forest, 33,000 white GIs died in combat (with another 10,000 dying from exposure and disease). And it doesn't mean a thing now.

Then one generation ago the u.s. empire threw a 500,000-man expeditionary force that was the heart of the u.s. military into a protracted, eleven-year war to stop Communist-led national liberation movements in three Southeast Asian countries. To their white surprise, they lost big time and 58,000 GIs and Marines and sailors and airmen lost their lives as well (though to be sure they each got an engraved line on that spiffy black wall in Washington—'cause in America there's always a prize in every box of crackerjacks). And it doesn't mean a thing now.

Today, in contrast, the u.s. bubble empire, with its heavy-technology storm troopers, struts and preens itself in decadent ecstasy whenever they can recapture any small, poverty-stricken Third World capitalist neo-colony (often done in a fake war, as in Afghanistan and Iraq, with cooperating bribed warlords and generals). Hollywood invasions of Haiti, Afghanistan, Panama, tiny Philippine islands, or dysfunctional oil-field dictatorships mark the true level of their beat power now. But if a few hundred or a few thousand of its mercenary techno-legion GIs get whacked, then the whole society is weeping and wailing.

Privileged amerikkka is too soft to slug it out anymore. We might say that the u.s. empire is less like a great military power in the old sense and more like a superbly-armed private mafia for a gated suburb. Its power is very dangerous on a tactical level—like a SWAT team blowing down your front door will really put some concern on your mind—but strategically it is more and more dysfunctional and immobilized.

To be the lone "Superpower" left is not necessarily to be superduper nor even to be on the rise. What is rising instead is the new stage of capitalist production & distribution—what everyone too-simply calls "Globalization."

4. Anti-War & The Nature of the War

The Anti-War movement doesn't understand, but these are completely different wars than in the 1960s or 1970s. Now we have neo-colonial wars. Not wars of good vs. evil, not wars of oppressed vs. oppressor. And certainly not liberation wars.

They are wars within the capitalist world hierarchy, between the bloated metropolis and its own vicious neo-colonial subordinates. If the manager and the foreman in your factory lose it and started shooting at each other you'd want to get yourself & the other workers out of harm's way. But, basically, as Dr. Phil always says, "We don't have a dog in this fight!" If they killed each other off without harming anyone else, that would be too fine to be true—as Habte Selassie said joyfully on public radio about the 1980s war between the British empire and the Argentine military junta, "Let the blood flow!" The political problem with the still-confused Anti-War activists right now is that they keep wanting to side with the foreman. Groan. 'Cause we're seeing lots of fights now where both sides are the capitalistic enemy, even though one side are "natives."

Imperial stormtroopers must descend on neo-colonial nations one after another. This isn't a sign of success but of growing failure, of system breakdown. Their own barely launched neo-colonial states, many hardly older than your local used car lot (like, i'm older personally than the nation of Pakistan or the Republic of Iraq—or the Israeli Fourth Reich, for that matter), are crumbling. Often these nations have lost much of their artificial inner cohesion. As the hundreds of millions of dispossessed without real jobs or agricultural land keep rising, as capitalist exploitation screws tighter and tighter on the very poorest, as capitalism itself forcibly breaks up all the old ways of life while State parasitism is protected with death squads and torture chambers, social upheaval can no longer be contained within limits or borders. To be able to control any square mile of territory you want anywhere in the world—by crushing weight of military hardware—but to control less and less outside of that, is not victory.

Globalized capitalism is also pirates with speedboats and AK-47s attacking freighters and oil tankers at sea (thousands of ships have been captured in the last decade, quiet as it's kept) & Brazilian cities where one-third of regularly employed men are security guards. Pakistan's pro-Western military regime admits that its own intelligence and security agency cannot be trusted because it is infiltrated by islamic fascist sympathizers. Nor can they rely on their corrupt and ineffectual police. So the hunt for Al-Qaeda and Taliban cells in Pakistan is being led by f.b.i. agents, who are emerging as the main secret police in Third World nation after nation. This is beautiful, a capitalist recall even better than Ford & Firestone having to admit their murderous rip-off & eat their bogus SUV tires. The u.s. empire is having to recall their own bogus neo-colonial states. Underline that.

Because America has a global presence and is everywhere, it can also be attacked anywhere, from Kenya to Colombia to Afghanistan, and can no longer actually be defended. Just as with the importation of labor and mass travel, no enemy can be kept outside the national walls. Not Central Asians out of Moscow nor anyone at all out of New York City. That's why "airport security" is such an elaborate pantomime, like the changing of the guard at buckingham palace or the appearance of Democratic presidential candidates at the NAACP convention—it's just for the show.

The white middle-class Anti-War movement that sprang up spontaneously here was both very new and very familiar, bad politics and all. Many thousands of all ages came into dissenting political commitment for the first time. One sixteen-year-old who was arrested by police in the mass illegal blockage & occupation of Chicago's Lake Shore Drive highway during rush hour said after getting out, "This is the greatest thing that's ever happened to me!" We were laughing, but we really understood that—it's one thing to hear about history but a whole different experience to be breaking rules and making a little history yourself. That in a white movement just born, without the years of shock & awe that the old Anti–Vietnam War movement went through, without Black revolutionary teaching (today's Black cultural nationalism and liberalism is just the empty box without the cereal), stale liberal politics are only to be expected. No need for us to go into any details or indictments.

No, the political problem isn't with new anti-war activists starting their cycle of reinventing the training wheel, it is with the shallow discount anti-imperialism that prevails. The Anti-War slogan "No Blood For Oil" has been so useful because it points the finger at selfish capitalistic motives in a broad cartoon way that folks from many different viewpoints can feel comfortable with. Like "Make Peace Not War" or "One Man One Vote" or "Have It Your Way." But being catchy & convenient doesn't make any of it true.

This is an example of how an essentially misleading idea first crafted by the capitalist Right was happily swallowed by the white liberal-marxist-anarchist crowd (there's as much or as little difference between these three brands of the same thing as between coke, pepsi, and rc), without them noticing what was up. This is an idea planted by the capitalists themselves, so it can hardly be a bold exposé on our part to use it in propaganda. In the buildup to the first Gulf War, it was the Bush Sr. Administration and the captive u.s. media who kept broadcasting how much control of the world's oil was at stake. As Bush 41 said, he wasn't going to let 25% of the

USA = #1
TERRORIST

petroleum needed by "civilization" be left under the control of some "little dictator." (Unlike the Kuwaiti dictatorship or the dictatorships in Saudi Arabia or Nigeria?) Ever since, it's all been wars for oil, according to the unthinking left of the metropolis.

If you could believe that the u.s. once invaded Vietnam because they wanted to own more white rice, or that the c.i.a. invaded the Bay of Pigs because they wanted more sugar cane, then this petromania is the vulgar materialist conspiracy theory made for you!

White Anti-War activists don't really understand what the words "capitalist world system" mean, or that Iraq has always been an integrated part of it (Arabs never created Iraq, which was constructed as a pseudo-nation by the British Empire after WWI). So long as oil was a commodity, it belonged to world capitalism not to Saddam Hussein. Was Saddam going to eat the oil with his morning cornflakes? Or refuse to sell it so he could not equip his regime with porn videos and tanks and palaces and mercedes? Not a minute went by that Saddam and his vicious little dictatorship (which was just an approved local ghetto franchise for world capitalism) weren't cheerfully selling the Western petroleum corporations all the oil they could. What else were they going to do with it? If outright occupation of Baghdad was so essential to imperialist control of oil, why didn't the Bush dynasty bother to do it in 1991? Duh.

It isn't that there is any lack of good people, sincere and intelligent, in the opposition to the u.s. war machine. It's that these are movements that by their very nature now are bankrupt & corrupted. Like the old social-democratic parties of Western Europe, which were born in militant working-class struggle from the bottom against autocratic regimes in the 19th century, but which by the start of World War I had become an institutionalized safety valve despite their mass working-class base.

5. Imperialism Itself Being Morphed

Certainly, the Whitest House would love it if all the world's petroleum was totally owned by u.s. corporations, or if all the world's computers were made in Silicon Valley. Or all the world's cars made in Detroit. And Mobil or IBM would love it, too, that's the must-keep-moving-to-breathe nature of shark-like capitalist competition. But they aren't making their actual plans based on that unreal fantasy. Nor are Halliburton or Wall Street depending on any fantasy world oil monopoly.

Because Globalization is erasing the duplication of national economies, Britain, for example, no longer owns its own auto industry at all but has its factories owned by Ford, Honda, GM, Toyota, BMW, and Nissan—and now China's Shanghai Automobile corporation. On the other hand, two of the three largest world petroleum corporations are British. National economies are no longer symmetrical and parallel, as they were in the bygone 20th-century daze of brother national imperialisms, before neo-colonial "Globalization."

Oil in international capitalist discourse right now is their metaphor standing for all key globalized commodities (just as nuclear weapons were once their illusory symbol for military supremacy). While petroleum is important economically, it is no more so than soybeans or rare industrial minerals or migratory labor or narcotics or many other major commodities which capitalist civilization can't do without and which the ruling class therefore needs to control. Oil is certainly much less important a commodity than women. White liberal/leftists and Black liberal cultural nationalists together (and they have so much in common politically) have been shouting their tired clichés about how the world conflict was over oil, but, as Butch Lee said recently, "What is starting to emerge is a world war 4 over who shall own women. If you haven't understood that, your daughters will."

The Iraq wars don't begin with oil, they begin in neo-colonial "Globalization." Iraq was invaded and Saddam's local franchise was overthrown not for oil (and certainly not because of any threat that they posed to Saks Fifth Avenue). It was conquered just so that the Bush regime could do it. Not p.r. campaigns to justify a war—as radicals unthinkingly echo liberals in saying—but a war that is the p.r. campaign. As an advertisement to the Third World that the u.s. empire was still able to destroy any nation-state that opposed it (and, not least of all, to project Bush W. 43 as the macho-macho man swinging his khaki-painted thang for the all-important elections). As *N.Y. Times* foreign affairs columnist Thomas L. Friedman said in his column titled "Because We Could":

> "The 'real reason' for this war, which was never stated, was that after 9/11 America needed to hit someone in the Muslim world ... Smashing Saudi Arabia or Syria would have been fine. But we hit Saddam for one simple reason: *because we could* ... " (emphasis in original)

Two things are going on here. The first is that as neo-colonial "Globalization" developed it morphed the nature of world conflict. We know that the distance between the formerly all-powerful imperialist powers and the Third World, between high-tech societies and low-tech societies, has broken down. Just as the distance between military and civilian has dissolved (in WWI 90% of the casualties were soldiers, in the latest wars 90% of the casualties are civilians, mostly women & children). And if imperialism has made technology and migrating multiethnic populations and modern warfare ever-present in global life, then how can you prevent any ex-soldier from driving towards Oklahoma City with a truck-load of ammonium nitrate fertilizer? Or a group of educated, multilingual Arab men from boarding a large jetliner in Boston?

So it's no surprise that the Noriegas and Saddams and Osamas of this new stage of capitalism were wanting to be big business themselves. The neo-colonies want to become players in their own right. In 1990 Saddam was given private permission by the Bush 41 regime to go for the Northernmost oil fields of Kuwait, which were in disputed territory. Saddam greedily overreached his playpen, and that was destabilizing to the u.s. empire's Middle Eastern back yard. The Iraq wars have never been about owning some oil directly (since imperialism owns it all, directly and indirectly) but about starting surgical restructuring to bring the entire region and all its population under reconditioned & tighter u.s. imperial occupation and closer imperial administration. In doing so, the u.s. empire would, of course, try to tap into Iraqi oil revenues as much as they can. That's not a secret. No different than the IRS and my paycheck, only on a global scale.

The second thing that is going down is that neo-colonial "Globalization" is erasing the economic foundations of the old imperialist national empires. That's why there's only one stumbling military "Superpower" left. It says enough that half the military expenditures for the entire world are by the u.s. military.

Some comrades have been heavily pointing out that this empire thing is not new to America. That the u.s. was always an empire from day one. Always invading, colonizing, always occupying other peoples and nations. But we have to be careful that even with this valuable insight we don't

get misled by the past, that an old truth doesn't accidentally obscure our vision of the new situation. The old white euro-settler society that was America is being ruthlessly torn down & remade, still stubbornly rooted in its stolen lands but no longer dominant on a world scale or even necessarily in North America. Like every other capitalist power, America is contributing its DNA to a world capitalism of a new type. We need to explore what the declining u.s. empire is evolving towards, and where the firing line is.

The old national imperialisms of the 20th-century Great Powers—Britain, France, Germany, the u.s., Russia, and Japan—were profit-making machines for their national ruling classes. Each jealously held various territories, home nations, colonies and neo-colonies, which were both captive markets for its industries and exclusive suppliers of raw materials. Since the entire globe and all of its inhabitants were divided up among the imperialist nations, the desperate need to gain markets and raw materials from rival nations forced the capitalist world into two unprecedented World Wars with each other. This arrangement of national imperialist competition defined world economics and world politics for most of the century. But that's no longer true on the ground. That's why the gigantic river of federal funny money pouring into the largely useless u.s. techno-military can only be financed by equally gigantic loans from abroad.

Imperialist war no longer pays for itself. One-third of all u.s. Treasury bond purchasing in 2003 to finance the Bush imperial deficit is from ... China! So the Beijing "Communist" regime and its surging capitalist class are the primary financial backers of the u.s. empire's strategy of endless loser war? Do you notice any problems in this situation? Picture some suits in a big barrel about to go over Niagara Falls.

6. National Rivalries Remain But Are Swallowed Into New World Order

Right now one of Bush 43's accusations against North Korea's Stalinist monarchy is that it has made transgressive exporting of souped-up versions of Scud missiles a major business (this trade, according to Western intelligence officials, earned $560 million in 2003, over 3% of North Korea's total GNP). Less publicized is that North Korea's silent partner in its missile business is the capitalist government of Egypt, the u.s. empire's largest neo-colonial "ally" in the Arab world. The Egyptian military regime provided North Korea with its first Scuds to take apart & reverse-engineer, lent technical help and is its partner in the advanced arms sales venture. The "friend" (the Egyptian regime is the 2nd largest recipient of u.s. foreign aid) and the "enemy" (the North Korean regime is rogue state No. 1, & is under constant threat of u.s. attack) aren't worlds apart but are working together on the same side.

Even pinning down a real national enemy in the old Pearl Harbor sense is difficult, except in Washington's made-for-tv phony wars. Since with neo-colonial "Globalization" the u.s. empire and its capitalist rivals and enemies interpenetrate each other and develop within each other. While the Republican Party right wing is screaming about China as the main threat to evaporating u.s. military hegemony over the Pacific, major defense contractors like Boeing and Hughes are also becoming key aerospace contractors in and for the new capitalist China. In that role these two giant corporations "accidentally" gave their Chinese selves the technology of the advanced u.s. ICBMs, so that the Chinese military could leap into a new generation of nuclear intercontinental ballistic missiles (both corporations just agreed to pay fines in the many millions of dollars to settle federal charges on this little boo-boo which was kept out of the TV News and front-page headlines).

The Chinese and u.s. empires are rivals but also increasingly partners, like the u.s. and France or Putin's Great Russia and the reunified Germany. For that matter, president Bush's younger brother Neil has joined Jiang Mianheng, the son of former Chinese "Communist" president Jiang Zemin, on the board of Jiang's new Grace semiconductor corporation in China, uniting a new generation of u.s. and Chinese capitalist dynasties. Just as General Motors has asked China's Shanghai Automobile Corporation to be its partner in taking over South Korea's large Daewoo auto corporation. As that small possum peering out of the swamp observed, "We have met the enemy, and they is us."

7. Now "Anarcho-Capitalism" & Fascism as a World Player

Is the imperialism which was formerly national in form, collapsing/consolidating into one global super-state or super-empire, as Tony Negri posits in his work *Empire*? (And as the Bush regime wishes.) The former Italian theorist of the armed workers' "autonomia" rebellion (now a Roman Catholic advocate of bourgeois democracy) sees a simpler, starker, more class conscious world in which every little mass struggle must visibly be against one final world capitalist state. This sounds nifty, and some aspects of it are obviously true, but it's way too simplistic and vaguely optimistic. Many are drawn to this idea of a global super-state because unconsciously it reinvokes the familiar, only on a larger scale. But things aren't that stable. Not one unified world empire but, for the next period, "anarcho-capitalism" as a new order of disorder. Not one world mega-nation but many more small states, semi-autonomous areas and many, many more armies and para-military mafias.

Neo-colonial "Globalization" is taking a crowbar to the old capitalist class structure, that's for sure. The relationship between the big capital of world banks and transnational corporations, and their former home nations and former subject classes, is splintering. The growth in the economy is in these transnational corporations, who are constantly churning and shifting economic relationships—bankrupting many smaller capitalists and farmers and entire local economies.

So smaller local bourgeoisies and petit-bourgeoisies are now trying to recapture their "abandoned" regions and neo-colonies and are starting "anti-imperialist" campaigns and wars of morphed nationalism against global imperialism. These struggles—which everywhere attract mass support from the dispossessed male classes—can range politically from neo-fascist and clerical fascist to the authoritarian left, but are usually far-right. These are intra-capitalist wars of local capitalist insurgencies trying to win back control of "their" nations from the Great Powers.

So the u.s. empire is actually being attacked in a series of conflicts by popular clerical-fascist movements in the former Third World, as at the same time a growing neo-fascist opposition is being "normalized" within the Western bourgeois democracies. Two expressions of the same trend.

You can see this legitimation of pro-fascist sentiment once lightly camouflaged in the u.s. Anti-War activities, where joint demonstrations with far-right Muslim groups who advocate the enslavement of women and genocide against ethnic minorities is common—and where anyone who questions allying with islamic clerical fascism is attacked as "racist."

This unexpected "normalization" and mass acceptance of widely different forms of neo-fascism is the most significant political development in current world politics.

8. "The Most Important Election Of Our Lifetime"

It's a symptom of the left's own system failure that we have not let ourselves understand even the largest elephants of political phenomena.

Like the 2004 elections. We saw two main left-of-center lines. Many were pulled in by the sincere desperation of many progressives, into the electoral war to oust the Bush regime, into "Anybody But Bush" or "Vote or Die" grassroots campaigns for Mr. Ketchuphead. If this most openly evil and warmongering and "fascist" administration couldn't be thrown out, many believed, then what hope was there for any humane future? Giving this election a strong drama of Armageddon.

Others took the more radical line that Bush & Kerry were two similar heads to one imperialist monster. That supporting Kerry was just a well-meaning but futile detour, a waste of the time and energy of "the working class." Both these sincere opposite positions contain trace elements of truth but are untrue, especially for revolutionaries. Moreover, although opposite in outward form, both positions come from the same viewpoint. Radicals still view the 2004 elections from the standpoint of civilians, as though their left were a "Consumers Report" for better political supermarket shopping.

The 2004 election was an important victory for revolutionaries here, the most important in many years (all the sweeter because in our very weak state we can only get the fruit that falls from the tree). It is axiomatic in war that success depends in large part on using the systematic mistakes

and incompetence of the enemy. While civilians may wish hopelessly for the "best" capitalist government, we revolutionaries need incompetence in the seats of power—and the Bush royal family has raised hubris and incompetence to an art form. It is a sign, actually, of system failure, like Czar Nick in Russia lurching suicidally into World War I.

Bush and Mr. Ketchuphead are obviously far from the same, no matter what left rhetoric may say. The Gores and Kerrys are state managers, can more or less manage or mangle the sinking welfare state, but they can't build mass popular movements to save their lives (or as Maureen Dowd once wittily remarked, why be for Gore "who can't even win when he's won?"). While Bush & his right crew can successfully ride the white euro-settler majority despite shooting the bottom out of the u.s. national boat, but couldn't manage a hot dog stand. If revolutionaries here could actually choose the general staff of our opposition, we couldn't dream up a better choice from our point of view. Ah, more years of stupid adventures, trampling over the loyal middle classes & mismanaged takeovers—it's political bliss (reminds me of the flip of that old Black Muslim song, "Black Man's heaven is a white man's hell").

Actually, neither the Clinton nor Bush factions of the u.s. ruling class are nationalists in the old sense. They both use populism, nationalism & chauvinism as political tools, but both camps have effectively abandoned the old "America." Both have global political frameworks in mind to match the globalization of the transnational corporations. But while the Clinton faction are "Globalists," using trade and covert action to fuse nations and regions—as in NAFTA and the WTO—the Bush faction has been truly bold in trying to force the global economy into one world empire by imposing a de facto world army and a single world ideology of their own (despite the frontier act, this type of empire more closely resembles the old Ottoman empire in approach than traditional u.s. imperialism).

While the good old u.s.a. is being drained of resources for this attempted world occupation—like a disposable battery—by rulers who obviously care nothing even about their own commercial airlines or industries or national parks or health systems. Since they believe that successful people of the transcontinental capitalist class should live in a privatized strata of their own high above nations or national infrastructures (as Cheney amusingly commented, he sympathizes with the frustrations of lesser businessmen using commercial airlines, although he never uses them himself).

To make it plain: Earlier stages of u.s. imperialism economically enriched the father country. After World War I and World War II, for instance, the u.s. share of world industry & world markets sharply rose. Starting with Vietnam this changed. This new attempt at a global state may be headquartered in Washington and draw on u.s. national resources, but its conflicts no longer bring new wealth home to the increasingly precarious, debt-ridden home society.

Maybe most important of all, the election marked the return of the dead white men and their loyal women, the settler majority. They are being permitted to fight to take their now-shrunken white nation back. The limited time of racial-class concessions and maneuvers needed by the ruling class—and enforced on an unwilling white majority by the State—to subdue and coopt and dissolve the Black Revolution of the 1960s, is over.

This is the real "post–civil rights" era, not the phony slogan, where "White America" step-by-step returns to a version of its normal hateful settler self. But the contradiction here is, this is happening in a world capitalist context where such societies are officially disapproved of and even banned. Like ethnic genocidal Greater Serbia, "White America" is trying to adjust, just as it did in inventing Segregation in the lynching years after the late 19th-century Black Reconstruction experiment. And at long last, a sophisticated final solution to their "Black problem" is now running after 400 years. But discussions about this have been sharply censored on all sides and among all "Races."

9. TRANSITIONS

i started these notes in March 2003 right after the u.s. tanks rolled unopposed into Baghdad, and everyone was talking about an overpowering new world empire. It seemed important then to correct the eagerness to get drawn offside and then to tell lies & claim easy victories. After a few pages, though, i stopped because so many basic questions were being pulled to the surface. Then came months of using my spare time to gather materials and start outlines for a significantly larger paper on the split in the u.s. ruling class over neo-colonial "Globalization," as well as the Bush regime's radical vision of overblown world empire different from the historic u.s. imperialism. The plan was to discuss how opposing ruling class factions dealt with insurgency & opposition, and internal conflicts about the changing role of the u.s. military establishment.

However, it became apparent that in my very limited time such an ambitious paper would never happen. So, instead, i decided to quickly jot down some notes, however inadequate, just to share ideas and questions (things like the transformation of the u.s. state or the social basis of conspiracy theories were excluded due to lack of time). i apologize for the rough and incomplete nature of these notes.

This is a very different time for Maoists. The struggles of the oppressed have never stopped for one heartbeat, of course, despite the collapse of the world left or the conversion to capitalism of the anti-colonial leadership of color. "Necessity knows no laws." As the most developed form of communism in the 20th century, Maoist parties and struggles born from Maoism span the divide between old & new. The NPA in the Philippines, "Shining Path" in Peru, and the new guerrilla army/party in Nepal are major national liberation insurgencies ostensibly drawing on the example of the Chinese Communist Party during its 1930s–40s guerrilla years. As is the fragmented Naxalite movement in the West Bengal area of India. But many old guerrilla insurgencies have gradually become mired in intractable scenarios as the world political-military situation has changed around them. And, perhaps as a consequence, questions have gradually arisen about the class politics of their wars.

Old forms of revolutionary struggle, however valid in their day, are being replaced by new forms arising from the changing class awareness. The most influential new examples of insurgencies of the oppressed both come from Maoist party roots, the Zapatistas in Chiapas and the Revolutionary Association of the Women of Afghanistan. Neither is anything like a traditional Maoist M-L party, obviously. But both are creatively rooted in the basic Maoist principle that the oppressed have the right to take the struggle & society itself directly into their own hands (as opposed to Stalinist papal hierarchies or social-democratic legalistic reform movements). Lenin's strategic advice holds true: When there is a political problem we can't solve, we solve it by going deeper, further down into the classes of the oppressed. Everywhere in the periphery we see new "horizontal struggles" break out, as in the unemployed workers movement in Argentina who are tired of being "represented" and sold out. Everywhere the oppressed are erasing borders and slowly remaking nations as surely as the capitalists are.

It is in the Global South, in the tumultuous neo-colonial periphery of the Third World, that the new revolutionary experiments are being born. It is there that the strategic offensives will break out. Everywhere both the far right and the left are testing out power boundaries, building semi-autonomous zones of their own. None of this is in any final form, as the transition into a dramatically different world is under way. For Maoists, Yenan is far behind us now, and yet still lies ahead of us

Theory Mao Tossed to Us (2017)

Like a hand grenade of ideas thrown from the distance into our skirmishes, when Mao's iconic writings from the 1920s–30s were finally translated and widely disseminated here in the 1950s–60s, revolutionary theory on the lumpen/proletariat underwent a major shift. We still haven't come to grips with the confusion of that change, even though the blast zone is far behind us on the highway now.

While appearing to follow the form of the Marx & Engels class analysis of the stormy petrel of the lumpen/proletariat, Mao's theoretical take represented a big remodeling job. A sharper turn, in fact, than i personally could hold onto or understand back then. Mao Z most famously explained the

* This is a very simplified and abbreviated version of the opening of "Mao Z's Revolutionary Laboratory & The Lumpen/Proletariat," which is the only English-language work we know of which traces and analyzes in useful detail Mao and his party's actual work with the lumpen, and how that evolved with their political theory. "Mao Z's Revolutionary Laboratory & The Lumpen/Proletariat" is short book-length itself, but is the second part within a larger volume, *The "Dangerous Class" and Revolutionary Theory: Thoughts On the Making of the Lumpen/Proletariat* (Kersplebedeb, 2017). Readers interested in following up this practical experience of millions of people in struggle over many years together, should definitely read the complete version in J. Sakai's *The "Dangerous Class" and Revolutionary Theory.*

lumpen/proletariat's difference from all other classes in his analysis of Chinese society in 1926:

> "Apart from all these, there is a fairly large *lumpen*-proletariat, made up of peasants who have lost their land and handicraftsmen who cannot get work. They lead the most precarious existence of all. In every part of the country they have their secret societies ... One of China's most difficult problems is how to handle these people. Brave fighters, but apt to be destructive, they can become a revolutionary force if given proper guidance."[1]

Influenced by reading Mao, electrified to recognize themselves in his terse description of the lumpen/proletariat, the Black Panthers used it to unlock the most radical advance of the 1960s wave here. According to the BPP's Huey Newton and Bobby Seale, the lumpen were politically leading the u.s. revolution, while after victory the task of building the new socialist society would be taken up by the working class. Thousands of Black youth poured into the extreme danger zone that was the Party. For the left not to recognize the conscious role of the lumpen/proletariat there is to let old 19th-century dogma dim revolutionary theory. Which was the precise same old bureaucratic politics that Mao himself was struggling against so long ago in his own revolution.

Mao Z's terse last line summing up the lumpen for the revolution, became famous among many revs in the 1960s–70s. From Anti-War organizers to the Black Panthers who quoted it frequently, the line reverberating and influencing far beyond the much smaller ranks of those who called themselves "Maoists." It seemed so basic, it didn't occur to would-be revolutionaries like myself that it wasn't anywhere near as simple as it seemed, and that in fact i didn't fully understand it at all.

Mao Z's starting analysis accepted the lumpen as ordinary people, not as primarily "dangerous" or exotic. Our guy wasn't afraid of them. Humanizing them in his analysis,

Mao was painting there with broad brushstrokes, in optimistic colors, of the lumpen as victims shaped by poverty and oppression—thus as potential revolutionary tinder. This concise, seemingly easy to understand explanation of Mao's was a pretty radical change of class understanding for Marxists back then. It reflected a newer understanding of realities out in the capitalist periphery.

The other thing that many of us didn't grasp, is that Mao's words weren't just another theory, like Marx or Bakunin had. Mao's theories were in a whole different ballpark from those earlier comrades. Not because he was necessarily any more observant, but because his theory was shaped by the political experiences of millions of lumpen over almost *two generations in China from the early 1900s to the 1940s. These ideas had been reforged over and over on the anvil of oppressed people's experience*, up to and including all-out revolutionary war, year after year. Understanding paid for in many human lives, and which carried that more than one individual's personal weight to it.

What our guy Mao Z knew even then, subtly coloring those first words in 1926 when he called them a potential "revolutionary force," was that the lumpen played a key role in the revolutionary process for him. They weren't just bit players or minor actors on the large stage of overturning society. The lumpen in China were a major, and even at some times and places a *decisive* factor, in the mass revolutionary struggle that actually took place. Whether that fit anyone's theory or not. They burst through all that. That's what becomes clearer when analyzing in depth the class politics of the Chinese revolutionary experience.

The "Vagabond Army"

Over and over, in the struggle in those early years, Mao Z ran into and found common cause with lumpen/proletarian fighters. Retreating after the disastrous, ambitious, 1927 "Autumn Harvest Uprising" during the first year of the open civil war, the small core of a thousand revolutionary soldiers led by Mao took shelter upon the Chingkangshan mountain range, an elevated and remote plateau that was a traditional refuge for bandits and other fugitives. They were only a tenth of the forces that uprising had started with, and Mao Z had been disavowed by the Central Committee and stripped of his party leadership positions. Not that it had made much difference to those revolutionaries resting and regaining strength on the mountains. They were being schooled in learning how to survive as guerrillas 101.

The "red" survivors ran into two bandit chiefs who were said to be Triad secret society members—Wang Tso and Yuan Wen-t'sai—with their little armies. Both of them former bandits turned army unit commanders of the new modern capitalist national army, turned back to bandit leaders. Their bands quickly became "red" and joined Mao's small army on the mountain, which increased then from one to three "regiments" (later, after Mao's main force left the area, they were rumored to have reverted to banditry again; in any case both chiefs were killed in the constant fighting of that time, as so many were).[2]

Starting the next Spring of 1928, other "red" forces began converging with Mao's as the new Red Army began to take shape. General Chu Teh (*Zhu De* in the new translation system) became the commander-in-chief of the rapidly growing central Red Army, with Mao Z as the chief political officer, in a historic partnership that shifted the center of gravity of the entire revolutionary leadership to the distant universe of mass guerrilla war in the countryside. Chu Teh was then the more famous, as a noted mercenary general, and the force—with its many tens of thousands of soldiers—was often called "the Chu-Mao army" in the Chinese newspapers and by the public.

A career military officer, in difficult circumstances Chu Teh had won battlefield promotion to general, and was a star in Chinese military circles. Holding powerful capitalist government offices that came with a high income from the customary bribes and graft, Chu Teh soon had a mansion, a harem with several wives as well as concubines, and a heavy opium habit. Before he conquered his long-time addiction to put everything else away and become a revolutionary. It's no surprise that Chu Teh was also a senior member of the lumpen/proletarian Elder Brothers, a tie he freely admitted actively sustaining and using in his Communist guerrilla years.[3]

The Elder Brothers were the dominant lumpen secret society in the key Yangtze valley region. Many members came to hold responsible positions in the local revolutionary movement and the insurgent Red military.

In those first years of the Red Army, when the whole democratic movement was reeling on the defensive, retreating under constant attack, forced under that great repressive pressure to transform into an illegal mass movement of undergrounds and partisan organizers and rebel militias and soldiers by the many thousands—or perish—the lumpen/proletariat were the indispensible social base for the revolutionaries. Not simply some useful people, but temporarily the key strata, maybe not according to anyone's admitted political doctrine but in the actual real time situation.

At the party's 1929 Gutian conference, two years after the Red Army's founding, Mao Z's report on their political-military situation bluntly said that their military's "roving banditism" and other such political problems had their root in the reality that *"the lumpen-proletariat constitute the majority in the Red Army"* (while in those years of rebuilding right after the Autumn Harvest uprising, Mao also had reported that *"the soldiers of peasant or working class origin in the Fourth Army in the Border Region constitute an extreme minority."*).

Lumpen/proletarian soldiers were the definite *majority* of the many thousands of revolutionary fighters under his leadership. Although neither Mao Z nor the rest of the party leadership were eager to broadcast this heretical and scandalous situation.[4]

Peasant China Throws Millions Into the Game

This major revolutionary role for the lumpen was only normal, we should say, in the context of China then. Since the same surprising class configuration had been responsible for the much larger mass movement which the new revolution drew its lifeblood from. A giant peasant rebellion in the form of militant Peasant Associations had broken out in 1926 across Southern China, centered in the expansive rural countryside of Hunan Province and contiguous areas, and comprising at least 4.5 million peasants.

In reporting on the new rebellion in the countryside, Mao Z *didn't* place the Communist Party at the center of events, because they weren't. Although the relatively small numbers of Communist cadres would try to hold village meetings and inspire the peasants to start local branches of the associations, before quickly moving on as they usually had to. Instead, he placed as the key instigators a new grouping of the most oppressed themselves—which he referred to as the *"utterly destitute."*

This was difficult to pin down on the surface, because the party was reporting from the countryside through a filter. Bluntly, closeting the lumpen as much as possible. Because the major role of the lumpen in the revolution was so counter to established Marxist doctrine, both Mao Zedong and the party itself worked to lessen the flashy guest appearances of their lumpen/proletariat on late-night tv. Remember, this was a time when Mao Z was being heavily attacked within the party for recognizing the radical potential of lumpen outlaws. Party leader Li Li-san even explicitly criticized him for the sin of *"guerrillaism infected by the viewpoint of the lumpenproletariat."*[5]

In Mao's 1927 "Report on an Investigation of the Peasant Movement in Hunan," referring to surveys which showed the overall shape of the movement, Mao mentions one in Changsha county, which counted the poor peasants as 70% of the Peasant Associations' membership. Which Mao thought representative for the overall membership of the militant Peasant Associations in Hunan province. Mao then added a significant point, that **there was a sub-category of the very most poor, the "utterly destitute," which accounted for 20% of the peasant movement's total members.**

Even more, Mao goes on to say that almost all the grassroots leadership at the local level were poor peasants and especially the very poorest. In fact, according to Mao, in one of the best-surveyed areas with mature peasant organizations, it was shown that "... of the officials in the township associations in Hengshan County **the utterly destitute comprise 50 per cent** ..." There's no question that this newly identified social strata he named *"the utterly destitute"* played a key leadership role in the militant movement, apparently far beyond their size in the population. But who were they?

In fact, the *"utterly destitute"* were our old friends the rural lumpen/proletariat all over again. The Communist Party central committee editorial group supervising the later republishing of Mao's writings admitted that by the *"utterly destitute,"* Mao specifically meant two groups together: the "rural *lumpen*-proletariat" and the "rural proletariat." The second was only a tiny fig leaf. What was really happening was that the rural lumpen themselves were playing a big grassroots leadership role in the rural uprising that would transform all China. A good day, for outcasts and outlaws.

It seems that everywhere Mao looked in those early days of the 20th century in rural China, the lumpen/proletariat were involved when battles against the rulers broke out.

That this was true of the most important mass movement in China's history—the peasant movement which became the popular base of anti-capitalist guerrilla war and eventual revolution—only throws more fuel onto our theoretical camp fire.[6]

It was not all positive report cards. As the revolutionary war developed, in 1939 Mao Z himself warned party cadres that it was in the nature of the lumpen to *"waver"* and *"vacillate"* between revolution and counter-revolution. At the same time, however, he reaffirmed that at the root most lumpen/proletarians still remained innocent victims of oppression who needed the revolution's help in liberating and reforming themselves. Less positively, he warned: *"While one portion is easily brought over by the reactionary forces, the other portion has the possibility of participating in the revolution."*[7]

Notes to Theory Mao Tossed To Us

1. Mao Tse-tung. "Analysis of the Classes in Chinese Society." In *Selected Works of Mao Tse-tung*. Vol. 1. Foreign Languages Press, 1965. Peking. Page 19.

2. See Mao's own account of that time in: Edgar Snow. *Red Star Over China*. First Revised and Enlarged Edition. Grove Press, 1968. Pages 163–171; also Stuart R. Schram. "Mao Tse-tung and Secret Societies." In *China Quarterly* No. 27. July–September 1966.

3. Phillip C.C. Huang. "The Jiangxi Period: An Introduction." In *China Research Monographs Number Thirteen. Chinese Communists and Rural Society 1927–1934*. Center for Chinese Studies, University of California at Berkeley. August 1978. Pages 11–13; Agnes Smedley. *The Great Road: The Life and Times of Chu Teh*. Monthly Review, 1972. N.Y. Pages 88–89; Snow. Op cit. Pages 333–334.

4. Mao Tse-tung. "On Correcting Mistaken Ideas in the Party." In *Selected Works of Mao Tse-tung*. Vol. 1. Page 114; Schram. Op cit.

5. John E. Rue. *Mao Tse-Tung in Opposition 1927–1935*. Hoover Institution, 1966. Stanford. Page 99.

6. Mao Tse-tung. "Report on an Investigation of the Peasant Movement in Hunan." In *Selected Works of Mao Tse-tung*. Volume 1. Peking. 1965. Page 33; Mao Zedong. *Report From Xunwu*. Stanford University Press, 1990. Pages 116 and 122.

7. For all other sources please see the complete version of this chapter in "Mao Z's Revolutionary Laboratory & the Lumpen/Proletariat," in the book *The "Dangerous Class" and Revolutionary Theory: Thoughts On the Making pf the Lumpen/ Proletariat* (Kersplebedeb, 2017).

Gen. Richard Stilwell

"Pseudo-Gangs" (S1, 1983)

In war both sides must try to carry out bold plans. The imperialists as well as the guerrillas build with elements of surprise and deception. This is one part of gaining the initiative, life and death in military matters.

On the tactical level we can see this in the heavy imperialist use of "pseudo-gangs" in counter-insurgency. "Pseudo-gangs" are small units of captured or surrendered guerrillas, who are "turned" by the imperialists and sent back into the underground to pretend at still being revolutionaries. The "pseudo-gang" sets up assassinations and traps, causes confusions, and also provides an ongoing depth of intelligence to the imperialists. It was during the "Mau Mau" rebellion of 1952–56 in Kenya that the imperialist security forces first promoted this tactic in a major way.* The leading imperialist theorist on "pseudo-gang" tactics, now-famous Brigadier General Frank Kitson of the British Army, learned his trade as a young officer in Kenya.

* The term "Mau Mau," which has disputed origins, was invented and popularized by the British authorities. The Kenyan people back then never used this term, and usually called their uprising simply "The Movement." The organized fighters were named the Land & Freedom Armies.

Insurgency In Kenya

The background of the 1952–56 Kenya revolution shows the development of "pseudo-gangs" as one integral part of the whole imperialist counter-insurgency. The uprising was primarily based among the "KEM" peoples (Kikuyu and the related Embu and Meru peoples) in the Central Province. At the time of the uprising they numbered one-third of the Afrikan population of Kenya. These 1½ million Afrikans in the Central Province had borne the worst of the colonial oppression. By the eve of the revolution the Kikuyu were increasingly landless, a million people pent up on 2,000 square miles of tribal reservations (called the Reserves by the British) while the 30,000 European settlers directly occupied 12,000 square miles of the best farmlands.

Afrikan workers earned an average wage of $73 per year, including food and housing. The contract laborers on the settler plantations were paid with a few coins each month and being allowed to raise their own food on a 1½ acre plot. In return each Afrikan family signed a three-year contract obliging the entire family, including children, to give the settlers 270 days of work each year. No Afrikan could leave their area or be absent from the plantation overnight without his "master's" permission. For landless Kikuyu real income had fallen by 30–40% during the fifty-year colonial period. By 1950 the Afrikan living standards in Kenya were going down rapidly as war-torn Britain needed more and more capital to reindustrialize (just like in the U.S. Empire today).

The anti-colonial revolution in Kenya was a mass uprising by the hungry and oppressed. The goal was "Land and Freedom," national liberation and the ouster of the European settlers. Two events had also precipitated the uprising. One was the refusal of the new "socialist" Labour Party government in England to grant independence to the Afrikan colonies. This ended the faint hopes that the colonial system could be nonviolently reformed or that "friends" in Britain would give freedom to Afrikans.

The second event was an attack against Afrikan children. The Beecher Report plan (named after its missionary author) was being imposed despite universal Afrikan protests. Under this 75% of all Afrikan school children were to be forced out of school after the 4th grade. Another 18% would leave school after the 6th grade. This would have ensured the settlers a continued reserve army of semi-educated Afrikan child labor. This scheme stirred up deep anger among the masses, who had made great sacrifices to give their children what little education was available to them. The feelings were so strong that during the war Afrikan schoolmasters who followed the government plan were targets of assassination. While the imperialist propaganda pictured the guerrillas as "blood-thirsty savages" running wild, we can better understand the heart of the Kikuyu fighters by one of the popular songs they sung in the forest:

"Neither your unsatisfied wants
Nor your difficulties will kill you.
Without eyes to see the tears of the children
It matters not whether one is foolish or clever.

"If Mumbi's children are not educated
Then neither the European
Nor the Asian will lose sleep
Worrying about how to satisfy their needs.*

"This is a time for sharing. Kikuyus arise!
Let us help the children with their difficulties
For they are the ones who will take our places.

"The need for a spear is gone
Replaced by the need for a pen.
For our enemies today
Fight with words ..."

* Gikuyu and Mumbi were the legendary father and mother, the founding parents, of the Kikuyu peoples.

The armed struggle had great mass support, perhaps close to the highest degree that could be imagined. This was necessary since the fighters had very little in the way of modern weapons or political/military preparation. At peak strength the great majority of the guerrillas had only simis, the traditional Kikuyu sword. The homemade guns constructed from half- and three-quarter-inch waterpipe and the sprinkling of "precision" (as they were called) rifles, pistols, and shotguns bought on the black market or seized in attacks equipped only some 20% of the guerrillas. Ammunition was initially so scarce that the Kikuyu women forced into prostitution by colonialism secretly charged puppet troops one bullet each; this slender supply being one necessary source for the new Land & Freedom Armies.

There were almost 20,000 fighters. This was a very large number, considering the Kikuyu population of under 1½ million. By official British estimates 90% of the Kikuyu actively supported the struggle. When the Movement called upon Kikuyu to boycott the Nairobi bus system, to give up frequenting Asian cafes, and to stop using European beer and cigarettes, the masses responded. The underground Movement was so all-pervasive that the puppet Kikuyu Home Guards were at first heavily infiltrated. General Kitson accidentally reveals this in describing a late-night "native" dance he attended:

> "The assembled company represented a pretty fair cross-section of the sort of Afrikans with whom we did business. All our own men were there ... three or four tribal policemen were happily drinking away with the Afrikan foreman of a big European farm. This man was a great personality in the area, a pillar of the Christian Church and leader of an enthusiastic band of Kikuyu Guard. Four months later we discovered that he was also a member of the Mau Mau Central Committee ..."

In the first year of military struggle, starting in the Winter of 1952–53, guerrillas were in the ascendancy—assassinating puppet officials, capturing police posts, and forcing the British Army units back out of the forests. This initial success proved the potential of Afrikan power, but it was also somewhat misleading. While the revolutionary zeal of the people was high, there were important contradictions within the nationalist movement.

The nationalist movement was divided into two political tendencies. One was headed by Jomo Kenyatta, beyond any doubt the main independence leader and hero to the Kikuyu peoples. Kenyatta was the leading representative of his class, the European-educated Afrikan petty bourgeoisie. Their program was parliamentary democracy for Afrikans, which meant civil rights, equality with settlers in business and land ownership, and eventually an Afrikan majority government. To do this Kenyatta and his associates had led their banned Kikuyu Central Association (KCA) in the 1940s to begin a secret campaign of oathing—of having each Kikuyu take a sacred oath to regain their land and freedom.

By 1952 the KCA, although in theory legally banned by the colonial authorities, was conducting mass rallies of 20,000 to 30,000 Kikuyu, with the black, red, and green Afrikan flag waving from the speaker's platform. Jomo Kenyatta's strategy was to slowly build momentum toward campaigns of mass civil disobedience, just as Gandhi had done in India, to nonviolently urge the British out. As a legal, mass united front the KCA had organized the Kenyan African Union, which embraced all the other Afrikan peoples as well. This was the public movement that most Afrikans and most Europeans knew of.

But within this nationalist stirring there was another more secret organization, which became the actual leading nucleus of the uprising. This was a revolutionary political tendency, centered in the Afrikan proletariat and set upon the course of armed struggle. On May 16, 1950, the Afrikan and Asian workers in Nairobi (the colony's capital) began a nine-day general strike, which stopped all economic activity in the city. The 100,000 strikers were protesting the British repression against their new nationalist unions (which had openly demanded independence). The strike spread to Mombasa and elsewhere. Using troops and mass arrests the British finally crushed the political general strike.

This set-back was not unexpected, and only consolidated the resolve of the Afrikan working-class leadership to organize armed struggle for liberation.

While the new underground conspiracy included Kikuyu from almost all classes in Nairobi, from peddlars and unemployed youth and street criminals to small merchants, it was primarily the workers in two unions, the transport workers and the domestic and hotel workers.* In June 1951 the young revolutionaries took over the large Nairobi chapter of the moderate Kenya African Union (KAU). Within the next year they would secretly win over control of the KAU local committees in much of central Kenya, unable to fully take over the KAU National Executive because of Jomo Kenyatta's great prestige.

In the Summer of 1951 the revolutionaries established their clandestine Central Committee as the supreme leadership of the rapidly growing network of underground cells. Small armed teams were started to provide security and eliminate informers. The Central Committee took Jomo Kenyatta's oathing campaign, which had been going on with rising response, and raised it to a new level with the "Warrior's Oath." This new, second oath ceremony secretly pledged one to join the armed struggle as a fighter and was administered on a surprise basis. Once a Kikuyu was honored by being invited to take the "Warrior's Oath," he had to either do so on the spot or be immediately executed. It was a

* Unlike the AFL-CIO–type imperialist unions, these nationalist Afrikan unions were highly militant associations led by political workers.

selective national draft. This then was the armed movement that the British called "Mau Mau," a nationalist movement initially led by the young Afrikan proletariat.

Armed propaganda had started, most particularly in assassinations of prominent Kikuyu puppets. All this placed Jomo Kenyatta and the Afrikan intelligentsia in a difficult position. The British enforced collective punishment (seizure of livestock, etc.) on Kikuyu villages where armed propaganda had been most visible. Kenyatta had been warned by the colonial authorities to join the puppet chiefs in attacking the "Mau Mau" terrorism—or else. In the Summer of 1952 Kenyatta and his petty bourgeois group of KCA leaders began publicly denouncing the "Mau Mau" guerrillas at large rallies. This was a serious crisis, since Kenyatta was the beloved hero of the Kikuyu peoples, and even most fighters thought of him as their ultimate leader.

The Central Committee decided to try and hold together the political tendencies by coopting Kenyatta as the figurehead of their revolution. In a secret meeting Kenyatta was introduced to the Central Committee; to his surprise he found out not only that most were working-class leaders in "his" organization, but that the illegal Central Committee had drafted him as a member. Although angry, Kenyatta went along. His disagreement with the armed struggle was so evident, however, that his execution as a traitor was discussed later. Kenyatta's arrest and removal from Kenya by the British saved him, and preserved his public position as the No. 1 leader of the independence struggle.

This is a sharp example of the incomplete political consolidation of the Movement. In fact, Kenyatta's own class did not fully participate in the Revolution (although they became its main beneficiaries). The British-educated Afrikan petty bourgeoisie, while of course desiring civil rights and later independence, was in the main loyal to British imperialism. They clung to their precarious positions as minor officials, as clerks and schoolteachers. Those petty bourgeois who did give support to the revolution did so primarily for tactical reasons, to save themselves from reprisals and keep a foot in both camps.

This had a strategic effect upon the struggle. There were almost no intellectuals among the over 15,000 fighters in the main Land & Freedom Armies in the forest; the most educated person among them had two years of high school. This mass guerrilla struggle was poorly armed politically, with no revolutionary science available to the fighters. The revolution as a whole was not socialist. While there had been a few socialists among the Nairobi unions, they were among the first arrested. Without revolutionary science, without the advances and lessons that had been won in the revolutions of many nations, the Kikuyu movement could make only the most improvised and spontaneous plans. This was decisive in their defeat, outmaneuvered both politically and militarily by imperialism.

Events reached a turning point with the assassination of Chief Waruhiu on October 6, 1952. He had been one of the highest ranking puppets. That night spontaneous beer parties were held all over Central Province in celebration.

Imperialist authority had been so clearly undermined that the British declared a State of Emergency and began wide-scale repression. Local underground committees fought back, thousands of young men fled to the forests, and the war had been fully joined.

The nationalist underground was reorganized starting in January 1953 to wartime roles. There were two sectors, the Passive Wing of support committees (buying arms, supplying food, etc.) and the Active Wing comprising the seven Land and Freedom Armies. Hope was bright in Afrikan eyes. The revolt was spreading, including to the Kamba (who were 12% of the Afrikan peoples). This was especially significant, as Kamba recruits were used by the imperialists as a main element in the puppet police and military. The Movement was so widespread, almost universal, that its activities seemed unstoppable. Afrikans expected an intense but short war, in which their numerical advantage of 100-to-1 over the settlers would inevitably bring them victory. One Land and Freedom Army commander recalls:

> "We had to defeat the Europeans, I continued to reason. There were 60,000 Europeans against six million Africans. Each European had to fight againt 100 Africans. It did not matter if he killed half of them and finally be killed himself, making sure that the survivors would share the land that had been used by the European, cast down the colonial rule and form an African government ...
>
> "My knowledge had been swept together with the thousands of ignorant warriors whose focus was only the Kenya settlers. I had ignored the fact that the colonial system from United Kingdom was the source of our exploitation which we were determined to eliminate."

Counter-Insurgency in Kenya

British imperialism gradually assembled a military force of over 50,000 troops. There was the Kenya Regiment of local settlers and some elite British infantry battalions, but the total of European police and soldiers was not large. Most of the imperialist forces were puppet Afrikan troops. There were six battalions of Kings African Rifles (regular colonial infantry), local Home Guards and thousands of Turkana and Somali tribal police brought in from other British colonies.

Weakened by World War II, and also fighting in wars in the Middle East, Korea, and Malaysia, British imperialism could not afford to assemble any overpowering concentration of strength. In spite of their useless handful of old armored cars, cannon and World War II bombers, the technological gap between the imperialists and the revolutionary fighters was not qualitatively significant. In the forested mountainside or Nairobi slum street a grenade, a shotgun, or even a simi in the hands of a guerrilla was more potent than a British tank.

Imperialism's advantage in the war was a matter of professional strategy and modern organization; with these imperialism regained the strategic initiative. While there have been several books written by British officers implying that "pseudo-gangs" and Afrikan guerrillas "turning" defeated the uprising, this is not true. "Pseudo-gangs" were not primary in counter-insurgency, but only secondary. Their tactical importance in some situations can only be evaluated by first understanding the overall situation of counter-insurgency.

Imperialist counter-insurgency operations exposed the urban revolutionary infrastructure and destroyed the organized political leadership. This was the key step. The British security forces had the advantage of wielding a well-practiced level of violence that Afrikans didn't anticipate. Few oppressed peoples, even the revolutionaries, believe that imperialism really will apply massive repression overnight. This unwillingness to face the impending destruction of "normal" life allows imperialist security forces to so often get in the decisive blows early.

In October 1952 the British began "Operation Jock Scott," a preemptive campaign of arresting the nationalist leaders to forestall the armed struggle. Within a month some 8,000 Afrikans and been arrested, moderate and revolutionary alike—Jomo Kenyatta was among the first and most prominent of the detainees. The entire Central Committee was arrested. This first blow damaged, but did not completely cripple the Movement. A new Central Committee was formed, and the liberation war was fully launched. So unsuccessful were the imperialists at first that an inspecting British Parliamentary Delegation reported critically in January 1954:

> "... the influence of Mau Mau in the Kikuyu area, except in certain localities, has not declined; it has,

> on the contrary, increased ... In Nairobi, which is one of the most important centres in Africa, the situation is both grave and acute. Mau Mau orders are carried out in the heart of the city, Mau Mau 'courts' sit in judgment and their sentences are carried out by gangsters."

So the Movement not only survived in the forested mountains but right in the colonial capital. It was, in fact, in the city where the political organization was the best developed. In Nairobi the underground center obtained arms, ammunition, medical supplies and food for the forest guerrillas, while also waging urban guerrilla warfare and recruiting new fighters for the growing forest armies.

Although the local settlers and the visiting British politicians were worried that "Mau Mau" had the military initiative, in part this was because the colonial authorities were buying time; major preparations, including the training of thousands of new puppet police, were underway for strategic counter-blows against the rebellion.

On April 24, 1954, an army of 25,000 imperialist soldiers and police suddenly cordoned off all the Afrikan areas of Nairobi. This was "Operation Anvil." Sweeping each street and building, the security forces herded the entire 100,000 person Afrikan population before them into a large field, where they were held and individually screened. 15,000 Afrikans were then detained in concentration camps, including all suspected nationalists and even all known union members. Relatives of the detainees were forced to leave Nairobi. The entire new Central Committee was arrested, and the underground was effectively hamstrung by this operation. At one stroke the political leadership of the revolution was removed and the major center of organization smashed.

Parallel operations took place in other urban areas. In the White Highlands (the settler plantation districts) over 100,000 Kikuyu were forcibly uprooted and expelled. General terror was used, since the imperialists had correctly concluded that the entire Kikuyu peoples were against them. Some 77,000 Afrikans were eventually detained in the coming months in concentration camps. Torture was casually and commonly administered. Prisoners were subject to severe beatings, rape, castration, and other mutilation. Over 1,000 Afrikans were officially tried in colonial courts and executed (in contrast, the British had executed only eight of Begin's fascist-Zionist terrorists in Palestine).

It was in the countryside that the imperialists next demonstrated the effectiveness of massive force against the unprepared. In June 1954 the "villagization program" took hold, forcibly uprooting over 1 million Kikuyu in the tribal reservations. The entire Kikuyu population was forced to move into new guarded compounds, under close confinement by the police Their subsistence farming was disrupted, livestock lost. Both men and women had to spend much of their time on unpaid, forced labor gangs, cutting down brush and doing military construction. This deliberately lowered food production below the minimum for survival, so that no surplus foods existed to supply the forest Land and Freedom Armies. Thousands of Kikuyu children and aged died from starvation and disease.

Puppet troops were encouraged to victimize the general Kikuyu population at will, robbing homes, seizing livestock, beating and abusing women. Thousands and thousands of Afrikans were shot down or hacked apart by puppet troops and local settlers, with the uncounted bodies simpiy being thrown away. The British claim to have killed 11,503 guerrillas during combat, but the total of Afrikans killed has often been estimated as high as 50,000.

These strategic counter-blows effectively defeated the 1952–56 revolution. The Land and Freedom Armies were still thousands strong, but were cut off from both political leadership and from their base of support among the masses. In the heavily forested mountainsides of the Aberdale and Mt. Kenya areas the guerrillas could temporarily evade the security forces, but were unable to replace their losses or resupply themselves. They had lost the strategic initiative. Efforts were made to recreate political structures in the forests with new mass patriotic organizations and new leadership bodies such as the Kenya Parliament. In the growing confusion these could not work. Guerrilla armies were suspicious and independent of each other; under the tightening imperialist pressure these too kept breaking down for survival into smaller and smaller autonomous units. The capture in October 1956 of Dedan Kimathi, the leading military commander and one of the last of the guerrilla hardcore, marked the final end of the revolution.

The revolution of 1952–56, even in defeat, profoundly shook up and changed East Afrika. Local European settlers proved unable without major reinforcements to hold down the Afrikan masses, who were determined to struggle for national independence and justice. Rumors of new oaths and new preparations for guerrilla war arose. British imperialism could not afford an endless series of such escalating rebellions. The revolution forced the dismantling of the old British colonial empire in East Afrika and the concession of independence. That this set the stage for the rise of the new neo-colonialisrn in no way lessened the heroic accomplishments of the young fighters who had sacrificed so freely. Most of all, the Kenya Revolution was not an end but a beginning, a foundation on which all succeeding Afrikan liberation movements have built.

The Use of "Pseudo-Gangs"

Operation Anvil was followed in December 1954 by Operation Hammer, a classic imperialist annihilation campaign to destroy the cut-off Land and Freedom Armies. The Aberdale forest was surrounded and bombed day and night, while a division of British troops searched through it in force. This big sweep was an admitted failure. Even in the thousands the Afrikan guerrillas easily filtered past the lines of awkward European troops crashing through the forest. After a whole month of intensive forest operations the imperialists had netted only 161 guerrillas killed or taken prisoner. It was in these circumstances that the "pseudo-gang" tactic (the British called the Kikuyu guerrilla units "gangs" to deny their political character) came into the foreground.

It all began in March 1954 with the capture of a single Afrikan guerrilla known to us only as "George." During long interrogation Gen. Kitson (then a captain in army intelligence) persuaded George to "turn." As Kitson tells it:

> "After completing the interrogation we took George out on a patrol and he pointed out several huts near the forest edge where his gang used to go for supplies. He went into one pretending to still be in the gang and the owner gave him some interesting bits of news. Over the next few days we did the same thing in other areas where George's gang was known to work,

Operation Anvil

> making up a suitable story each time to account for George's presence. On one occasion a contact made in this way told George that a supply group from his gang was lying up nearby. George went and met them and led them back to where we lay in wait so that we ... killed or captured all the members of this group. We had in fact done something far more important than that: we had at last broken through the great divide ..."

Soon it became too difficult for George to explain why he was always alone. To be more convincing, he coached eight puppet Afrikan police how to impersonate guerrillas. Suitably dressed and armed with simis and home-made guns, these men pretended to be the rest of his unit, staying in the background while George did the talking. This was the first "pseudo-gang" in Kenya. At first the "pseudo-gangs" were direct death-squad Phoenix-type units, setting up guerrillas for army traps, or, if they could lull them into letting down their guard, shooting down their newly-met "brothers." New traitors were recruited so that the "pseudo-gang" members would all be experienced forest "veterans," known and trusted. Intelligence-gathering quickly became an equal function, and often some guerrillas were left unharmed by the "pseudo-gang" if they seemed to be a good source of news about the revolutionary Armies further away.

Then an even greater conceptual breakthrough came to the imperialist security forces. Instead of merely lurking on the edges of the Movement, why couldn't they *become* the Movement? Gen. Kitson says that it began with the problem of a very efficient guerrilla unit in Thika District, which had corrected some seventy puppets in the previous six months:

> "The main reason for the survival of these terrorists was that we had been unable to make contact with our pseudo-gang. We knew who the terrorists' supporters were and we sent various members of our

Didan Kimathi

team to meet them pretending to be visitors from Nairobi or emissaries from the forest. Whatever the story the local Mau Mau committee received them courteously and promised to arrange a meeting with the gang. But a meeting never took place.

"Eventually the Military Intelligence Officer for Thika District devised a long-term plan. Near to the area in which the gang operated were a number of farms which had no Mau Mau committee on them because they'd all been arrested some months earlier. He decided to introduce a pseudo-gang who would tell the laborers that they had been forced out of their normal area in Kiambu. Our gang would ask for support and encourage the formation of the normal chain of committees to provide it. Once the system was operating freely he would arrest all the supporters of the real gang from the other group of farms. He hoped that the real gang would be forced into getting supplies from the committees which he had set up to support our pseudo-gang. Our gang would then be well within their rights to demand a meeting with the terrorists in order to co-ordinate operations."

This plan worked perfectly, with the "pseudo-gang" organizing a whole network of secret support committees among the Afrikan laborers. Soon the real guerrillas, now convinced of the "pseudo-gang's" authenticity, agreed to meet with the "pseudo-gang," and were wiped out in a police ambush. The imperialist security forces were very pleased by this "immense success." Secret "pseudo-gang" operations were set up by a new police Special Forces command in each district. These "pseudo-gangs" built their own base of support, becoming "warrior's oath" administrators and recruiting eager Afrikan youth straight into their contaminated pseudo-movement. This positively confirmed who was disloyal and neutralized them while using them as a front to kill the revolution.

By the war's end, in 1956, roughly half of the last several hundred guerrillas holding out were actually "pseudo-gangs." Having started as straight hunter-killer teams using disguise to get within killing range of guerrillas, the "pseudos" finally evolved into a complex, fulltime pseudo-movement. The settler police officer who ran the pseudo-movement recalls:

> "The task of keeping every man in our force recognizably active, that is to say acceptable to the remnant hostile gangs as comrades-in-arms, was extraordinarily difficult, and as much work and time had to be devoted to this extremely important aspect of our technique as was devoted to the actual hunting of Mau Mau. We had to get all our teams seen in the forest from time to time; we had to get their members to write letters and keep up the chain of correspondence in the jungle; we had to keep their food stores going. You could not remove half the Mau Mau from the forest and expect the subsequent absence of hideouts, letters, traps and many other signs of Mau Mau activity to pass unnoticed by the other half.
>
> "Often we were able to arrange meetings in the forest where our teams would confer with hostile Mau Mau. Having proved their loyalty to the cause and extracted all the information they possibly could without giving the game away, our men would withdraw ... and the way would be paved for more operations."

The question naturally arises of who these "turned" guerrillas were, and how did the imperialists twist them around? The security forces love to play up "turned" revolutionaries, implying that they can always intimidate or buy many freedom fighters. This contemptuous propaganda is very deliberate, since they know that this degrades the image of the liberation struggle. Such propaganda blows can be even more damaging than temporary defeat itself.

Actually very few Kenyan guerrillas betrayed their revolution. At their largest, in June 1956, the "pseudo-gangs" involved only ninety traitors out of over 15,000 forest guerrillas. In every struggle we have always seen some who "turned" out of weakness or ambition. This was true in China, Mozambique, and Vietnam as well. Even in defeat and when confronted with execution, Afrikan guerrillas (most of them teenage youth) remained true to their people and their revolution.

"Pseudo-gang" traitors were carefully hand-picked by the security forces. Gen. Kitson learned from experience that guerrillas with patriotic convictions were resistant to his scheme: "... it was best to rule out people who had joined Mau Mau because they were fanatically keen on the movement politically." What Gen. Kitson looked for were Afrikans who had the same mentality that he himself had. These he could trust. As he put it:

> "By far the best were the Africans who joined the gangs from a spirit of adventure ... Tired of their drab lives on farms or in the Reserves, they thought that it would be fun to be a gangster and carry a pistol and kill their acquaintances. Their outlook was not far from that of many young men of spirit anywhere else in the world and they were the easiest to handle because they were the easiest to satisfy."

Gen. Kitson once asked an Afrikan traitor who had become a "pseudo-gang" leader about George, the very first of them:

> "'I know why you joined our organization,' I said, 'but what about George?'
>
> "'George is different,' he answered. 'George does not mind about the Mau Mau or the Government and he certainly does not care who wins. George just likes excitement. He wants to walk around with a pistol and get plenty of loot. He changed sides because he

> could do all this better with you and be more comfortable at the same time.'"

The Afrikan revolutionary forces were aware of potential problems from these unreliable types, but in the political disorganization were unable to firmly deal with it. The Movement called these lumpen "Komerera," a Kikuyu word for "criminals in hiding." They were a problem to the Land and Freedom Armies, particularly when military pressure forced fighters into autonomous, smaller units. Komerera were always straying off from the main Armies, trying to escape political discipline, and often interested in raiding the closest Afrikan farms for food, women, and money so that they could lay up in the forest. While the Armies tried to find and redraft komerera back into the regular fighting ranks, this only preserved outward unity while also preserving the contradictions. These problems infected whole Armies eventually.

It was a mark of Gen. Kitson's professionalism that even as a young captain, fresh from England, he was able to understand the opportunity that the komerera gave him. Kitson didn't let his bigotry (his team spoke of "taming" Afrikans) blind him to the possibility of winning over and using unknown Afrikan guerrillas to penetrate back into the heart of the rebellion. His "pseudo-gang" system in Kenya earned him medals and a swift promotion to Major. From Kenya he went to Malaya (building "pseudo-gangs" there as well) to the Middle East with the UN peace-keeping forces, and on to General's rank and a place as one of imperialism's top counter-insurgency commanders.

The Rand Corp. (the major U.S. Defense Department "think tank") recognized Kitson's role as a counter-insurgency theorist by inviting him to be one of the participants in their 1962 counter-insurgency planning conference (to prepare for Vietnam). His reputation was crowned by the publication in 1971 of *Low-Intensity Operations,* a theoretical study for the Imperial General Staff and a semi-official primer for

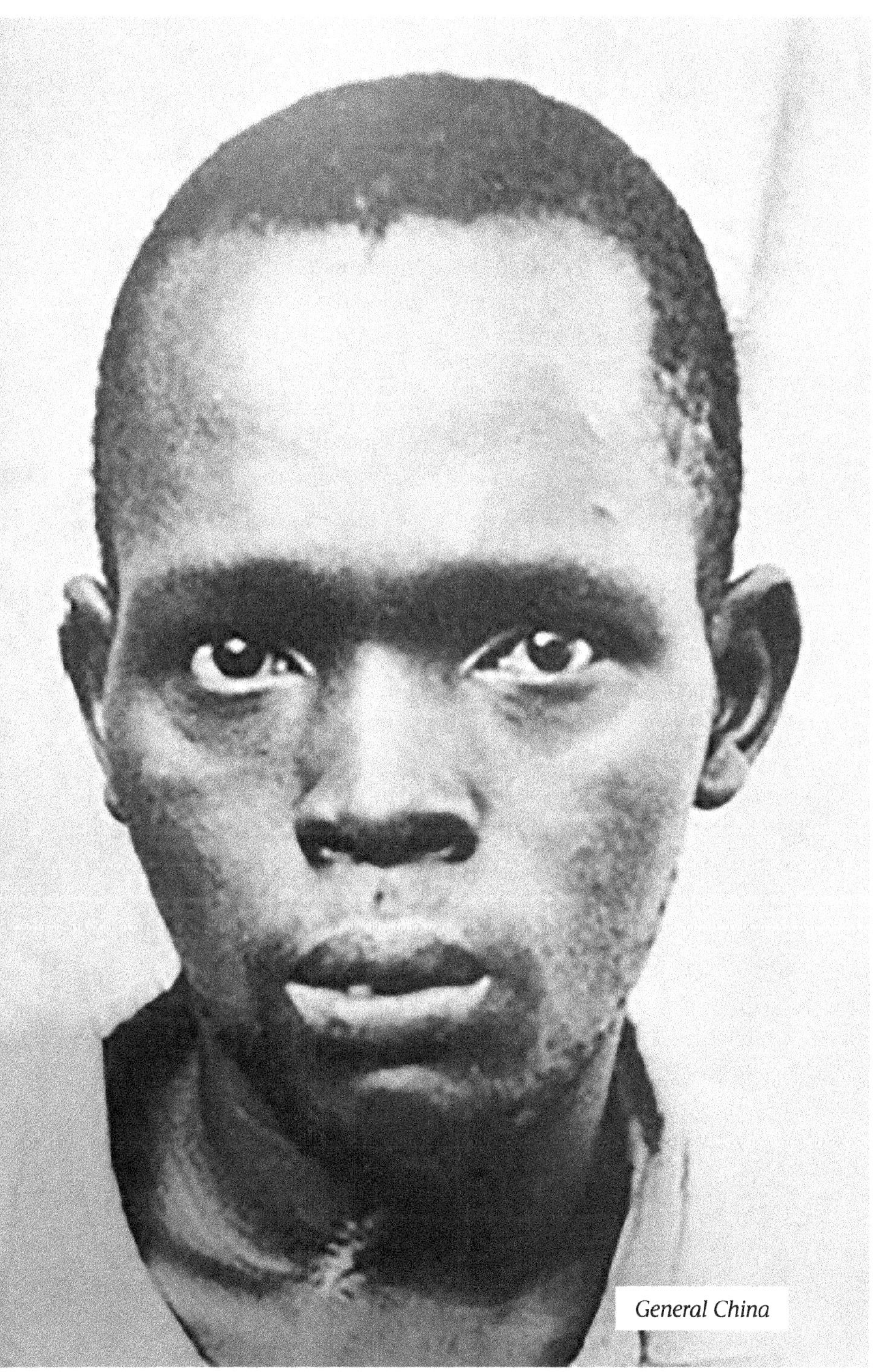

General China

British Army officers. Since this study was technical and written only for a military readership, neither Kitson nor his superiors expected it to attract any public attention. To their regret, it did.

Gen Kitson's tendency toward boldness put the Army in an awkward position, because the special usefulness of his study was that it discussed these matters in a relatively open way. So that Gen. Kitson recommended that the British Army be engaged in peacetime to use counter-insurgency tactics against the British trade unions and other reform movements at home! Further, he also recommended that Army counter-insurgency officers be integrated into all civilian decision-making on social problems, from the local town level on up.

This wouldn't pose any political problems, Gen. Kitson wrote, since it would be kept secret from the British public. Once this all-too-revealing study was discovered by the British Labour Party, there was a very embarrassing furor over it in Parliament and the media.

While Gen. Kitson's study was too honest and too publicized for the imperialists, there is no doubt that it represented the official thinking of the imperialist security forces on both sides of the Atlantic. The "Introduction" in this book is by Gen. Sir Michael Carver, as Chief of the British Imperial General Staff. This high-level endorsement is continued in the study's "Foreword," which is by U.S. Army Gen. Richard Stilwell. This is more interesting than it appears.

Gen. Kitson's admiring colleague, U.S. Gen. Richard Stilwell, is identified in the book as U.S. Army Deputy Chief of Staff. This is a high ranking connection, indeed. But the U.S. Army's Gen. Stilwell is much more than that. He is the most important counter-insurgency planner and administrator in the Pentagon. In 1964–65 Stilwell was Chief of Staff (MACV) for all U.S. forces occupying Vietnam. After that he was head of the CIA counter-insurgency effort in Thailand. Gen. Stilwell's entire career has been linked to covert counter-insurgency operations. In the 1950s we know that he was officially an obscure military attache, but in reality was the secret commander of all CIA military operations in the Far East. In that role, in 1952 Stilwell organized the last U.S. invasion of China—the disastrous offensive by Gen. Li Mi's 10,000-man puppet Kuomintang army across the Burma-China border.

According to the *N.Y. Times,* May 11, 1983, Gen. Stilwell was the "prime mover" in the creation of the Army Intelligence Support Activity, a new, secret counter-insurgency force that helped rescue U.S. Gen. Dozier from the Red Brigades in Italy, and is active now in El Salvador and Nicaragua (and elsewhere). The *N.Y. Times* says of Gen. Kitson's Amerikan colleague: "Now retired, General Stilwell is the Deputy Under Secretary of Defense for Policy and, in that capacity, plays a leading role in intelligence, counterintelligence and security policies." It is clear, then, that Gen. Kitson is close to the highest levels of the U.S. counter-insurgency command, and writes of it with certain knowledge.

This is important to ascertain, because one of the noticeable cover-ups in Gen. Kitson's study relates to the U.S. He wrote: **"A more elaborate operation might involve the building up of a pseudo-gang from captured insurgents and the cultivation by them of a local supporters' committee in a particular area ... There is some evidence to the effect that pseudo-gangs of ultra-militant black nationalists are operating now in the United States."**

While Gen. Kitson obviously believed that only his fellow security officers would read this revealing comment, he properly had to formally deny that this information was officially leaked from his Pentagon colleagues (such as Gen. Stilwell). So Gen. Kitson's study says that his source of information on that was a book by a white pacifist professor in Philadelphia. This Euro-Amerikan professor, who is a former Civil Rights supporter and an advocate of nonviolent integrationism, claims in one line of a book that he had heard unspecified "rumors" discrediting some unknown armed Black nationalists as "pseudos." This is the lightest of smokescreens, since it is obvious that a close imperialist colleague of top Pentagon and CIA officials doesn't depend upon "rumors" allegedly heard by a pacifist college professor to know about U.S. counter-insurgency operations. It is interesting that a leading U.S. counter-insurgency official was pushing Gen. Kitson's "pseudo-gang" theories. Perhaps the experience of Kenya has practical application for us today.

"Pseudo-Gangs" In Perspective

"Pseudo-gangs" are not invincible weapons, but like all imperialist tactics are effective within certain strategic constraints. In Kenya the strategic situation favored their use. There the movement was ideologically underdeveloped, and, after the first blows, without effective overall leadership. The fighters were increasingly disunited as the war progressed—both politically and organizationally—and were broken up into small, isolated, self-governing collectives or units. This describes a near-ideal situation for "pseudo-gang" tactics to penetrate and spread.

In Vietnam, which is almost the polar opposite in terms of strong communist leadership and strategic unity, similar imperialist tactics got absolutely nowhere. "Turned" Vietnamese guerrillas, such as the "Kit Carson Scouts" attempted by the U.S. Marines, were useless as a whole. Even Gen. Frank Kitson, the best-known practitioner of "pseudo-gangs," was unable to advance one inch with his expertise against the Irish Republican Army. Sent to Belfast with elite British troops, Gen. Kitson predicted that they would completely eliminate the IRA and finish the war—by 1975. The IRA is still laughing.

Of course, there is no iron wall between strategic situation and tactics. One influences the other, and vice-versa. There is at least one hypothetical framework in which "pseudo-gang" tactics can have major strategic consequences. This is when the "pseudo-gangs" *become* the movement, organizing a pseudo-movement of underground community committees, new recruits, etc., all out of honest supporters of the revolution. So that an entire pseudo-movement exists (in competition with the original movement) which looks authentic, is mostly made up of honest elements, but which conceals at its heart the imperialist security forces. In such a process the security forces *create* movement leaders—of their own. This has certain implications, particularly in the more sophisticated "encapsulated-gang" tactics.

In Kenya the security forces had recruited two minor guerrilla officers, Gati and Hungu. Both had taken an active role in a faction fight wherein they and other opportunists had tried to divide the Armies along the lines of illiterate vs. literate. They were both opposed to the existing commanders (who could read and write) and sought to whip up resentment among the fighters against those who could read. If they took over, Gati, Hungu and their friends had hoped to make a deal with the British Army. Instead, these two went over to the authorities alone.

The security forces quickly promoted them as "leaders." The authorities offered big rewards for their capture, put them on the "most wanted" list, said that they had shot down police, and in every way gave them a "revolutionary" image. Then, backed up by "pseudo-gangs," Gati and Hungu were reinserted into the guerrillas to become major revolutionary leaders, to undermine the already-difficult efforts of the real leadership. Once such a pseudo-movement operation gains entry into the struggle it can have strategic consequences.

BE A
MAN
AMON
MEN

From South Afrika to Puerto Rico to Mississippi (S1, 1983)

On September 28, 1978, Jay Mallin, the "Latin America/Terrorism Editor" of *Soldier of Fortune* magazine, was in Puerto Rico at a secret imperialist counter-insurgency conference. That conference was hosted by the Puerto Rican Attorney General's office, under the supervision of the U.S. Dept. of Justice. For three days puppet police and government officials were given intensive instruction by counter-insurgency experts from different countries on how to repress the Puerto Rican Independence Movement. And one of the main lecturers was Mr. Jay Mallin.

What is this hidden connection between police in Puerto Rico and *Soldier of Fortune,* the main recruiting and news magazine for right-wing white mercenaries? For that matter, who is Jay Mallin? These questions help to bring to light more about how U.S. imperialism really operates.

Both the U.S. Government and the press have always pictured the white mercenaries as a disapproved-of "extremist fringe." The mercenaries are pictured as a few gun-crazy private "adventurers," colorful but unimportant. Now we find out that an editor for *Soldier of Fortune,* which was the No. 1 instrument of mercenary recruitment for the defeated settler regime of "Rhodesia," has been giving secret indoctrination to officers of the Puerto Rican puppet police.

Mr. Jay Mallin's career, once brought into the daylight, is not that of any "extremist fringe" or "adventurer." Mallin lives in Coral Gables, Florida, and is a researcher at the Center for Advanced International Studies, University of Miami. This university has also cooperated in his academic cover by publishing several of Mallin's books on guerrilla warfare. Before that Mallin was Havana correspondent for *Time* magazine for ten years before being expelled in 1962. He still handles special Latin Amerikan assignments for *Time*.

It is important to clearly understand that Mr. Jay Mallin is himself not a mercenary, not a soldier, and not an "adventurer." **He is a right-wing political propagandist.** And his work stretches everywhere U.S. imperialism goes into battle. In 1965 President Lyndon Johnson had 15,000 U.S. troops invading the Dominican Republic in his bloody warm-up for Vietnam. Naturally U.S imperialism had touched off much world-wide criticism and anger by this Grenada-like invasion.

Afterwards Doubleday & Co., a major New York publisher, came right out with a book on how international communist takeover conspiracies about the Dominican Republic completely justified the U S. invasion. The book was called *The Truth About the Dominican Republic*—written by none other than our Mr. Jay Mallin. How convenient for U.S. imperialism then that an "independent" book was being widely sold backing up its repressive crimes.

It will be no surprise to learn that the book was a U.S. Government propaganda project. Jay Mallin had been secretly approached by the U.S. Government and signed to a contract under which he agreed to write that book for them. Mallin received the usual author's royalties on book sales from Doubleday & Co., plus an extra payment from the Government of $2,368.

U.S. State Department officials gave Mallin classified documents to work from, and even edited his manuscript. *The Truth About the Dominican Republic* was 100% imperialist propaganda, secretly initiated, paid for, supervised, approved, and distributed by Washington. The U.S. Information Agency purchased 25,000 copies from Doubleday to give out to students in other nations. Jay Mallin was undoubtedly expressing his own right-wing opinions, but, more fundamentally, he was a minor employee of the U.S. Government counter-insurgency machinery.

Mallin has a great many "respectable" connections. When kidnappings of U.S. executives became common in Latin Amerika and Europe in 1973, Burns International Security Services brought in Mallin to give lectures on guerrilla movements to departing businessmen. His main connection, however, has been to the front-line forces in counter-insurgency.

While Washington denies any relationship to the armed white right, to "extremist" groups such as the Minutemen, to mercenaries and *Soldier of Fortune* magazine, S.O.F. editor Jay Mallin has been welcome everywhere within the U.S. military. And welcome on an official basis. He has written on terrorism for the Marine Corps. At Fort Bragg's U.S. Army Institute for Military Assistance (where the CIA and U.S. Special Forces give Latin Amerikan puppet soldiers counter-insurgency training), Mallin has been an invited lecturer. He has even taken part in seminars at the Pentagon.

Perhaps Mallin's closest connection had been to the U.S. Air Force. He has been a "regular contributor" (as that journal says) to *Air University Review,* "The Professional Journal of the United States Air Force."

Although it has attracted little public attention, the U.S.A.F. maintains a permanent counter-insurgency force, a small elite trained both as aircrew and assault commandos. This force is headquartered at the Special Operations School, Eglin Air Force Base in Florida. Elements of this hand-picked counter-insurgency force have operated in many nations in Afrika, in El Salvador, Guatemala, Iran, and dozens of other countries. **In fact these "Special Operations" Air Force commandos took part in the Government raid on the Republic of New Afrika's children's school outside Jackson, Mississippi in 1981.** Jay Mallin has been a political lecturer for the Eglin AFB counter-insurgency school and has often been a guest there since the early days of the 1960s (when it was named the Special Air Warfare Center).

We should not look upon Jay Mallin himself as personally important or special in some mysterious way. He is just one of thousands of voices orchestrated by Washington. His job has been to give out imperialist indoctrination. His words are the same worn, anti-communist tirade we are well aware of, painting every popular struggle as a tentacle of the Soviet international conspiracy, painting freedom fighters as "terrorists." Mallin always insists on more military action, more invasions, more repression as the thing for Amerika to do.

As a typical example of his right-wing indoctrination, one of his raps on Cuba calls on White Amerika to recover its misplaced manhood: "All that is required from America is a genuine determination to get rid of Castro. Once the decision is made Castro will be overthrown, but the decision had not been forthcoming. Throughout these critical years, United States policy towards Cuba has been a reflection of overall policy towards the hemisphere, a policy characterized by hesitation, indecision, and lack of understanding of *Latinos* and their countries. Too often America has acted as if it had a guilty conscience, and therefore had to keep turning its cheek. *Latinos* respect *machismo* in a man and in a nation."

This swaggering, reactionary nonsense should not be confused with U.S. imperialism's actual strategy. Mallin's writings on Cuba, for example, express nothing of the strategy used by the CIA's "Operation Mongoose" in its attempt to turn back the Cuban Revolution in the 1960s. In an identical way, Mallin's ranting against what he portrays as the perverse evil of today's guerrilla warfare is also obvious nonsense! "Terrorism is a disease of modern society, a virus growing in an ill body ... The actions of terrorists, however, cannot be measured in the way other acts of war or revolution are appraised. Urban guerrillas do not march to the same drumner as regular soldiers, or even rural guerrillas."

So the simplistic work of Jay Mallin only reflects a part of what the imperialists and their commanders actually think. The larger issues of neo-colonialism and real counter-insurgency strategy are far above his level. Even in the area of mass propaganda Jay Mallin is insignificant (certainly so compared to the Moral Majority or Jesse Jackson). **His specific role is basic political indoctrination of U.S. imperialism's front-line soldiers against national liberation, keeping them motivated and "ready to go."** This is the strand that ties together Jay Mallin's diverse connections.

U.S. Imperialism maintains a multiplicity of armed forces—some military, some police, and some supposedly unofficial and para-military—but all are carefully taught to think the same. Both U.S. Air Force officers reading *Air University Review* and Klansmen reading *Soldier of Fortune* got similar political indoctrination from Jay Mallin. As did Puerto Rican police officers, white mercenaries in South Afrika, U.S. "Green Berets" operating in Central Amerika, and many others.

It is just as if Jay Mallin were an employee of a central imperialist military indoctrination bureau. Only it is clearly in U.S. Imperialism's interest to hide the connections. Just as in 1965 the U.S. Government tried to hide the fact that Mallin's book supporting the Dominican Republic invasion was a secret CIA project from start to finish. As the CIA Chief of Cover and Commercial Staff told a Senate Committee in 1976: "We need a variety of mechanisms. We need a variety of cooperating personnel and organizations in the private sector." U.S. Imperialism wants to conceal their overall command and coordination of all the diverse repressive forces of imperialism. From South Afrika to Puerto Rico to Mississippi.

What Happened to the Zimbabwe Revolution (S1, 1984)

In hard times we must face hard truths.

We must stop viewing armed struggle in a romanticized and deliberately simple-minded way. The same thing applies to national movements. There are three reasons why this is imperative.

1. With no practical, communist understanding of what is going on in liberation wars between oppressed and oppressor nations, solidarity work is very underdeveloped.

2. Since in the real world things are not so simple as comrades here in the U.S. desperately try to believe, quite often imperialism is several jumps ahead of us. All too often the "movement" has been raising funds or holding rallies for what in reality is an ally of U.S. imperialism.

3. A romanticized and ignorant view of armed struggle in Afrika, Asia, and Latin Amerika may be fine for a cheerleader team, but when comrades who suffer from this infection try to do armed activity themselves they naturally do so in a romanticized and ignorant way. Ours is now a road partially blocked with political-military wrecks in the first hundred yards. It is not an accident that people who failed to see the decisive political-military problems of their own work in recent years are still uncritical of their support of President Robert Mugabe of Zimbabwe. It is not an accident that those who learned nothing from Zimbabwe are ignorant about El Salvador. At some point repeated ignorance is not innocent, but is a deliberate choice in politics.

Recent developments in Southern Afrika have been a blow. Many comrades are surprised and upset at the South Afrikan government's success at maneuvering socialist Mozambique and Angola into cooperation with it. Once new liberated nations bordering white apartheid South Afrika were thought to be a launching pad for a decisive war to liberate South Afrika. Now, Mozambique has apparently been bent into some limited cooperation with the apartheid regime, becoming a buffer state to keep Black South Afrikan guerrillas disengaged in exile.

These contradictions did not grow overnight, but have been ten years in the making. **The "key" event was when U.S. imperialism stopped the Zimbabwean Revolution.** How imperialism stopped this revolution must be understood—not only for its own sake, but because of what it tells us about the larger situation. **Imperialism did so by penetrating the liberation movement itself**, making a neo-colonial alliance with the petty-bourgeois leadership. Class unites with class. Neo-colonialism used the armed struggle against itself, having the Zimbabwe freedom fighters unknowingly bring into power imperialism's own agents. This regime of Prime Minister Robert Mugabe and his ZANU-PF party shields itself by using the socialist and national liberation identity of the movement it betrayed and struck down.

These contradictions are class contradictions within the oppressed nations. To not understand them is to not see the class and national factors that imperialism—quite concretely including the CIA—tries to use in **neo-colonial counter-insurgency**. The imperialist experience gained in suppressing the '60s movement in the New Afrikan ghettos here was used in Zimbabwe. We can say that if you don't understand Zimbabwe, that you probably don't yet understand Amerika.

I. The Generals of Neo-Colonialism

The search for a neo-colonial weapon to kill the Zimbabwe Revolution began with a political sttruggle within U.S. imperialism. While we are most familiar with imperialism's traditional strategy—keeping the Afrikan masses down through the repressive settler-colonial regime—this is not imperialism's only option. **Many imperialist officers in the CIA, the State Department, the Council on Foreign Relations, the planning staffs of many multi-national corporations, saw the long-term necessity of indigenous neo-colonialism rather than European settler-colonialism in Afrika. Even in the form of "neo-socialism."**

There has been an intense policy struggle within the imperialist camp between those who favor the traditional option of military repression and those who favor the neo-colonial option of embracing and subverting the national liberation movements. (Imperialism actually uses both weapons, and neither will ever completely replace the other.) Within the imperialist state a so-called radical grouping on Afrikan strategy formed during the 1970s.

W. Anthony Lake

Until 1976 the most visible member of this tendency was W. Anthony Lake, a career State Department officer. He was the perfect, almost stereotype, elite liberal: a product of private schools, of Harvard, Cambridge, and Yale. By 1970 Lake had served in Saigon and had advanced to the White House. He was Special Assistant to Henry Kissinger on the National Security Council staff. In a surprising move Lake openly broke with the Nixon-Kissinger conservative line, resigning in protest over the destabilization of Cambodia.

Although in exile from government, W. Anthony Lake rose still higher in imperialist policy-making circles. He became a focus in the preparations for new imperialist strategy in Afrika. Lake became a familiar figure in discussions in the Rockefeller-based Council on Foreign Relations. In 1971–72 he was foreign policy coordinator for U.S. Senator Muskie's Presidential campaign. At a time when most foreign policy attention was fixed on Southeast Asia, Lake argued for the importance of Afrika to U.S. world interests.

As director of the Special Rhodesia Project of the Carnegie Endowment for International Peace, Lake organized Congressional liberals against U.S. support for the Smith regime of "Rhodesia." He had become, in an insider's sense, a foreign policy star. So much so that in 1973 conservative William Safire, writing in his *New York Times* column on "The Next Kissinger," said that "a liberal-activist President might go for Anthony Lake as his foreign policy advisor."

In 1977 such a "liberal-activist President" did come to power. And the new Carter Administration was faced with a crisis in Zimbabwe. The old Nixon-Kissinger policy of relying on the European settlers of "Rhodesia" had failed. Afrikan guerrillas were knocking out imperialist defenses, mobilizing the masses, and on the verge of unconditional military victory. The CIA reported that the Smith regime had only a short time to live. Another U.S. fiasco was near in the chain of humiliating defeats that stretched from Vietnam to Angola.

The Carter Administration charged into the crisis, pushing through a sharp change in strategy. There was an accompanying shake-up in personnel. W. Anthony Lake came back as State Department Director of Policy Planning. Richard M. Moose became Assistant Secretary of State for Afrika. A former Lake ally on the National Security Council staff in 1969,

Moose was a key mover within the Senate Foreign Relations Committee staff in cutting off funding for Kissinger's ill-fated 1976 war in Angola. "Rhodesian" settler officials, bitter at their abandonment by Washington, started the double-entendre that "The Moose drinks in the Lake."

The *Washington Post* reported: **"The Carter Administration, emphasizing its bolder support for Black majority rule in Afrika, is replacing the top officers at the State Department's Bureau of African Affairs ... Two of the present three Deputy Assistant Secretaries in the African Bureau also are scheduled for replacement, informed sources said, with a fourth deputy to be added on economic policy. Officials deny 'any purge' ..."**

Although the small group quickly reshaping U.S. Afrika strategy was chaired by Vice-President Mondale, the real star was UN Ambassador Andy Young. For years, as a Civil Rights leader, Young had visited Afrika as a fellow activist and friend of liberation struggles. He had international stature as one of the Rev. Martin Luther King Jr.'s chief aides in King's Southern Christian Leadership Conference (SCLC). In South Afrika the authorities had allowed him to meet with an imprisoned Robert Sobukwe, the founder of the Pan Africanist Congress. Young took Sobukwe's two children back into his own home in Atlanta; they were raised as part of his family. These well-publicized personal ties to Mother Afrika made Young the best possible advance-man for imperialism's courtship of Afrikans. This was not just a cosmetic touch. The Andy Youngs and Jesse Jacksons have a practical understanding of mass Third World movements that a Kissinger will never have.

Led by Andy Young and W. Anthony Lake, the small Carter Administration group on Afrika strategy laid down a realistic view of imperialism's options. Two key points in their assessment were: **1. U.S. imperialism, irregardless of what anyone thinks, is unable to defeat communism in Southern Afrika by military means; 2. U.S.**

strategy on Afrika must take into account the ever-present danger of mass uprisings in New Afrikan ghettoes here. These points were interrelated, in fact.

Of the three existing military options, two had failed and the third was too dangerous to use. The settler-colonial regimes had been militarily broken in Portuguese Angola, Guinea-Bissau, and Mozambique. Settler-colonialism in "Rhodesia" was losing its war, and South Afrika, the last settler-colonial fortress, thought the "Rhodesian" situation so hopeless that it had been looking for a neo-colonial solution since 1974. Kissinger's fantasy of CIA mercenary armies substituting for the U.S. Army and Marines had been totally smashed in Laos, Cambodia, and Angola. The third military option, of direct intervention à la Vietnam, was suicidal in Afrika.

Andy Young said it all: "I see no situation in which we would have to come in on the side of the South Africans ... **You'd have a civil war at home.** Maybe I ought not to say that, but I really believe it. **An armed force that is 30 percent Black isn't going to fight on the side of the South Africans.**"

So U.S. imperialism's ultimate option of superpower invasion was ruled out because of their fear of Afrikan mutiny and **"civil war at home."** This was not only Andy Young

Andy Young, Security Council [United Nations, New York]

speaking. The intelligent white elements of the imperialist forces shared this concern. They take seriously the revolutionary possibilities of the New Afrikan masses. The Rockefeller Commission on "Critical Choices" wrote on Afrika policy: "Among other considerations, Americans should recognize that the effects of a major race war in Afrika would extend far beyond that continent, with the ominous prospect of encouraging further racial polarization in the United States."

W. Anthony Lake perceptively said: "One should also consider the possible impact on our society if a racial conflict in Southern Africa were to escalate dramatically, **if televised reports of Black and white bloodshed were to become even fractionally as familiar to American living rooms as the bloodletting in Indochina became in the 1960s. In short, the domestic divisiveness of the issue makes Southern Rhodesia all the more dangerous a problem for the United States.**"

So the Carter Administration pursued the search for a "peaceful," neo-colonial solution. By publicly pulling away from the white settler-colonial regimes, by publicly claiming to support the goals of the liberation struggles, U.S. imperialism was repositioning itself to find Afrikan allies. Their goal was to disarm the guerrillas, stop the revolutionary process, and usher in pro-Western, bourgeois Afrikan governments. **This would also help reinforce the same politics here in the New Afrikan communities.** Zimbabwe, Andy Young insisted, was "the key."

This broad turn towards co-optive neo-colonialism was also shared by the other regimes involved in Zimbabwe, by Britain and South Afrika. There were significant differences between them, however. The South Afrikan regime wanted a puppet Afrikan government under its hegemony. Britain wanted the most bourgeois Afrikan regime, stable and protective of British investments, that it could set up, providing that at least part of the guerrilla leadership was involved (since London understood that no regime without those credentials could defuse the liberation war.)

U.S. imperialism had, for once, the most sophisticated strategy. On the surface, Washington would call for Afrikan majority rule in Zimbabwe—and then let Britain take the leadership (as the former colonial power) in international negotiations. This modest attitude was unusual coming from Washington. One of Lake's criticism's of Kissinger's Afrika strategy was that "Super-K" had foolishly catapulted U.S. imperialism into the spotlight as the No. 1 power, the No. 1 ally of South Afrika, the No. 1 Western power fighting in Angola and Zimbabwe. Out of which U.S. imperialism only got further exposed as the No. 1 enemy of liberation. And lost the wars, too.

Lake's line on Zimbabwe was to let Britain run the risks and take the responsibility: "The aim was a low posture on the issue; Washington would follow London's lead and try to hide behind British skirts in the face of African pressures for more forceful action against the Smith regime." **All the while Andy Young, as chief U.S. negotiator on the issue, would openly sympathize with the Zimbabwe freedom fighters while building relationships.**

This was the innovative thrust of U.S. imperialism's new Southern Afrika strategy. While white settler South Afrika wanted an Afrikan puppet who had no involvement in liberation, while Britain wanted the most bourgeois Afrikan leaders it could install, Young and Lake gambled that U.S. imperialism could win over the main guerrilla leadership itself—that of the ZANU-PF Party. After all, who could better cover for neo-colonial betrayal than the political leadership of the guerrilla armies?

Andy Young was counting on several hidden factors working for imperialism within the Zimbabwe Revolution. The first was that, just as in the U.S. Empire, Afrikan national independence movements contain within them different classes and political forces. Much of the Afrikan petty-bourgeois leadership has always wanted, first and foremost, the "freedom" to become capitalists and Europeanized. Young's most remembered quote is about this not-so-secret attraction: **"At the junction of Jomo Kenyatta Avenue and Uhuru Avenue in Nairobi I saw a sign. It read: 'Kentucky Fried Chicken.'"**

In March 1980, Andy Young wrote very happily on how the emerging petty-bourgeois leadership in Zimbabwe "will join a Southern Africa bloc that has been very pro-United States and anxious to establish economic ties to the West ... everyone will be a winner." This, he said, included even the guerrilla leadership everyone in the West thought was so radical:

> "Zimbabwe will begin with a greater per-capita trained Black leadership and a larger Black middle class than any other African nation at the time of independence ... One burly bearded guerrilla leader pulled me aside during negotiation attempts in Malta in 1978 and, as I prepared to be attacked as a 'tool of imperialism,' he quietly asked: 'What **really** happened to the Oakland Raiders? They were supposed to be in the Super Bowl!' Like many of his fellows he had studied in America for nine years and had made many friends there. Later I was able to identify at least 30 Patriotic Front freedom fighters with post-graduate degrees from American universities."

The other hidden factor Young was counting on was the front-line Afrikan states. While U.S. imperialism could not reach the 30,000 Zimbabwe guerrillas, it might be able to get the host Afrikan states to disarm the guerrillas. In June 1977 Andy Young was interviewed on Public TV's *MacNeil-Lehrer Report*. He dramatically said that the Smith regime could fall within 18 months, and that plans were needed to deal with the new Afrikan government that would emerge.

Most important, said Young, was that joint plans to disarm the liberation forces had to be made with the front-line states: "These plans cannot be just British and American ... I think we cannot deal with these problems 5,000 miles away. **The people there on the border are going to have to**

take responsibility for dismantling the guerrilla army ..." That month Presidents Carter and Julius Nyerere of Tanzania had made a private understanding to cut short the Zimbabwe liberation war by international negotiations and bourgeois elections. We will cover this in detail later.

So in the critical year of 1977 the U.S. and Britain brought increasing pressure on the Smith regime to transfer power, while working to identify imperialism with the guerrillas. Young said that Washington just wanted **"to unwrite some real neglect and outright wrong-doing on the part of much of the West."** British Foreign Secretary David Owen praised the Zimbabwe guerrillas as **"essentially men of good will driven to take up arms."** Field Marshal Sir Michael Carver flew into Zimbabwe to become British Commissioner. Carver, who had commanded counter-insurgency operations against "Mau-Mau" in Kenya, announced: **"What I am basically committed to is that Rhodesia will become a basically Black country run primarily by Black Africans for the benefit primarily of Black Africans."** The imperialists even had their thugs trying to sound like the liberation movement. The neo-colonial operation to deep-freeze the Zimbabwe Revolution had been launched.

II. Installing the Neo-Colonial Agents

For U.S. imperialism to deflect the revolutionary war it was necessary for their hidden agents to subvert the liberation army. This was done in 1977, when a surprise coup installed Robert Mugabe and his clique over the ZIPA fighters. Mugabe pretends to have been the political leader of the liberation war, a pose that helped his ZANU-PF party into power and still helps cover for them. But Mugabe himself, who was imprisoned from 1964–74, did no political writing and had no communication with the liberation cadres, had nothing to do with building the guerrilla forces or guiding the war.

He was, in fact, practically unknown by them until 1975.

Imperialist strategy was simple: **to co-opt the war, deflecting its political aims from liberation to bourgeois democracy** ("majority rule"), grant Afrikan government as quickly as possible so as to stop the growth of socialist consciousness. As one major history of the liberation war put it: "To prevent the radicalization of the Zimbabwean nationalist movement through armed struggle, Kissinger had to remove the cause of the war by making Smith concede majority rule. The Rhodesian leader, with his narrow vision of world realities, was not only expendable but had become a liability ... For the longer the war went on ... the more radical the guerrillas would become." Kissinger's "Afrika shuttle" negotiations failed in 1975, since his reactionary bent kept him from breaking with Smith. Now a new U.S. Carter administration was moving to co-opt the liberation struggle.

For this strategy Mugabe was the perfect tool. He was a prominent Afrikan teacher and nationalist politician, who had always been close to liberal church circles as a "Christian socialist." Moreover, his tactical sense had always led him to pose as a "militant" or socialist, while in practice his concept of independence was precisely what Washington wanted—Afrikan "majority rule" in the form of bourgeois government.

In 1960 Mugabe, as the "militant" nationalist, had offered to pledge loyalty to "Rhodesia" if a new constitution gave him and other petty-bourgeois Afrikan politicians half the seats in the settler parliament. As late as 1975 Mugabe had agreed to the abortive South Afrikan "Détente" plan to promise Zimbabweans voting rights after five years—in return for which the ZANU and ZAPU guerrillas would be disarmed. During the proposed five-year pacification period only the settler army and police would be armed. Mugabe, like many other petty-bourgeois nationalist politicians, was always drawn to reformist deals.

In 1975 he avoided re-arrest by escaping to Mozambique, where he joined the ZANU military camps. Despite his old

1963 rank as ZANU Secretary-General, the army refused to accept him as their political leader. Four senior ZANU military commanders finally issued a statement friendly to Mugabe, but which explicitly limited his role to being a "middleman" (their word) in communications with the discredited bourgeois politicians. Yet there was no doubt Mugabe's star was rising. In January 1976 Mugabe flew to London, where the British Broadcasting Corporation interviewed him at length on their *Focus on Africa* show. This popular radio program was beamed all over southern Afrika. Mugabe posed on the show as the "militant" defender of the guerrillas, attacking President Kaunda of Zambia for arresting and repressing ZANU fighters. This dramatic broadcast, which was the self-admitted "breakthrough" in Mugabe's career, was, of course, arranged.

At that time the liberation war had undergone an important change. A new army, formed under Tanazanian-Mozambican directives from both ZANU and ZAPU (but actually almost totally from ZANU), had reopened the suspended liberation war on a greater scale than ever before. **ZIPA (Zimbabwe People's Army) was also more radical than its earlier parent bodies.** New commanders had replaced the older ZANU commanders, while thousands of fresh fighters were being led to conduct a more political war. ZIPA published its own revolutionary journal. Women fighters were not only joining the fighting (instead of being only ammunition porters), but in a move against male chauvinism all training instructors were women fighters. ZIPA began organizing drives for the first time into areas of Zimbabwe far inland, away from the Mozambique border. The war spread as never before, on a far larger scale.

In March 1976 *Africa* magazine reported that: "A highly confidential study carried out by Major General Walls, the Rhodesian Chief of the Security Forces, explicitly warns that Rhodesia alone cannot contain a guerrilla offensive for much longer." In many rural areas the settler forces could no longer even mount patrols. Settler bases were attacked repeatedly. **The fighters could see that unconditional military victory was definitely coming**. Fortified with this knowledge, the ZIPA command and the cadres rejected any imperialist deals, "talks" on compromises with imperialism, and all of the petty-bourgeois nationalist politicians who so desperately wanted to cut the revolution off. This absolutely included Mugabe and the other old ZANU politicians.

The ZIPA command began publicly moving to form a new revolutionary party out of the fighters themselves. ZIPA started appointing its own international representatives abroad, requested that all OAU solidarity funds come directly to its camps, and reluctantly sent its own separate delegation to sit alongside the old parties, ZANU, ZAPU, ANC, at the October 1976 international negotiations at Geneva. Mugabe and his clique were frightened, frantically issuing orders to the fighters which were all ignored. This was the most radical development of the independence struggle, although the ZIPA command was not itself a communist vanguard.

We should be precise on how much influence the Mugabe clique had on the army—almost none. While the ZIPA cadres had at first looked upon the old ZANU Supreme Council as still their political leadership, once they discovered that the old ZANU politicians were in favor of an imperialist deal to stop the revolution, they repudiated them. The old ZANU leaders were at first unable to even get permission to enter the military camps. Even when Josiah Tongogara, Mugabe's factional ally and the famous head of the ZANU military, got into the Mozambique camps he was unable to persuade fighters to desert the ZIPA political line. Tongogara had a long friendship with Samora Machel and other FRELIMO leaders, and they encouraged the ZIPA guerrillas to get together with him. Yet even with this pressure, **after an entire month in the camps of lobbying and intrigues by Tongogara and other Mugabe clique leaders, the majority of the revolutionary army still refused to accept that leadership**.

What is primary is that it is the Afrikan masses who created the armed struggle, and it is they who always wanted to reclaim their land without any imperialist compromises or neo-colonial conditions. So in the 1960s, before Nkomo or Mugabe or any of the petty-bourgeois nationalist politicians had organized any armed activity, the Zimbabwe masses repeatedly staged violent urban uprisings and general strikes. The petty-bourgeois politicians learned to use, by rote, socialist and Pan-Afrikanist slogans, but only to appease the liberation activists. The ZIPA commanders, who used "Marxist-Leninist" rhetoric just as Mugabe and Nkomo did, were not really more advanced. **The important thing is that many Zimbabwe fighters wanted war to unconditional victory and socialism**—that's why as long as the ZIPA commanders stuck to that program they had the support of the army. And it was within the ranks of the fighters that the first communist political consciousness was being born. That's why U.S. imperialism had to stop the war, even if that meant abandoning their settler puppets.

At that time the role of the front-line states again became pivotal. We should give some background: the five front-line states—Zambia, Mozambique, Tanzania, Angola, and Botswana—were the hosts for the Zimbabwe liberation forces. Military bases, training camps, HQs, and civilian refugee camps all were on their territory. And it was from two bordering states—Zambia and Mozambique—that the fighters infiltrated back into Zimbabwe. FRELIMO in Mozambique had closer ties still to ZANU, whose troops it had trained and still fought beside in both Mozambique and Zimbabwe itself.

But the front-line regimes also had their own agendas. Born with distorted colonial economies linked to "Rhodesia" and South Afrika, Zambia and Mozambique lost millions of dollars from disruption of trade ties to the settlers. Both also suffered political-economic instability as the war spilled over into their national territories. For these reasons both conservative Zambian President Kaunda and socialist Mozambican President Samora Machel wanted a Zimbabwean settlement as quickly as possible. The wishes of the front-line states were usually orders, since both Zambia and Mozambique used their power to make the Zimbabwe movement do what they were told.

For example: in 1975 the front-line states halted the Zimbabwe armed struggle altogether. Zambian President Kaunda and South Afrikan General van den Bergh (chief of the infamous Bureau of State Security) had worked out a "Rhodesian" sell-out settlement in October 1974. When ZANU Chairman Herbert Chitepo complained to the OAU, Zambian officials told ZANU they would **"use muscle to crush ZANU."** On March 18, 1975, Chitepo was assassinated by a car bomb. **On this pretext the front-line states stopped the war**; arresting and, if necessary, killing the Zimbabwe cadre who resisted.

In Tanzania, Mozambique, and Zambia the ZANU guerrillas were disarmed and confined to their camps. In both Zambia and Tanzania all the Zimbabwe liberation offices were closed. Zambian police did mass arrests of ZANU officials, members and relatives, torturing many to extract confessions. Three ZANU military commanders who escaped into Mozambique were arrested by FRELIMO and returned to Zambian imprisonment. **Cut off, most of the Zimbabwe guerrillas inside the country were killed in renewed counter-insurgency offensives. By late 1975 less than fifty guerrillas were still active in Zimbabwe**. The "Rhodesian" regime was overjoyed.

But the "détente" sell-out collapsed in late 1975, as "Rhodesian" Prime Minister Ian Smith stupidly refused any watering-down of settler rule. Tanzanian President Julius Nyerere and Mozambique's Samora Machel decided that the Zimbabwe war had to restart. They rearmed and turned loose the thousands of impatient Zimbabwe fighters, reorganizing them into the new ZIPA.

By January 1977 both Mozambican and Tanzanian governments were angry that the new ZIPA had become so radical, that fighters were refusing to go along with the U.S.-British negotiated deal that the front-line states wanted. Tanzania started arresting ZIPA political cadre, forbidding political education classes in the training camps. In Mozambique an unsuspecting ZIPA command were arrested by FRELIMO. All members of the ZIPA Military Committee were arrested except its chairman, Rex Nhongo, who had secretly gone over to the Mugabe faction. FRELIMO also arrested all the ZIPA Provincial Commanders, Base Commanders, Sector Commanders, and many General Staff members. Units were broken up and hundreds of ZIPA fighters executed. Once again the front-line states had disrupted the liberation war in order to enforce their policies on the Zimbabwe struggle.

So the Mugabe clique, unable to voluntarily gain leadership over the guerrillas, had been given command only by FRELIMO's armed intervention. Mugabe, Machel, and Tongogara have all admitted precisely this in published accounts. We must recall that Andy Young emphasized how U.S. imperialism had to get **the front-line states, as the only possible option, to disarm the revolutionary fighters.** U.S. imperialism's scenario turned out to be an accurate guide to events.

III. The CIA and ZANU-PF

We can begin examining CIA penetration in Zimbabwe by referring to a remarkable book: *Struggle for Zimbabwe* by David Martin and Phyllis Johnson, two British and Canadian reporters specializing in Afrika. This book is nothing less than the history of the liberation war according to Mugabe, Tongogara, and their clique. First published in 1981, the second edition (printed in the U.S. by Monthly Review and in Afrika by Zimbabwe House) has an introductory endorsement by President Mugabe himself. This, then, is an authorized, semi-official ZANU-PF account of the struggle. In Martin and Johnson's "acknowledgements" the authors reveal that: "Among those who gave much valuable time for interviews and reading parts of the manuscript were the Prime Minister, Robert Mugabe, and his colleagues ... Thanks are due to the Ford Foundation which agreed to fund the final expenses for completion of the book ..." Why would the Ford Foundation pay for the writing of a British book which favorably pictures "Marxist-Leninist" Robert Mugabe and his allies as the "liberators" of Zimbabwe?

There is a curious hole in this history which starts to explain the Ford Foundation's friendly interest—the CIA. **The CIA almost never appears at all in this semi-official, pro-Mugabe history of the Zimbabwe struggle**. Outside of a one-line mention of CIA participation in an abortive U.S. foreign aid project, the **only** mention of the CIA is very strange. In telling about Kissinger's talks with "Rhodesian" Prime Minister Smith in September 1976, the book says:

> "The United States had theoretically withdrawn official links with Rhodesia in 1969, but the CIA, with the full knowledge of their Rhodesian counterparts, had maintained **a fullscale operation in Rhodesia**. Kissinger, by referring to 'our own intelligence links,' confirmed this clandestine operation, and this embarrassed the CIA who had told the President and State Department that they had withdrawn from Rhodesia." (our emphasis)

We are supposed to believe that the U.S. Government, including the White House, was innocently unaware of CIA counter-insurgency operations in Zimbabwe (although the authors can't explain how Henry Kissinger then knew about it). The imperialists certainly would like us to believe such lies. It is starting to get clearer why the Ford Foundation paid for this book. And the CIA's "**fullscale operation in Rhodesia**"—why do the authors fail to write even one word about it? This book, endorsed by President Mugabe, makes it appear as though the CIA played little or no role in the Zimbabwe struggle. That certainly is the impression we're left with.

Both the authors and President Mugabe know full-well that the CIA is a dedicated enemy of the Zimbabwe Revolution, and has long been very active there. Why are they concealing this? The CIA's "fullscale operation" in Zimbabwe had three basic components: covert military aid to the Smith regime; intelligence-gathering; subversion-penetration operations against the liberation movement. The first component needs little explanation, being the familiar Bay of Pigs, El Salvador–type military operation. In Zimbabwe the CIA, acting directly or through the South Afrikan settler regime, furnished the tiny "Rhodesian" military (the settler security forces were smaller than the New York Police Dept.) with hundreds of key specialists in counter-insurgency war: unit commanders, pilots, helicopter mechanics, interrogation experts. This was the most openly menacing part of CIA operations in Zimbabwe, but was ultimately the least dangerous. In direct confrontation the Zimbabwe masses exposed the CIA as a paper tiger.

The CIA's intelligence and penetration operations were and are much more successful. In a variety of areas the CIA uses front-groups to monitor—and if possible to subvert—Zimbabwean politics. Afrikan trade unions in Zimbabwe were co-optive instruments legally sanctioned and regulated by the settler-colonial regime. Their No. 1 task was to persuade Afrikan workers not to strike (which was illegal, of course) or take part in the liberation struggle. As pay for pacifying the Afrikan workers, their union officials got to occupy one of the few petty-bourgeois positions open back then to Afrikans. Imperialism encouraged the Afrikan petty-bourgeoisie to open up many, many small competing unions (like "Mom and Pop" grocery stores) to disunite and confuse workers. By independence there were 52 Zimbabwean unions with an average membership of only 3,800.

These dummy unions were actually very modern—in a bourgeois, AFL-CIO style. They emphasized, just as in the

U.S., an involved grievance procedure, emphasis on "bread-and-butter" issues, tactical focus on wage negotiations. This should only be expected, since all these dummy unions were subsidized and in large part used by the CIA. Both to get intelligence and to keep workers without any real organization. One of many instruments used by the CIA was the "International Confederation of Free Trade Unions" (ICFTU), the anti-communist union organization of the NATO powers. The ICTFU is led by the U.S. AFL-CIO and has a long, documented history of collaboration as a CIA instrument. An ICTFU official admitted in Zimbabwe in 1971: **"It is probably true that this country has received in recent years more international trade union assistance than any other country on the Afrikan continent ... There is not a union here which has not received assistance either directly or indirectly."** While Afrikan workers in Zimbabwe fought their oppressors with waves of strikes, even in the face of gunfire and mass firings, their pro-Western unions opposed these and played

only a negative role. This is the result of one tentacle of "full-scale operation in Rhodesia" by the CIA.

General intelligence-gathering about the liberation movement is done using many instruments, with "academic cover" being the first level. U.S. imperialism, which had long left Afrika primarily to the main colonial occupiers, began to build up its intelligence net in the mid-1950s to catch up. In 1954 the CIA and American Metal Climax, the main U.S. minerals corporation in Zimbabwe, set up the African-American Institute to supervise brainwashing of Afrikan students, research on Afrikan liberation, and other such tasks. That same year William O. Brown shifted from the U.S. State Department Bureau of Intelligence to become the first head of the Boston University Afrikan Studies Program. In 1956 CIA Deputy Director Max Millikan shifted to the directorship of the CIA-funded MIT Center for International Affairs, a major research center on Afrikan liberation movements.

Since the CIA cannot act openly in Afrika, it pushed the creation of these university Afrikan Studies Programs. Since then, Afrika has been criss-crossed by U.S. "researchers," "political scientists," "doctoral candidates," trying to interview liberation cadres and "research" guerrilla movements. It is widely known where such information goes.

CIA funding for such intelligence-gathering had to be "laundered." For this the Government turned to the minerals corporations and, most notably, the private foundations. The Ford Foundation is the main funding instrument for covert CIA intelligence using "private sector" personnel in Afrika. In fact, the Ford Foundation is the primary source of funds for most of the major U.S. Afrikan Studies programs. This foundation also funds numerous scholarship programs so that Afrikan students can be indoctrinated in the U.S. Extensive links to the CIA have always been present: for example, Richard Bissell was on the Ford Foundation staff when he served as CIA Deputy Director. Edwin Land (whose Polaroid Corporation's police services in South Afrika are well-publicized) was simultaneously a

Joshua Nkomo, left, and Robert Mugabe leaving peace talks in Geneva in 1976. Photograph: Dieter Endlicher/AP

member of the Foundation Board and a member of the U.S. Foreign Intelligence Advisory Board. **This shows us why the Ford Foundation was willing to fund an authorized, pro-Mugabe book on Zimbabwe that strongly downplayed the role of the CIA—and explicitly white-washed general U.S. Government involvement with any such CIA activity.**

* * *

The CIA's search for critical penetration into the Zimbabwe armed struggle found success. In 1977 the CIA reached a secret agreement to support the Mugabe/ZANU-PF party to become the next government. This decision became known, of course, to the CIA's local co-workers in Zimbabwe, the "Rhodesian" Special Branch (political police). In consternation the "Rhodesian" intelligence men told many of their closest Amerikan friends. One of these was right-wing author Robin Moore (of *The Green Berets* fame), who lived in Salisbury as "self-appointed ambassador" from the U.S. right. Moore wrote:

> "Reliable African sources are charging that the CIA is backing Robert Mugabe, although it seems odd that the U.S. would back an avowed Marxist ... the link between the CIA and the Mugabe camp, working out of the United States, is said to be Karanga tribesman Edson Zvobgo. Zvobgo, a Rhodesian teacher of political science and at one time detained for terrorist sympathies, has established university connections in the United States as a cover for his political activities."

Luckily for the CIA and their Zimbabwean friends, Moore's comments were ignored as just the crazy mud-slinging of the white supremacist right-wing. Edison Zvobgo is currently the Zimbabwean Minister for Legal and Parliamentary Affairs, a Member of Parliament, member of the ZANU Central Committee, and one of Mugabe's closest allies. Zvobgo and Mugabe have been close since their early days in the nationalist movement; at the founding of the Gwelo Congress of ZANU in 1963, Edison Zvobgo was elected Deputy to Mugabe as ZANU Secretary-General. Zvobgo, like almost all the other ZANU and ZAPU leaders, was arrested and imprisoned in 1964. He was, along with ZANU President Sithole (who later betrayed the revolution in prison), in the historic automobile full of ZANU leaders caught carrying dynamite into the capitol. At first glace Zvobgo might appear to be just like any other older revolutionary cadre in the Third World, like the many Vietnamese officials who underwent long imprisonment by the French in their struggle's early years.

His relationship to U.S. imperialism surfaces when we look at his elite, petty-bourgeois career in the U.S. Beginning college at Pius XII University College in Lesotho, Zvobgo transferred to Tufts University in Massachusetts. Then came his return to Zimbabwe in 1963, followed by his arrest the next year. While most of the liberation detainees were held until late 1974 and early 1975, British pressure forced them to release a few early in 1971—most notably Edison Zvobgo and his cousin, Michael Mwema (also a founding ZANU Central Committee member).

Zvobgo briefly played a role in the founding of the ANC in 1972, before leaving to Zambia to begin exile. Once in Zambia he demonstrated how useful a move his release had been. In 1972 the ZANU guerrillas were just restarting their war after the 1969–72 "silent years" of retraining and base-building. But they were almost without support internationally except for China. The families of the fighters in Zambia often had no food. Zvobgo, as a leader with some familiarity with the international scene, was asked to lead fund-raising and support for the fighters. He refused, saying that he had "sacrificed enough." (His cousin went even further, betraying the movement and being expelled from ZANU.) Now, Zvobgo said, he was moving to Amerika to give his family a better life.

It was at this time that Zvobgo was recruited to work for the CIA. Eddison Zvobgo was an unusual ex-convict and revolutionary exile. The Afrikan Bureau of the U.S. State Department arranged U.S. residency papers not only for Zvobgo and his immediate family, but also for other adult relatives. All got INS work permits. We can assure you that prominent Third World revolutionaries do not ordinarily get such a warm welcome from U.S. imperialism.

Zvobgo was instantly admitted to the Fletcher School of Law and Diplomacy at Tufts. This has a certain significance. Fletcher is the elite training ground for U.S. imperialism in international diplomacy and affairs (with a tuition alone of over $8,000 per year). It has a "hawkish" orientation, as we can tell by a recent report that an equal number of 1984 graduates will join the CIA as will join the State Department. U.S. Ambassador to El Salvador Thomas Pickering is a

Fletcher graduate, as were the two U.S. Ambassadors before him. The foreign trainees are all those being groomed for the international pro-U.S. elite. Argentina's current Economics Minister, leading his government back to a tight U.S. relationship after the Falklands fiasco, is another Fletcher alumnus. As is Edison Zvobgo, supposedly an Afrikan "anti-imperialist."

Zvobgo graduated from Fletcher in 1974. Promptly he was admitted to Harvard Law School. By 1975 he was Professor of Law at Lewis University in Illinois, living in an expensive suburban house, driving an expensive new car. Quite a distance to travel in only three years after leaving prison in Zimbabwe. He had an influential "Uncle."

The CIA's small investment in Zvobgo paid off in 1975–76. A split in ZANU provided an opportunity for Zvobgo to reenter the leadership of the movement. He immediately began agitating for Robert Mugabe's elevation to ZANU President. Most important of all, as Zvobgo became active again he regularly flew back to Afrika, visiting guerrilla camps in Zambia, Tanzania, and Mozambique. The CIA had been worried about the new, more radical ZIPA guerrillas. Since once in camp each fighter adopts a "war name" to protect his family and cover his background, the CIA had no idea who not only the ordinary fighters were, but in many cases no idea who new commanders and political commissars were. Moreover, they were uncertain as to the new ideological currents. Zvobgo, under the cover of "chats" with U.S. State Dept. Afrika Bureau officials, transmitted to the CIA regular reports on the guerrillas. This was security identification information: real family names and background, political tendencies, friends, military position and unit, and so on. Zvobgo helped arrange for Robert Mugabe and the U.S. Government to reach a secret understanding.

Even before the 1979 Lancaster House Conference in London, at which Zvobgo was a ZANU-PF delegate, he had become increasingly active pushing a pro-U.S. orientation within the liberation movement. Naturally, these neo-colonial ideas had to be packaged in a militant-sounding way. Mugabe and Zvobgo moved the party's journal, *Zimbabwe News*, to Illinois, USA. This may appear like an odd place to headquarter a Zimbabwe liberation activity, but it allowed editor Zvobgo to change the politics without interference. In the January–May 1976 issue Zvobgo, in a signed editorial, appealed for U.S. imperialism to support Mugabe's ZANU-PF party. He wrote then:

> "What policy should America adopt—if it wants to (a) succeed, (b) to be respected and hopefully (c) to be loved in Southern Africa? We suggest the following—
>
> "On Zimbabwe: Support ZANU and its armed forces in their armed struggle against the Ian Smith racist regime. Discard Joshua Nkomo, Bishop Muzorewa and Ndabaningi Sithole ... There are no other options available for the U.S. if it is tired of supporting losers. The current American policy of supporting settlers is going to hurt. Union Carbide, AMAX, Foote Minerals and other American corporations now sustaining the regime are going to receive short-swift treatment from a revolutionary Zimbabwean Government—on account of U.S. myopic policies."

There is only one way to interpret this surprisingly upfront message: 1) That U.S. imperialism might **"succeed"** and even be **"loved"** in Afrika by supporting ZANU-PF against the Smith regime—this says to the fighters that U.S. imperialism might become their "loved" ally, instead of an enemy. 2) That the fighters should want U.S. imperialism to back ZANU-PF against Nkomo, Muzorewa, Sithole and other Afrikan politicians—this says that superpower intervention in the affairs of the Zimbabwe people is OK if it's backing ZANU-PF. 3) That the U.S. minerals corporations will be "hurt" after liberation not because all exploiters will be expropriated, but only because of wrong U.S. government "myopic policies"—this says that a changed U.S. policy will protect imperialist investments. At the same time Zvobgo was telling U.S. corporations that large cash contributions to ZANU-PF would be remembered after independence. Imperialism was in command, with CIA penetration reaching the political center of the people's movement.

IV. Civil Rights Instead of Liberation = Neo-Colonialism

Zimbabwe's liberation war was formally ended in November 1979, at Lancaster House in London. A neo-colonial settlement was inevitable. The purpose of the British-U.S. conference was not to free Zimbabwe, since liberation through unconditional military victory was at hand. We should remember that even as early as 1977 British Foreign Secretary Crosland told NATO that the guerrillas would inevitably win unless there was an imperialist settlement:

> **"... there would be no doubt over who would eventually win on the battlefield. But if the issue were settled on the battlefield it would seriously lessen the chance of bringing about a moderate African regime in Rhodesia and would open the way for more radical solutions ..."**

So the only purpose of the conference was to enforce a pro-imperialist deal. And the fix was in. The front-line states, having eliminated any guerrilla grouping resisting a settlement, were still demanding peace on almost any terms. Mugabe had committed himself as well, needing an international agreement to explain why ZANU-PF couldn't deliver on its war-time promises. Tongogara said: **"We just have to have a settlement. We can't go back empty-handed."**

Although imperialism had lost the military war, it thus held the whip hand at the bargaining table. Mugabe's pathetic little request for a few radical points he could use to cover-up the sellout was sternly rejected by British Lord

Carrington. The final result was outrageous: Afrikan government by bourgeois elections, protection for all capitalist investments, all settler plantations to keep the land they actually occupy except through cash government purchase, all settler police, army, land, and officials to have guaranteed pensions paid by the new Afrikan government, no changes to the constitution for ten years except through unanimous Afrikan and settler vote in the Parliament.

The revolution was stopped short of victory. The Zimbabwe masses ended the oppressive settler rule, but did not get their land back, could not expropriate the imperialist holdings, could not, in fact, solve their urgent class needs. But the new Afrikan elite saw their own class prosperity coming. And the front-line states mistakenly thought that this imperialist deal meant stability and economic recovery. President Samora Machel hailed Conservative Margaret Thatcher as **"the best British Prime Minister for 15 years because she had the courage to solve the Rhodesia problem. Our aims for Zimbabwe were the same. It was just our tactics that differed."** British imperialism and the Mozambique Government had the same "aims," only different "tactics."

The Martin and Johnson *Struggle for Zimbabwe* explicitly erases liberation and socialism as goals for the freedom fighters. ZANU-PF's **main** goal, this Mugabe-authorized account says, was bourgeois elections. They describe the Lancaster House negotiations:

> "There was only one way to end the war, and that was to agree to a new internally acceptable constitution and to the holding of new British-supervised elections. Once an independence constitution had been agreed on there was really no way out for either side. The main principles the guerrillas had been fighting for—one man one vote elections, majority rule and independence—were all contained in it and even if the constitution was flawed on points of detail and

> obnoxious in some of its racial provisions, the fact remained that the main reason for going to war had been removed ..."

Neo-colonial civil rights meant that the new petty-bourgeois elite would soon be cabinet ministers. Josiah Tongogara as a youth had to leave for Zambia in search of education and opportunity. There he finally gained a "good" job for an Afrikan—bar manager at a white club. We can sense his joy at Lancaster House, as this now-powerful general looked forward to a bourgeois life. Before reporters he proposed that since he and "Rhodesian" Prime Minister Ian Smith came

Villagers are searched before entering one of Rhodesia's "protected villages"

from the same home area, that they should team up and watch out for "their" area's interests in Parliament. In fact, Tongogara fondly recalled Smith's mother:

> "Tongogara impressed Smith with his open approach, and even asked about his mother who used to give him candy as a child when his father worked on Smith's father's farm: 'If I get home while the old lady is still alive,' he said, 'that would be one of the greatest things for me—to say hello, ask her about the sweets and whether she still has got some more for me.'"

In that same vein Mugabe and U.S. imperialism—now loved by ZANU-PF—traded endorsements. Andy Young in his *N.Y. Times* column, "Zimbabwe Holds the Key," indicated U.S. favor of Mugabe in the upcoming elections. While Young put down Joshua Nkomo and ZAPU (**"Joshua Nkomo seems to be the implied, if secret, favorite of the British, the Russians, Ian D. Smith and South Afrika."**), he boosted Robert Mugabe: "Robert Mugabe's Zimbabwe Afrikan Liberation Army is credited with most of the military success that led ultimately to control of much of the countryside ... when I asked a British Foreign Office delegation, 'Which of the black leaders would you trust to run your family business in your absence?' they unanimously named Mr. Mugabe ..." What a recommendation.

After his party's victory in the April 1980 elections, Mugabe had a very friendly visit to the U.S. In Harlem thousands cheered as President Mugabe, practiced at using just the right words to imply Pan-Afrikanism and radicalism, said: "Long live our oneness—long live our struggle!" But in Washington, fulfilling his end to the love-fest, Mugabe endorsed U.S. President Carter for re-election in the warmest terms: "It is this admiration we feel for you that leads me to wish you well in the race you are running. **Unfortunately this race is being run in the United States. If he was running in our territory, he would be assured of vic-**

tory." Mugabe and Tongogara, finally free to express themselves, ended up embracing Jimmy Carter and Ian Smith.

The neo-colonial "oneness" was far more than diplomacy. Mugabe's ZANU-PF government began by announcing its loyalty to two of U.S. imperialism's main policies: protection of U.S. corporate investments and "détente" with the South Afrikan settler regime. Andy Young was right that "Zimbabwe Holds the Key"—today's Mozambique–apartheid regime accord just follows in Zimbabwe's footsteps. President Mugabe sent a message in his election victory press conference:

> "We cannot get them away even if we wanted to. The reality is that we have to co-exist with them, and co-exist on the basis of mutual recognition of the differences that exist between us. In other words, we should pledge ourselves, if South Africa does so on its part, to noninterference in South African affairs and they to noninterference in our affairs."

What Mugabe means by "noninterference in South African affairs" is really "noninterference" in the settler-colonial oppression. ZANU-PF, when its own movement was based in other nations, always swore to do likewise for Namibia and South Afrika. In one typical 1975 interview, Kumbirai Kangai (now Secretary of Labor) said: **"But once Zimbabwe is liberated, if we create a government which limits its concerns to the boundaries of Zimbabwe, then I think we will have sold out the whole cause. I believe it is our international obligation to continue in a concrete way to advance the struggle beyond the borders of Zimbabwe."** Now Kangai has a Mercedes and the South Afrikan guerrillas are barred from Zimbabwe. Washington is "loved" but the Afrikans who are trying to fight the Boers are not.

The CIA is pleased with ZANU-PF as well. To take one example we have already brought up: CIA contact with Zimbabwean unions has not been halted, but has intensified.

Robert Mugabe's brother Albert became the first General Secretary of the Zimbabwe Congress of Trade Unions. But a financial scandal broke out. On December 2, 1981, Albert Mugabe was found floating dead, fully dressed, in the deep end of his private swimming pool behind his ranch house. It is normal in ZANU-PF for "socialist" trade-union leaders to live the suburban European lifestyle. But when the temporary administrator delivered his report on the ZCTU, it was embarrassing to the neo-colonial regime: the ZCTU was totally bankrupt and being evicted from its offices; Albert Mugabe had kept no financial records, not even using checks—all funds were withdrawn by him and other officers in cash. The only good news was that the administrator said that the workers weren't paying their dues.

To keep the ZCTU offices together, the same old International Confederation of Free Trade Unions (ICFTU) stepped in to pay the officials' salaries. Why would the "AFL-CIA" pay to keep the ZCTU going? Because it is serving as a central agency for imperialist supervision of Zimbabwean workers. Recently, the African-American Labor Center (AALC) has been subsidizing ZCTU activities. The AALC was founded by the CIA to officially "encourage labour management co-operation to expand American capital investment in the African nations."

It was symbolic when the Mugabe regime made the guerrillas turn in their AK-47s and Kalashnikov rifles. The fighters were retrained by British imperialist instructors as regular army units, and rearmed with the NATO rifles used by the former settler army. People's Courts and other ties with the masses were ended; the fighters regrouped in new bases. They now are a standard capitalist army, living as parasites (soldiers earn three or four times what plantation laborers earn) whether they like it or not. Their role now is to police their own people. Again, we recall that in 1977 Andy Young said that the task in Zimbabwe was "dismantling the guerrilla army and retraining it to be a police force." For imperialism. This is the final success of neo-colonial subversion of the armed struggle.

The Zimbabwe masses made revolution. Shackled with worthless, petty-bourgeois leadership, still they struggled forward and gave their lives to liberation. If their revolution was deflected, it is also true that Zimbabwean life was transformed—and will never again be the same. Socialist ideas are openly discussed. The politics of popular change has been demonstrated to all. Settler-colonialism's suffocating death-mask has been smashed forever.

Many comrades here still give "solidarity" to ZANU-PF; this is the same as objectively covering for CIA-backed counterinsurgency because of ignorance (or in some cases opportunism). Some comrades know "something is wrong" with the new Zimbabwe regime, but are afraid to either question openly or investigate. The same phenomenon of a romanticized and deliberately simple-minded view applies to Mozambique–apartheid regime "détente." This just weakens us, since the difficulties of the real world can only be overcome, not ignored. We all in some measure share this infection. It is linked to the fear that unless we fix out minds only on the super-positive—"heroic" guerrillas, "communist" parties, "inevitable" victories—that we will get undermined and blown away by our own uncertainties. Scientific socialism is just that: critical, a weapon of the oppressed classes against the oppressing classes, a guide to practice. To change the world we must change ourselves.

CAPITALISM
IS A
DEAD
END

The Shape of Things to Come, Part II

Conclusion of an interview emailed back and forth into mid-2022

Kersplebedeb: We began this exchange in 2020 and are finishing it off in 2022. Biden is now president; you referred in the first part of this interview very much to Trump, but Trump failed to hold on for a second term, and he may not win or even run again in the future ...

J. Sakai: Am always going to focus on a Trump more than a Biden, since he was important in the new white breakout. Not Biden, who everyone knows is just another state manager/politician from the ruling class locker room. Even if our clown Trumpenfuhrer fades away personally like lumpen David Duke did, it's that Trump was the elected white power President of the settler colonial majority, not liberal corporatist Biden.

The fabled liberal future, in which people of color keep growing to be a new numerical majority of color over the white nation, is only an illusion. New Afrikans were a numerical majority in much of the Old South in the post–Civil War 1 Black Reconstruction era, and yet within a generation white settlers were the "majority" in total armed power race dictatorship over them everywhere there. We are simply going through an agonizing replay of that in a neo-colonial Batman costume.

Again, we have to start going beneath the immediate surface of politics into the underlying reality which first forms its coming shape. And as a necessary reminder, capitalism is a dangerously violent parent even to its own, and severe conflict and disloyalty between the ruling class and discarded u.s. euro-settler factions has happened before and will go on happening until the end.

Not since the fantasy capitalist Confederacy's total bloody loss in Civil War 1 and then the defeat of the rural Populist protest movement in the Plains states at the turn of the century, have some u.s. white popular classes taken such heavy body blows as in recent history. Although it occurs now in a different and much more difficult setting, that of the decline of u.s. empire within the growing dystopian arc of the capitalist system itself.

Remember, "America's" white classes are only privileged, not sacred or eternal. All too vulnerable their own selves to big capitalism's constantly growing "creative destruction" and ceaseless appetite for rolling everything back into yet greater capital accumulation. That's why they are always ready to jump to the right, to get back more of that settler privilege that they feel is their national birthright. Other versions of the right-wing "Make America Great Again" mass movement have happened before, and have experienced class political progress or defeat—or even in extreme cases, class whiteout. Nor have they themselves always been all that loyal to u.s. imperialism as their nation, when they felt their own desperate interests going in the opposite direction.

The naughty white working class of that Confederate South in the last Civil War, for example, ended up severely reduced in numbers, cut down like no-longer-needed herd animals by the end of the war. 13% of all white military-age men in the South had died in the few years of war, and even many more had been disabled (a year after the War ended, the state of Mississippi had to spend 20% of its revenues on artificial limbs). Some two million white Southerners were forced to migrate West and North looking for new jobs and new Indigenous land to steal to become really white again.[6]

The European conservative theorist of geopolitics, Friedrich Ratzel (who coined the ethnic nationalist slogan *lebensraum* made famous by "88"), visiting the u.s. South in 1874, was struck that he saw "no skilled workers, nor a vigorous white working class of any size worth mentioning." He compared even the largest u.s. Southern cities he visited back then to those large but backward cities of colonized agricultural societies, such as non-industrial Havana or Veracruz, that displayed "an incomplete, half-developed profile."[7] That reduced Southern white working class wouldn't even start to really recover until the 1930s New Deal and the bloodbath industrial bonanza of WW2.

Even the late-19th/early-20th-century political defeat of the precarious small farmers and laborers of the Midwestern Plains in their Populist political uprising, whose presidential candidate was Nebraska's William Jennings Bryan of "You shall not crucify mankind on a cross of gold" fame, also involved mass white class defeat.

Between 1890 and 1920, some u.s. Plains states of the Grain Belt saw widespread white demotion to tenant farmer status as well as actual large lower class removal, with many white bankrupt small farmers and jobless rural laborers forced on the road. Turned back in their attempted populist revolt by the iron walls of the railroad monopolies that controlled their crop sales, and the Wall Street financial interests that controlled their debt. While in one direction, some lingered to swell the anarchist IWW into the greatest rural radical labor organization "America" had ever known. In another direction, a surprising one million struggling rural Plains states whites in those years gave up on their loyalty to "America" altogether and moved camp across the border to remake their nationalistic identity as euro-settler Canadians. (Where some say their white settler anti-banking populism became one important seedbed for Canada's own social-democratic left.)[8]

Flash forward to more recent history. Even before they became u.s. citizens, early European immigrant "ethnics" such as the Irish had always been counted on to be mass cannon fodder for "America's" always-outward-moving military. So the fact that modern young white working-class men and boys took up the "FTA" spirit and joined the widespread mutinies against the Vietnam War in the 1960s, was a big shock to the u.s. ruling class.

At the same time, surreal as it may seem today, until the late 1970s a white postal letter carrier or union corporation factory guy could expect to own a home, support a wife and children on his single income, take family vacations—i.e., have some kind of lower middle-class lifestyle. Euro-american settlers got used to that real quick.

So white workers at that time not only expected middle-class incomes in union industries and trades, but increasingly refused to sacrifice themselves in imperialism's neocolonial invasions abroad. In other words, were of less and less use to the u.s. ruling class.

Little surprise what happened next. Today, now that the u.s. industrial working class has been mostly offshored and local blue collar wages here miniaturized, many white towns and communities that once had a movie theater, maybe a small nearby hospital, restaurants and clothing stores, are often left with none of these. Only a fast food outlet or two and some bars. Since 1979, the number of u.s. manufacturing jobs paying over $20 an hour has decreased by 60%. It is odd but normal now to take in a historic white working-class ex-industrial community that is like half-deserted, where a blue collar family you know is trying to squeeze every adult onto government disability and food stamps. It's the new "unions." It's not just clichés about Appalachia and the upper Midwest "rust belt"—a recent magazine article notes in passing that "Holyoke, Massachusetts, once home to more than 25 paper mills," is "now one of the poorest places in the state." Without pausing for any explanation, since it assumes we all get it.[9]

Today, everyone senses our landscape distorting into what feels like the bulging shape of an incipient "civil war" of some yet unnamed kind. Professors and capitalist writers and mass media use that phrase, which has even been debated in contesting *New York Times* columns. Is Civil War 2 in the cards being dealt us or not?

The capitalist media is choking on these words, but can't ever explain them. Because by not grounding political analysis in the u.s. empire's permanent settler colonialism, we can't get to the unresolvable contradiction of "America's" post-modern capitalism. That it needs both old colonialism but in camouflaged form, along with a contentious partial de-settlerization of society (or a tactical step back from outright white master-race rule of the biosphere). Which is all an inescapable part of the bitter jumbled neo-colonial capitalist retreat and rearrangement of all classes old and new—and the resultant neo-colonial wars and civil wars like Uyghur genocide and "Iraqistan"—and now with Ukraine emergency alarms inevitably ringing in all our senses.

Kersplebedeb: We are returning to the theme of globalization vs. nationalism, and the limitations of that framework. In that light, and given that you brought it up, what are we to make of the Ukraine war? Are we at some kind of turning point?

J. Sakai: This Ukraine war certainly might become one critical turning point, though it is too early yet to see its full widening circles of consequences. In one way it is a turning point for us because the u.s. left has more or less been united for this moment, only under Biden's leadership. Confused AOC can be his corporal now, "yessir!" Isn't that the political gut punch people didn't see coming?

When globalized economies became evident in the late 20th century, one of the first premature reactions in bourgeois political analysis was to jump us to the linear conclusion that now separate nations as old news would become unimportant, obsolete, and thus somehow would helplessly fade away. Yet the very reverse happened. Ditto tottering old empires and oligarch/plutocrat monopolies and bureaucrat state capitalism.

Sri Lanka's Hambantota International Port, whose 99-year lease was granted to China Merchants Port Holdings Co. Ltd.

Globalization is not some "no speed limits, no traffic laws" economic and cultural free for all, with the fabled "free market" being the sole guide to what anyone can do down and dirty in the scrum. *Capitalist globalization needs and is structured around extreme nationalism.* How else could they keep the world in order and us under their boot? That's why English is the mandatory language used by all pilots and air traffic controllers in world commercial aviation, just as a survey of the world's leading scientific journals found that all the top 50 such publications were in English. In countries such as Germany, France, and Spain, many more university academic papers are produced in English than in their native languages. Many E.U.-based transnational corporations have quietly adopted English as their mandatory language for all company-wide management communications. (All of which also advantages the U.K. and Canada, Ireland and Jamaica, New Zealand and Australia and so on, of course, keeping alive in diffused form the Anglo-Saxon world of the dead British Empire—but within a globalized capitalism. As Vlad the Invader himself bitterly nags us about over and over.)

The universality of identity and outlook that is now natural and needed to make our evolutionary future out of today's global crises, is also always under constant torque to be twisted into new narrowing capitalist forms. Globalization like everything else exists in contradiction and creates its opposites. "America" can hardly be the "lone superpower" of everything, when China's trade and investment in Africa are replacing Britain's and "America's," and when Iran is more powerful politically and militarily in the Middle East than either "America" or Russia. And when the biggest global cultural export of "America" isn't Hollywood anymore but New Afrikan hip hop.

In globalization the capitalist world is becoming more multi-polar but not in the least democratic or egalitarian—and why should it?—and also even more complicated than anyone expected. Like, the natural tendency is for big capitalist industry to concentrate, with duopolies now being seen as the steady end state. Such as Boeing and Airbus in jetliners. But the real trend is much more complex than that.

For instance, we are used to seeing the duopoly of either yellow u.s. Caterpillar or Japan's Komatsu in bulldozers and earth-moving vehicles on construction sites and highway projects in the u.s. as our bus drives by. But that's just here, for us locals. Worldwide is a truer more multi-polar picture. While Caterpillar and Komatsu are indeed the world's No. 1 and No. 2 in market share of heavy construction equipment, white "America's" beloved "Cat" has only a 13% world share. The three leading Chinese companies have a greater share of world sales together than "Cat" and green John Deere, the other major u.s. company, combined. And Swedish and South Korean and Swiss companies are taking real (for them as small countries) market shares of heavy construction machinery, too. One or two percent of the entire global market for an expensive manufactured commodity is not small change anymore.[10] Some companies specialize more in expensive but extra-heavily-built vehicles for Northern cold weather use, while others put more emphasis on less expensive and lighter equipment for use in flatland tropical climates. No matter how many "Cat" caps white men wear.

Not that many advantages do not persist from imperialism's previous configuration. Obviously, the u.s. dollar is the foundation currency for world capitalism, which every national treasury and local hedge fund must have access to. As such, the u.s. still enjoys cowboy leverage in the world financial system—at least for now.

And of course, "America's" FBI together with its elite special military units awkwardly function as globalization's makeshift neo-colonial super-duper police. Which is why the u.s. could arrest, move to New York, convict, and imprison the former commanding admiral of the Guinea-Bissau Navy. Which must have fascinated fellow Black inmates in their jail tier. Just as they are doing now with arrested Prime Minister Andrew Fahie, the elected leader of the British Virgin Islands. And former president Juan Orlando Hernandez of Costa Rica, who is also awaiting his u.s. trial. It was only an outraged revolt by the leadership of the Mexican Army that forced the FBI to release their recent chief commanding general from federal jail in New York. Under unique u.s. law, any person in the entire world from the UN Secretary General to Putin's maid can be arrested for alleged direct or indirect relationship to drug dealing or related money laundering, tried here, and imprisoned. Of course, the u.s. is primarily policing up its satraps and subordinates who run the neo-colonial states of the oppressed periphery.

What we see, once we start looking for it, is that "globalization vs. populist nationalism" may loom large in those publicized clashes that dominate our political news—but cannot be any fundamental contradiction of the system because the capitalist ruling class needs, uses and coordinates, and is behind both sides—both globalization and resurgent nationalism. Any more than you can say that big corporations versus state-incorporated trade unions are a principal class contradiction, when both forms of class activity are needed, shaped, and coordinated in symphony by the same ruling class and its state.

Checking off basics: nation-states are the way by which capitalist classes used to stake out and claim territorial class ownership of a particular human society and its lands as their exclusive property, as against all other rival capitalist classes. While under European feudalism there were shifting-in-shape-and-size aristocratic domains and principalities, but not nation-states as we know them (for instance, the present Normandy coast of France once spent more centuries as a feudal part of England than it has since as part of France).

Nation-states are where special bodies of armed men get uniforms that everyone must recognize as their license to kill and enforce overrule. Back in 1776 "America," the founding foreskins made massively violent racial enslaved labor openly legal and protected in national law and policy, as a necessary gear in the startup motor of its "infant empire's" capital accumulation. Copycatting patriarchy and the iron law of class society that no born woman may own her own body. Now, centuries later, the large but just-wetnursed Chinese "Red" state capitalist ruling class has similarly made its own mass enslaved and semi-enslaved proletariat, only in veiled form, legally and militarily chained for this same desperate cannibal hunger of startup capital accumulation.

Seen that way, a nation is an indispensable capitalist class instrument, encompassing both steering mechanism and hammer, even though as a form it is now outgrown historically by the humanity-wide development of population, production, and culture. i mean, some say there's nothing like Arabic Icelandic hip hop. Or Cambodian queer Southern Californian fiction.

Same with rusted old empires and poisoned oligarch countries, neo-colonial tribes, transitory lumpen states—any old collectivities which don't really fit barrier-leaping humanity anymore, but which addicted ruling classes cannot do without when they need a patch or a fix. It's as if economic and cultural globalization and the interweaving of the world's populations is the rising ocean, while now under the surface the sinking structures of antique empires and nations are thrashing about as residual dinosaurs. Like in the Covid-19 pandemic reality tv game, in which industrial high-tech nations like "America," China, Great Britain, Russia, and much of the EU couldn't stop dropping and fumbling away any effective public health response.

The more new crisis a capitalist faction is in, the more it wants to have some old nation around it as a safety blanket. Ditto its old races, genders, and religions. That capitalist nation-states across the board increasingly don't work and are breaking down from anyone's standpoint, is the central trick bag in our world's free-falling capitalist plummet.

There are overriding practical reasons for all this, because in endgame system failure not enough is getting repaired or replaced, being obsolete isn't aging out to be improved. It's *all* happening, the capitalistic living and the dying, coupling and competing in every ancient and newest way possible, but all doing their gig work and sex work in one big crowded room. Citizens hoarding toilet paper but also cryptocurrency, while their imperial state hoards its vintage 1950s-era B-52 bombers, as nations willy-nilly join in essential commodity supply chains together while also trying to rain irrational war and sabotage on each other—it's all the norm for capitalist system dysfunction now.

For what it's worth, my outsider opinion has been that the most conspicuous old capitalist imperial leaders—like the royal Clintons and oligarch Putin and China's potentate Xi Jinping—have been completely unable to cope with their own nations' piling up and up life and death problems. As the world capitalist system's unresolvable contradictions come more and more due. So all the Borises, Vladimirs, and Bidens are desperately overplaying their own hands in shaky ventures economic and military to somehow "win," as their ruling class and maybe even their populace remembers once doing.

i mean, the trash fires of fleeing u.s. troops in "Iraqistan" have hardly cooled, but big capitalism's rulers appear not to have learned a thing from that world's-longest-running Hollywood movie. These are truly unprecedented big power capitalist gambles in which all sides later turn out to have lost. Costly conflicts where afterwards they can't find a winner. Although, even if certain of nothing else, "America" is determined right now to fight to the last Ukrainian. That will certainly teach the world a lesson—only what is it?

Keep in mind that this global class system is gigantic, containing billions of people—and like one of their huge oil tankers can turn only in a wide slow arc. Like in Mexico and Central America, for example, this same turning point of a great downward arc of a falling nation coming apart started decades ago. Into the final cataclysm of the capitalist system's global fall and crash.

Welcome to the steadily spreading chaos that we all sense as the background of our new times. The societies that are capitalism's human structure coming apart from the stress of this neo-colonial era's overriding contradictions. Here we see ruling class interests as well as the autonomic survival reflexes of capitalist societies kicking in: all hands desperately ventilating and pumping chest compressions to aging forms of settlerism and ethnic nationalism. While more and more actors outta all classes are grabbing at pieces of their coming apart nations for themselves before it's too late. Fighting as well over the long ago installed on/off power switch by which one race or nationality can own or control others.

Kersplebedeb: So nations are breaking down, and as you say various players are "desperately overplaying their own hands in shaky ventures economic and military"—what comes to mind for me is that this has consequences in terms of warfare ...

J. Sakai: When the 19th-century military theorist von Clausewitz said that war was just the continuation of politics by other means, he deepened everyone's understanding of conflict, from the Pentagon to Chinese peasants. Likewise, at the turn of the 21st century, two Chinese military officers in an army unit assessing strategy published an extended paper/book on war in the neo-colonial era (although that is not a political term they are allowed to use). Which has again helped update the world's understanding. Peoples Liberation Army colonels Qiao Liang and Wang Xiangsui's 1999 *Unrestricted Warfare* gave articulated focus to changes which young capitalist military and intelligence and foreign policy officers had been increasingly debating. It became so significant in the spirited discussions on revolutionizing strategy and tactics among u.s. officers throughout the services, that eventually a branch of the CIA had to arrange its full translation and obscure commercial publication.

A word of caution: the Chinese officers did not discover any new military theory themselves, they were usefully summing up the many post-modern leaps actually going on in everyone's conflicts. Not only the Vietnamese guerrilla victory over "America's" most technologically advanced imperialist military in the world. But also then right back in turn, the CIA's White House men in Brooks Brothers suits inventing and financing a global Islamic religious jihad to foil Russia's attempted colonization of Afghanistan in the 1980s. To mention only the two most stand-out examples besides our own post-modern 9/11.

Their basic theme is that now the rules of warfare have changed, in that there no longer *are* any rules, at all. That warfare which was formerly given identity by official dec-

Mercenaries with Russian Wagner Group in Ukraine

larations of war between states, and form by armies of men in distinctive uniforms using lethal specifically military weapons against each other (the countless women and children raped and killed did not count), has broken through all bounds and limitations that used to try and safely divide military activity from civilian activity, war from peace.

The two Chinese officers recognized, in their *Unrestricted Warfare,* not only how quasi-state actors like the Republican Party or Al-Qaeda (my examples) can wage unorthodox violent conflict to piece together gradual dominance, but that now all combatants can weaponize a wide range of formerly civilian things, such as computer viruses, net browsers, and financial derivative tools. Ditto we can say to mass religions and drug mafias, corporations, and charities—like u.s.-occupied "Iraqistan" used their women's uplift non-profits as weapons right alongside their men's criminal ethnic militias, shotgun married by broad-minded Imperial Big Daddy just like that.

Since "the battlefield will be everywhere," the Chinese theorists predicted wars will not necessarily be declared as such, that there will be no diplomatic, legal, or moral limits at all, that "all the boundaries lying between the two worlds of war and non-war, of military and non-military, will soon be destroyed."

This directly relates to what we have seen over the past years in Ukraine, visibly starting in a new Russian war plan of gradual conquest by indirection, seen attempted even before Russia's "half-sandwich" 2014 military occupation of the Crimea and much of Ukraine's eastern Donbas region. Coming out of the oven unmistakably when Putin's man Viktor Yanukovych tried to take the Ukrainian Presidency and then suddenly steer their country back into a USSR-type remarriage with Moscow. This was all borrowed wholesale from China's *Unrestricted Warfare* by Gen. V. Gerasimov, Putin's main military strategist and supposedly the chief planner of today's 2022 invasion. Some articles, even in the mainstream u.s. media such as *Time* magazine and *The New York Times,* linked the invasion with these new concepts of unlimited warfare by misdirection:

> "Putin's strategy was one of unclarity, of blurry, gray movements in a fog of ambiguity, none of them rising to the level of war. American strategists sometimes call this the 'Gerasimov Doctrine,' after an essay published in 2013 by Valery Vasilyevich Gerasimov, the Russian army's chief of staff for the last ten years. 'The emphasis in methods of struggle,' Gerasimov observed, is on 'widespread use of political, economic, informational, humanitarian, and other non-military matters ... Overt use of force,' he advises, 'often under the guise of peacekeeping and crisis management, occurs only at a certain stage, primarily to achieve definitive success in the conflict.'"

That Putin's oligarch-state capitalism was already too weakened to carry out such advanced strategy as well as it wanted to in Ukraine, doesn't mean that the ideas themselves aren't increasingly organic to our moment. Armies are starting to supplement the role of expensive and scarce jet attack planes with flocks of bomb-carrying less expensive drones. Or recruiting thousands of smartphone-carrying civilians in the battle zone to act as your forward scouts and intelligence agents about enemy movements. Just like the New Afrikan struggle here is spontaneously doing on the battleground of the streets. Europe hasn't seen such a real-life quick testing war laboratory since the 1936 Spanish Civil War prepped big fascism for WW2. Which suggests, hmm ...

Kersplebedeb: I have seen these developments referred to elsewhere as "fourth generation warfare," and what you are describing certainly fits what seems to have become the norm over the past half-century. So the contradiction of capitalism surpassing the limitations of its historic nations, and the chaos that ensues from that, would be what is underlying these changes in how conflicts are being waged?

J. Sakai: We have to be careful to hold the lens of capitalist military theory the right way up, since it may seem to help us understand their wars—but is itself a blind alley. Capitalist militaries use terms like "fourth generation" war to systematize their own technical and managerial development. Starting with "first generation warfare," which to them was the forming of European state armies in the 1600s—who fought in the first rigid formations of soldiers using powered weapons (i.e. muskets and artillery). Today's "fourth generation warfare" is supposedly characterized by the mixing of regular and irregular forces and tactics, together with the strategic option of waging war directly upon unarmed civilian populations of the enemy, rather than targeting their more dangerous militaries.

How "new" and different this is, certainly sounds pretty questionable to revs, just being polite. i mean, we can test it using one well-established example that we all know about: at Wounded Knee in 1890, the Indigenous women, children, and elderly of the Lakota village (the young men were mostly elsewhere that day) were massacred without any quarter whatsoever, after the majority had disarmed themselves on demand by the invading Union Army cavalry troopers. It was also historic as a first Army enthusiastic field testing of white men's newly developed u.s. machine guns, which proved highly effective against unarmed women and children trying to hide behind tents. Fleeing Lakota were hunted and ridden down for miles by the victorious u.s. army troopers, a full twenty of whom later received Congressional Medals of Honor to prove that everything that the u.s. military does in its massacres small and large is exceptionally courageous and honorable.

This was one of the last signal battles of the historic euro-settler war to conquer the Plains Indians and Make "America" Great Again. In post-modern military terms, the technological triumph of the u.s. army's first machine guns and the elaborate propaganda awarding of the highest possible military honors by the "democratically-elected government," were as important moves as that 7th Cavalry's invasion of Indigenous lands itself.

So was trying out advanced "weapons of mass destruction" on unarmed civilians enough to qualify that 1890 day as good as "fourth generation warfare"? Or was it the Putinesque use of the "big lie," and super elaborate propaganda which publicized and played up their own war crimes but successfully blamed the victims for making it all so necessary, that would make it like "fourth generation warfare"? i think the point is evident.

These "generation" terms were coined as abstract generalizations by the u.s. capitalist military to use in their own managerial theory about capitalist conflict, but they are not accurate about our real world clashes themselves.

And now, since to blab about "fourth generation war" is only like some technocratic jargon to the general public, the u.s. national security community have been instead trying out a more fashionable video game-type term, "hyperwar," which means exactly the same thing.

We see "hyperwar" trotted out mostly when the house-broken u.s. media is reporting on Putin's unsavory wars. Obviously, like in Ukraine, where regular Russian army and marine units are sided there with retread veterans and paroled prisoners brought back as the privately uniformed Wagner Group, the more respectable face of an increasing mix of mercenary patch and fill units (such as Donbas Ukrainian town militias and companies of former Syrian army elite soldiers). While Russia uses its military weight advantage to do constant mass artillery and aerial bombardment not only of battlefields but also far beyond, trying to directly wipe out the target society itself. All this might be very striking, but is nothing that the u.s. military and other capitalist militaries haven't done themselves first, decades

or even generations ago (during the long Afghanistan occupation, on most u.s. military bases there "American" mercenaries, politely called "contractors," often outnumbered regular u.s. troops and aviation forces three or four to one).

Exotic sounding "hyperwar" might stand for some technical capitalist military configuration, but only obscures the actual military change and theory. While WW2, for example, is said by the u.s. capitalist military to mark the time where capitalism's "second generation war" evolved into the "third generation war" of Nazi blitzkriegs and motorized wars of fast non-linear maneuvering, this is only a narrow technocratic viewpoint. More importantly, to begin with, wars in the capitalist world have distinct and complex political identities and characteristics.

We can gain some perspective by reaching way back in time, to a nodal point of the wave of change that is coming over us right now. The 1935–45 Sino-Japanese war involving millions of combatants, eventually took place within and was to "Americans" mixed up with the global World War 2, where all the major imperialist powers divided into two camps, and fought it out at the admission price totaling at least 60 million lives lost to decide which capitalist nations would colonize everyone else, rule or ruin.

The importance to us now of that 1935–45 Sino-Japanese war, is that it was one of the first great neo-colonial wars, and helped usher in the present era of neo-colonial global economics and politics. When people use the term "neo-colonialism," they usually mean only some money-grubbing trick or crime, where a bribed politician helps some corporate giant of the imperialist metropolis ravage the labor and resources of some peripheral nation. It is so much more than that.

Neo-colonialism occupies a final period of capitalism of its own, where colonial empires and great powers fell, and the new freedom of every capitalist entity to forage and ravage disregarding nationalities and borders around the world became what we call globalization. What the all-enveloping

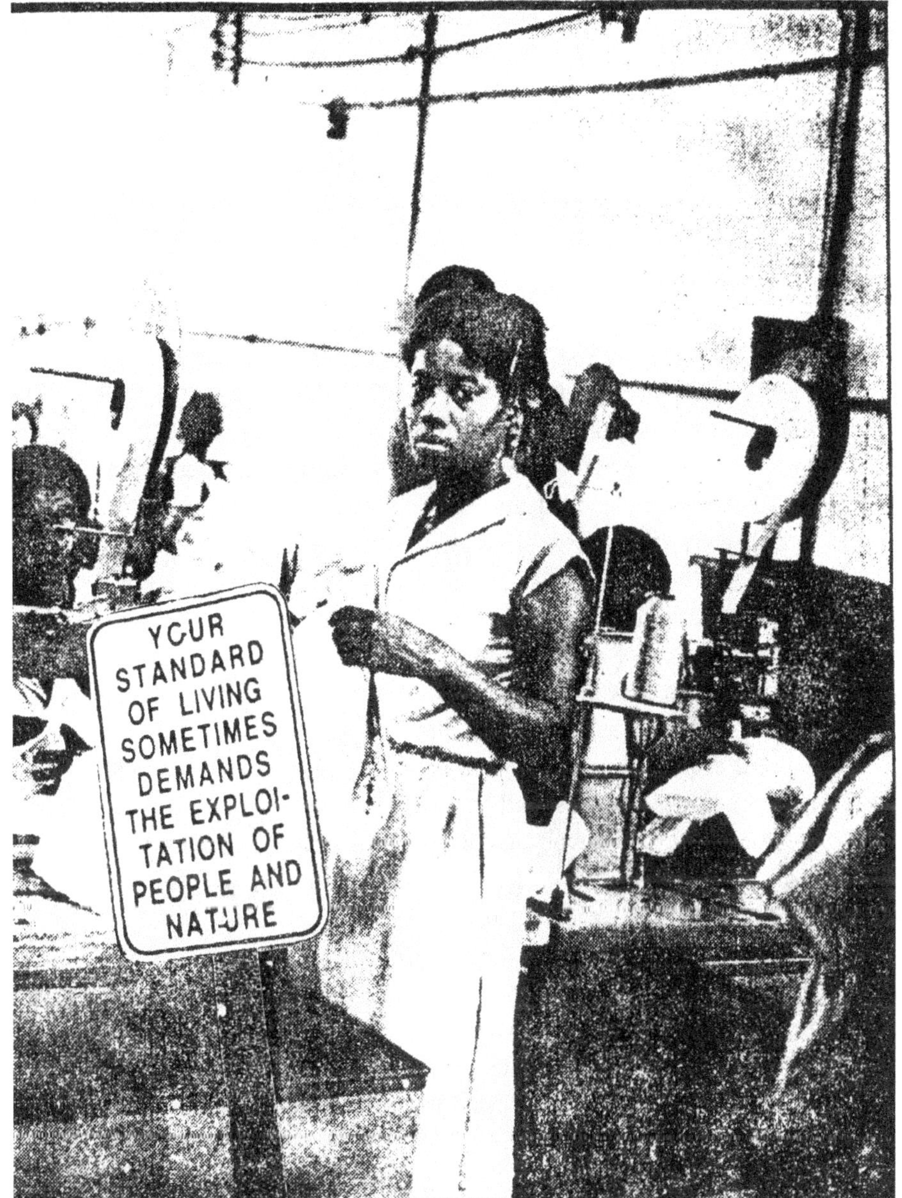
YOUR STANDARD OF LIVING SOMETIMES DEMANDS THE EXPLOITATION OF PEOPLE AND NATURE

effects of today's neo-colonial wars like in Ukraine and Ethiopia are to us, only serves to remind us of the shock wave caused by the Sino-Japanese war of the mid-20th century.

Revs saw the working out of the first successfully developed anti-capitalist revolutionary military practice and theory. The major 1935 Japanese imperialist invasion to make China a wholly owned and occupied Japanese colony, like Korea and Manchuria were then, was defeated in deliberately slowed protracted war by communist guerrilla forces famously represented by Mao Zedong's political-military teachings. Anti-capitalist revolutionaries who consciously took control of time itself. (While in a contrast we are familiar with, the global "lone superpower" u.s. empire in its Muslim "forever war," was enslaved and hag ridden by time). This is something capitalist conflict analysts rarely explain. Because in struggle politics is in command, not hardware nor techniques.

The ten-year Sino-Japanese war eventually became in part a theatre of global WW2, of course, but in itself it was one of the first great neo-colonial wars. Anti-capitalist revolutionaries understood this major strategic definition, while capitalist thinking worldwide did not, which meant it also didn't usefully understand the war there.

The obvious power of all-out Japanese capitalist invasion initially created a great wave of mass defeatism, even among young Chinese militants. China, after all, was famously derided as "the weak man of Asia." Whose last imperial dynasty had been unable to prevent Western imperialist nations and Japan from occupying China economically and militarily, with parts of the country even being garrisoned and directly governed by foreign capitalists, turning it into the world's largest neo-colony for the West and Japan. While Japan itself, with its battleships and modern mechanized army, had easily defeated the Russian Czarist empire in their decisive war of 1905. Emerging onto the level of a new great capitalist power as apparently overwhelmingly powerful as China was "weak."

The Communist revolutionaries reminded their people that far from being militarily invincible in China, as so many believed back then, the well-equipped Japanese fascist invaders were at an invisible but inescapable structural disadvantage to their ragged grassroots anti-capitalist opponents. As Mao pointed out, China was the greatest neo-colonial economic prize in the world. With no imperialist power being in the end willing to let one of their other imperialist rivals swallow it all up for themselves. No matter how much troops and equipment the Japanese fascists poured into China's vast land mass, other imperialist powers would bend the world around to prevent them from being victorious. This bleeding Achilles heel would in protracted struggle combine with revolutionizing the Chinese exploited and oppressed for a new kind of people's warfare, to prove fatal for the arrogant invaders, a skinny young wanted fugitive Mao accurately predicted.

(Not that Mao was omniscient about all warfare, any more than you or i could be. Used to muse about his dire postwar warning that guerrilla warfare in the Philippines could never succeed—since that capitalist neo-colony has generated armed insurgencies of almost every kind over and over for my entire lifetime and might keep trying til they get over. However unpublicized or unnoticed here in the metropolis, just like Mexico has been.)

More important than the system's professionals explaining the development of their capitalist warfare, is understanding the war we are in. Ukraine might be not simply a neo-colonial war—which it obviously is—but one of the major wars in the fall of the capitalist world-system. "Twilight" capitalism has forced the world on pain of destruction to learn new ways from it, to imitate it, for in the neo-colonial era it invariably teaches over and over all those it must keep intimate with both in production and systemic violence. New modes of production and conflict which leap over the limitations of old nation-state ways that only yesterday seemed invincible, embody how the retreat of the capitalist world-system puts everything we do and are through the grinding change mechanism of neo-colonialism.

Though this neo-colonial era pretends to do away with oppressor and thus also oppressed nations, it really only accelerates their interpenetration. Which has proven that capitalism cannot survive without colonialism. In a mere lifetime it has hollowed out the meaning of great national armies and industries on one hand, as on the other it drives hundreds of millions out of self-sufficient agriculture, handicraft production, and nature-based communities which functioned for centuries. Increasingly populating its computerized societies with reserve armies of labor that it piously and falsely identifies as some new phenomenon of "useless classes."

In a culture which makes a fetish of what is new, it is easy to forget that global capitalism's basic structures are to the contrary quite old. The two basic drives of the ceaseless accumulation of more and more capital but only to accumulate still more capital, together with the ceaseless dagger thrusts of "creative destruction," still compel capitalists and their class system to roll back and forth around the globe to now reconquer and recolonize and rape again the earth every day.

As though the displaced homeless proletariat and lumpen street masses of London and Paris in early 18th and 19th-century industrial capitalism were only the harbinger of capitalism's final shape. For our rulers, even in their new global clothing, have never changed their fundamental structural drives as a class being made up wholly of capital.

Always wiping each other out as entire corporations or entire industries or even whole economic regions in what the noted critical economist Joseph Schumpeter famously named "creative destruction," calling it the basic inner life cycle of capitalism. As Schumpeter said: *"The process of creative destruction is the essential fact about capitalism. It is what capitalism consists in and what every capitalist concern has got to live in."*[11]

While the class structure itself may wear more fashionable clothing, in important ways it is still much as it was centuries ago, except for the foretold wiping away of the peasantry into the global industrial marginalized working class. Only it now envelops the world and the main class sectors have become gigantic in their transcontinental size. The difference in scale changes things, as quantitative change past a critical point becomes qualitative change in its basic nature.

Remember, capitalist classes are never born united and rarely even pretend to be. Capitalist classes are always born with major political-economic internal battles and severe splits of their own. That's the normal, the ordinary routine of the world. Just as they were born as a top dog class outwardly fighting us—their workers—capitalists are born inwardly fighting each other tooth and nail to the death.

To give one example of changes wrought by the difference in scale: that there are, depending on who counts, loosely 700 to 900 u.s. billionaires today means that no one on Wall Street or Silicon Valley can be the "gatekeeper" anymore, selectively opening or closing the doors to the large sums of money needed to wage empire-wide political campaigns to wield the state. There's no J.P. Morgan or Rockefellers politically anymore. (Even without factoring in how the internet has transformed new political agitprop and reorganizing.) While journalists have spotlighted a tiny handful of white right-wing big donors such as Rebekah Mercer as the financial support for the Trump right's rise, this reaches the target but isn't in any way hitting the bullseye.

While most u.s. billionaires are fairly obscure white men keeping a low profile, there is a category we usually don't think of politically that for other reasons is more visible to us: owners of professional sports teams. So looking at the 31 privately-owned NFL teams, at least four billionaire pro football owners are known to be Trump backers. Just as the men of the Ricketts family, which controls TD Ameritrade and owns the Chicago Cubs baseball team, have been hardcore

Trump supporters (because their founding father is an open white power racist, the adult children have had to pledge that he is totally stonewalled from any management of their popular sports team).

Although Silicon Valley has used a progressive or even populist sheen as protective coloration, its actual ingrained hostility to people other than affluent white capitalist men has been proven over and over, and a number of its important figures are if anything to the right of Trump. Same same Wall Street and the financial elite. Now that flamboyantly goofy white power Trumpism has seeped into and become the hatchet's edge of the renewed GOP, regular big finance capitalist billionaires are publicly stepping forward as its special funders. Recently, to prepare for the 2022 GOP election campaigns, Ken Griffin of the large Citadel hedge fund donated $20 million to the party; as has Stephen Schwarzman, chairman of Blackstone, the world's largest hedge fund. While banking heir Timothy Mellon and insurance billionaire Patrick Ryan gave $10 million each. Nor are they the only ones.[12]

If "only" ten percent or so of u.s. billionaires would support an extended tear-the-house-down takeover by the white far right, that would still be a financial and political power base of close to a hundred u.s. billionaires.

While cosmopolitan multicultural transnational corporations encompass some of the ruling class, that is significantly less of a Jesus save factor for liberal democratic society than it is home-staged to appear. And as "America" in its overreaching culture promotes more and more frequent mass shootings to be its classier version of the suicide vest bombings of those backward much poorer societies, only lost-in-space liberals and progressives are left defending old government as legitimate.

Kersplebedeb: i am reading Immanuel Wallerstein, about the rise and fall of world systems. But i'm always unsure to what extent it makes sense to trace what is happening today backwards, as opposed to trying to understand it in the context of everything else happening today. Though the past does tend to feel more interesting.

J. Sakai: You remind me, oddly enough, of Malcolm X. Didn't he say, "Of all our studies, we have found history to be the most rewarding"? We always go back to our kitchen window to the past, to better understand. Because back in the past is where our present began, and that past is even now alive as a key part of our present. Everyone knows that.

But in the same way, our own present will be part of the future. We need at least a shaky smartphone photo of this future taking form now—a tentative look at its rough shape and a guide as to where revolutionaries will be at our work fighting in it. For now, constructing the outline of the future just using the clues already here in the present for us, if we can pick them out.

This is the anvil where revolutionary theory is being hammered out and tested still glowing hot. It's no secret that capitalism as a planetary system is in severe disjuncture. It's in everyone's conversations and supermarket lines. The other week, was browsing a women's vampires-and-werewolves paperback novel, when my eyes snagged on a line about a future Asian American Methodist bishop counseling a younger knight-wizard with a most non-biblical quotation: *"The old world is dying, and the new world struggles to be born: now is the time of monsters."* The young knight-wizard replies in her knowing ironic to the older woman: *"Although I doubt Antonio Gramsci had our kind of monsters in mind."*[13]

i had not expected a real-life 1920s communist anti-fascist prisoner's words foreseeing the raw *interregnum* awkwardly looming between old industrial capitalism and some new world-system, somehow dropped head-first into this fantasy novel landscape of post-apocalyptic supervillains and heroes (that was the first and last time he or his politics were mentioned there). But the mixing mix started to get more real when i heard that a writer in the pro-Trump conservative journal *American Greatness* had called on white men to now embrace their final metamorphosis for euro-capitalism: *"The decent know that they must become ruthless. They must become the stuff of nightmares. The good man must spare not a moment to train, in both body and mind, to become the monster that he may need to become in order to slay the monsters that prey upon the vulnerable."*[14]

This country gradually takes on terminal aspects of its modern doppelganger, the desperately dancing for time liberal democratic German Weimar republic which went all to H (spoiler alert: they really really didn't make it).

For us, "America's" own Civil War 2 can be a reality check, a flashing little warning light. With at last our very own amateur fight night: a comical "Munich Beer Hall Putsch," first-toe-in-the-water, January 6 test coup in the Capitol. Don't forget that between his 2016 triumph and his 2020 defeat, clown Trumpenfuhrer actually *gained* 1.5 million voters in Democratic sunny California. The whole capitalist system here is now misfiring against itself, parts breaking down one by one, no longer working as the dominant hegemony it once was. Even in the rich garden headquarters society of the imperialist metropolis.

Because the feeling is of crises no longer passing but only kept unresolved, multiplying, our left conversations have taken to peppering phrases with "twilight" and "late" when describing the capitalist system. There's a left cottage industry of intellectuals hesitantly but seriously writing about globalization deepening the crisis of world capitalism now. That so many differing radical theorists have turned their attention here is itself a signal flag. But revs need to search more directly into the gale.

Even if we weren't conscious of it, we have long been steeling ourselves for the demise of the capitalist world-system. Even if explicit revolutionary theory on the end of capitalism has been late coming and incomplete. Many of us from all sides have turned much more to culture than Depression economics in feeling our way into the future. But isn't that always true? As early as 1979, anti-capitalist literary critic H. Bruce Franklin pointed out that science fiction writing was then sampling the theme of the future as an apocalyptic dystopia, mistakenly confusing the end of capitalism for the end of farking everything. As he chipped in about the mindset of then-leading British SF author J.G. Ballard: *"it is easier to imagine the end of the world, than it is the end of capitalism."*[15]

This aspect of our imperialist culture sonar sensing the ping of possible real-life existential end game, but too frightened to face it except in a transposed fictional form, has grown to wide screen dimensions. As rampaging zombies destroying everything human became normal fixtures in movies and television. Or flip side, same coin, society threatened/saved by supervillains/heroes who without words or permissions appear to matter-of-factly replace ordinary humans as the only beings who can determine the fate of the world. As Kanye West stalks to grab the microphone from Taylor Swift, while millions of refugee people of color driven from their dying nation-states are trying to overrun and erase with the mass of their "useless" bodies the parking lot border lines of the wealthy Western metropolis. Or so oppressor culture in shock mixes the drinks.

Since every previously existing civilization and stage of history known to people has encountered its end times, the idea that present world capitalism might itself run out of time is not a recognition limited to some obscure fringe. Last year i was reading Irish novelist Sally Rooney's latest best-seller, when i ran aground right into a thick passage. Two main characters are young women who were BFFs at university and afterwards talk frequently though living in different places, by long emails ranging from relationship gossip across to serious intellectual discussions. So one emails the other:

> "Your paragraph about time reminded me of something I read online recently. Apparently in the Late Bronze Age, starting about 1,500 years before the Christian era, the Eastern Mediterranean region was characterized by a system of centralized palace governments, which redistributed money and goods through complex and specialized city economies. I read about this on Wikipedia. Trade routes were highly developed at this time and written languages emerged. Expensive luxury goods were produced and traded over huge distances—in the 1980s a single wrecked ship from the period was discovered off the coast of Turkey, carrying Egyptian jewelry, Greek pottery, blackwood from Sudan, Irish copper, pomegranates, ivory. Then, during a seventy-five year period from about 1225 to 1150 BCE, civilization collapsed. The great cities of the Eastern Mediterranean were destroyed or abandoned. Literacy all but died out, and entire writing systems were lost.
>
> "No one is sure why any of this happened, by the way. Wikipedia suggests a theory called 'general systems collapse', whereby 'centralization, specialization, complexity, and top-heavy political structure' made

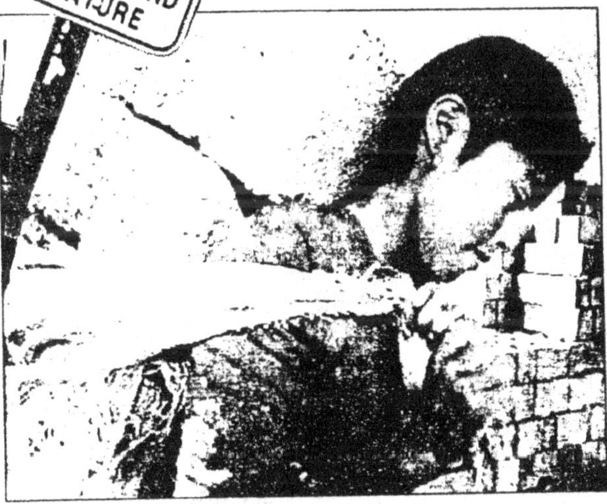

No childhood

A 9-year-old child (above) searches a garbage pile outside Quito, Ecuador, for objects he can sell, while a 13-year-old girl (left) carries cement blocks at a construction site. Thousands of children must work in Ecuador, where many people are poor and nearly half the population is under 18.

> Late Bronze Age civilization particularly vulnerable to breakdown. Another of the theories is headlined simply: 'Climate change'. I think this puts our present civilization in a kind of ominous light, don't you think? General systems collapse is not something I had ever really thought about as a possibility before. Of course I know in my brain that everything we tell ourselves about human civilization is a lie. But imagine having to find that out in real life."[16]

That jab in the head caught me by surprise. The novelist, who is a socialist, didn't have to make up any fictional "general systems collapse" theory—that developed theory on the possible lessons of the fall of Late Bronze Age Eastern Mediterranean societies exists, and the author of one scholarly book on the subject was even interviewed on a National Public Radio blog or something. Our obvious benefit from this idea is that it maybe opens our minds to considering how what we know are major problems in capitalism might even be much more.

What is pushing and hurrying us about is the ominous feeling that is lurking just behind everyone's shoulder now. A feeling that everything is somehow getting worse all the time, and that things only get worse and not better. In many countries, ours included, mass politics seem to be moving down the street towards a semi-fascist or maybe even fascist end, unless looming climate disaster gets us first. And no one seems to have any control over it. Like, no one is at the steering wheel.

It's as if the world is just sliding downhill towards X, and no matter how wide we try to open our eyes, somehow we can't encompass or take hold of it all. Even though the foreboding feels so damn big we should be able to see it with our naked eyes from across the solar system. Paradoxically it's too big for us to see.

Big economy/society "over-complexity" theory seems to make immediate sense—right now in this time of global supply-chain dysfunction, pandemic domino world upset, and unprecedented war and economic reprisals on everyone in general all at once—but is just one of a number of plausible theories explaining a near-term collapse of today's capitalist world-system. It is by far not even the most popular one right now, incidentally, though that doesn't make it wrong in my view. The most popular view would be global climate disaster, caused by relentless global warming from industrial capitalist civilization's greenhouse gas emissions. Even those who single out a different factor as the probable lever in tipping this world-system off into its final crash usually bring in climate disaster as a contributing factor for final system disaster. As the novel's character does herself in that weighty email.

What i've come to personally believe is that because today's capitalist crisis is so great, so enveloping of the entire system from horizon to horizon, it can be seen as many different crises or events, depending on what point or feature your eyes are focused on. All are probably real, but as parts of a greater final transformation of the capitalist world-system as a whole.

Not going to go over or even list all the different points of left opinion on the demise of capitalism. That's too big a detour to fit in here. But since my favorite interviewer/editor has raised the question of Immanuel Wallerstein's views on capitalist world-system change, let's use Wallerstein as an example to bounce off how my own views have developed here.

Left historical sociologist Immanuel Wallerstein was the most prominent developer of what is termed world-systems analysis or theory. Have read little of Wallerstein's thick basic writings myself, and certainly don't claim to understand them well enough to advocate yes or no. World-systems analysis tries to fuse all the varied Western academic fields such as sociology, history, anthropology, economics, astrology, and beyond into one theoryscope, trying to see how world-systems evolve and go through life cycles over long periods of time.[17] Wallerstein believed that every given world historic socio-economic system dies when its growth reaches its furthest limits (a variant away from Marx's historical materialist dictum that every type of historical society dies when it has exhausted its successive class role in further developing the means of production and distribution). And that capitalism's absolute need to always rake in capital accumulation and then double down again on even more capital accumulation has really reached its use-by date. As this world-system has effectively enveloped the entire globe and absorbed every human nation and people within it, and has thus hit its limits as a system.

Wallerstein saw this impact accentuating the current downward cycle of a regular "long wave" of the 50-year cycle of capitalist boom and ebb, first charted out by Soviet economist Nikolai Kondratiev. Which has now been finally disrupted in its cycle and is unable to rise up again, due to the lack of any new space or population to expand into and exploit more. This, he believed, has led to the system being "currently in the terminal stage of structural crisis," summing things up this way:

> "So, to resume, the modern world-system in which we are living cannot continue because it has moved too far from equilibrium, and no longer permits capitalists to accumulate capital endlessly ... We are consequently living in a structural crisis in which there is a struggle about the successor system. Although the outcome is unpredictable, we can feel sure that one side or the other will win out in the coming decades, and a new reasonably stable world-system (or set of world-systems) will be established."[18]

There is a generalized timeline being booted about by some serious analysts for the world-system's fall and full eclipse into *interregnum*. In this regard, Wallerstein and fellow historical sociologist Randall Collins won some academic cred in predicting endgame crisis, because in the 1970s they correctly predicted the fall in that next decade or so of the Soviet Union. And although they developed different views on causation—what will finally trigger the toppling of the capitalist world-system—their timeframes at least were essentially similar. Wallerstein earlier said that he saw the time of capitalist world-system collapse in "terminal transformation" occurring approximately in the 2030–2050 range.

Interestingly, both researchers believed that the accuracy of their individual predictions wasn't going to matter much. Because both agreed with the widely held view that our world is in a desperate race to stop and then to some degree reverse global warming—the great battle over greenhouse gas emissions and industrial age pollution. Which will calendar-wise soon unleash itself after other contradictions have shot their arrows, and which scientists predict will cause such physical and social destruction that the capitalist world will no longer be functional or usable as a system of social organization in any case. Whatever else most radical analysts who work to reveal capitalist endgame crisis may focus on, many of them also see capitalism's destructive blindness about the environment as bringing down on it the final, most physical, and least escapable fist in the 2050–2100 time period.

We note that Wallerstein believed that today's political struggle isn't actually over the fall of capitalism—which had already become a done deal in its early stages to him, fully in process—but over what future world hegemonic society will come to succeed it. Writing in the years before his death in 2019, he saw the future as "at best a 50–50 chance" between some new more democratic and more egalitarian world-system versus something highly repressive like fascism, which we all know hasn't waited for scholarly validation but is right now racing ahead of us everywhere.

My problem with all that has been that some left intellectuals might agree or not that this analysis or another one could be true, but what "proof" is that anyway? The 64 thousand dollar question applied here is how do we know that a systemic limit on accumulation is really going to finish off the capitalist system in the actually-existing now? Capitalism has gone through periods of no profits and big crisis before—like the 1929 Great Depression, for one—and didn't get that close to croaking. Got into emergency gear, went all crafty, reformed this while killing off that, sprinkled in some wars, and Bob's your uncle their capitalist profits were back. Capitalism has proven itself to be ruthlessly supple, capable of surprise strategies and reinventing itself to survive.

i mean, u.s. capitalism once way back in the mid-1860s went in just four quick years from having a vast chattel enslaved labor–based economy with millions of cheapest-possible unwaged workers, to suddenly no race-enslaved chattel property at all and the loss to many Southern capitalists of staggering amounts of one-half of their whole capital and business. But overall mister u.s. cap came out of it all bulging muscular. Ready to expand and conquer as never before.

So while i respect world-systems crisis analysis some, ditto other crisis analyses, wasn't sure that these theoretical predictions of capitalist system crash were firm and not jumping off-balance at clues. As our ever hopeful intellectual left has done so often before. (Though if there is a joker in the deck, it is certainly the already onrushing global climate change towards disaster.)

But my thoughts on this shifted gears when i started noticing something that i hadn't been hearing—that capitalism was actually destroying its own nation-states one after another. Some might be rebuilt later or not, but right now they are being gutted and taken down. This is an incalculable event. That's world changing beyond numbers.

To me the question of nations is so pivotal because that is how capitalism as a world-system has organized its societies structurally to do its work, apply its resources, and solve its problems. Nor is it true that in the absence of a functional capitalist nation, we can just jump in and go ahead with our neighbors to cheerfully and communally solve survival problems—check out Haiti for that one—because capitalism as its most bottom-line autonomic reflex will rather arrange to kill us all than let us remake our lives communally. Much of today's world can be explained by that one fact.

i initially ran into this understanding on the job—naturally, where else? When i first went to work at a suburban nursery around 9/11, the guys there provided a whole different learning experience about the world for me. That crew mostly came from a town in southern Mexico—largely happy young energetic teens and 20s, who came wading across the border or riding the coyote. We worked the garden season outdoors growing and loading into customers' SUVs, April until Christmas (selling fall plants then pumpkins and then Christmas trees and wreaths and all that is cash "plant" business, too). So they earned bucks to send home nine months a year, and then went home themselves to their vil to relax and play soccer every day and lord it up as young dudes who had some bit of u.s. cash for three nice months. Sweet to them.

It was all good until it wasn't. Year by year, their sky gradually darkened. At first the guys used to tell me that they weren't worried, since they had like a Mexican utopian vision. One married father told me that he knew his young son would be okay, since all Mexicans here had endless jobs for life—because for some strange reason in "America" none of the people liked to work (not saying it's true, just what they were saying). So Mexicans would gladly do all the real work. (Hey, in my favorite sushi joint all four sushi chefs are Latino, only the boss and cashier are Asian.) They and the u.s.a. were really only two parts of one body, like heart and lungs, they thought, and sometime soon white people would realize that and end all this border nonsense.

Not only did that dream not happen, instead nightmares, like ICE harassment and crazy white hate, shrunk the livable environment here all around them, while getting back for the start of the work season from Mexico got harder year by year. The coyotes got way more costly and unreliable (or were under more heat from the drug gangs to turn over their merchandise faster). Some guys quit, tired of the fear and figuring it wasn't worth the gamble.

The end finally came when the Mexican government, without an official word, abandoned the area their hometown was in, and big patches of dead state spread over it, like killed-off coral reef zones increasingly spill over the seabed. i mean, the state officials and police were still there and continued riding on top of all the ordinary people, but they were no longer in charge. A fickle criminal syndicate was now the actual state. A shadow state.

One of the guys described going home that last winter. All of a sudden on the main highway into town there was a roadblock complete with men with rifles. Their rules were simple: they did whatever they wanted and you obey or they kill you (the police carefully spent the day on the other side of town). If you were unlucky enough to be driving a newish car or truck, they motioned you out and took it, for keeps. You had to give them your dollars and if you had anything nice—like gifts you'd brought back from "America" for your family—they would take those, too. Laying on almost personal tariffs, just like a Trumpenfuhrer, only daylight naked not covered up in misdirection. No misunderstandings allowed there, that afternoon.

So the people in that town had their little society and bare little economy to live within, poorer but at home. But under this lumpen capitaloid shadow state there was erratic informal taxation and threat of killings always, and if you wanted to travel somewhere it was safest to take the bus and not have anything conspicuous with you. You shouldn't just drive around if you could avoid it, that wasn't safe. Those in our workplace up here who decided to stick with their "good" jobs, didn't go home anymore to Mexico each year—too much hassle and risk. They lived here so they had no safe home either place. Yes, Mexican criminal mafia is different but is also morally and functionally equivalent to ICE, the u.s government migration strong-arm agency. Crap = shite.

They weren't carefree smiling young guys on a work adventure anymore. Babylon is always so inviting, but in the end it's never fun.

Anyway, you know all this—it's nobody's secret that increasing sections of rural and even small city urban Mexico have been overrun or in part taken over by one drug cartel or criminal mafia or another in waves. It's bigger than the tired out "cops + robbers" or "poor colored people + plenty of crime" stereotypes that capitalist culture loves to stick in our sore heads. Just saying, because instead of mistakenly thinking i know something, picked up abstractly in the distance from the internet news, hearing it first hand from someone's life is when i started realizing the real, that capitalist nations that people lived in really were being essentially wiped out piece by piece, place by place. Holy crap, i thought. Makes sense on second thought: If the big guys like the u.s.a. and UK and Russia are all busy destroying even their own nations year by year—why not help everyone's neo-colonized peripheral nations come to go dead, too?

Of course, the u.s. empire—the home base of capitalist globalization—has pretty methodically been going around the world slowly, quietly rubbing troublesome nations jack out of existence for some time now. Oh, they still have well-paid representatives at the UN and on embassy row, and they are still on the little Rand McNally globe maps of the world. They may or may not be rebuilt some day, but right now they no longer exist as functioning societies with actual coherent governments. It isn't just Iraq and Afghanistan. They also did it to Libya and Somalia, and of course u.s.-cursed Haiti and Syria, the refugee exodus capital. Then there's sub-Saharan Africa's rapidly disintegrating nations no longer in the news, to say nothing of Ethiopia. Chinese diplomats brought this up once at an international gathering, the strange coincidence of countries being internally destroyed after the u.s. "helps" them.

We are starting to see that old Latin phrase *interregnum*—the dislocated space in time between two kings or reigns without a rule or particular order. And in coming years we will hear it more and more as the existing capitalist world-system is replaced with the uncertain wasteland of struggle over a future gone beyond it. What does that transitory landing zone start to look like? Going to take a specific road, and go into that Mexican crisis in a bit more detail. So grab a seat if you're into this informal map-reading.[19]

This summer, a killing in Mexico made headlines in their news and a little bit in ours. It sheds some negative light, some piercing darkness, which helps define the shape of this. Two old Jesuit Catholic priests, who had dedicated their last years to a small and poor mountain village in Chihuahua state along the border, were shot down along with a local tour guide who was desperately trying to find sanctuary in their church. The murderer is already named by police as a figure in organized crime; he had been set in a rage that day, townspeople said, first kidnapping and disappearing/kill-

Sinaloa gunmen pose for photo with kidnapped police officer

ing two brothers and burning down their house. Apparently because they and their amateur baseball team had just beat the rival team he had sponsored, as a local personage in a big drug cartel. A Chihuahua environmental activist told reporters simply: "He is a very bloodthirsty man."

Obviously, killing people isn't shocking anymore, but his targets were. Far off in the Vatican, Pope Francis himself said he was "dismayed" by the Jesuits' murders in their own church, and exclaimed on Twitter: "How many killings there are in Mexico!" For his part, the Mexican president said that the killings were "unacceptable." His prosecutors even offered a reward of $250,000 for information leading to an arrest. So an official big deal. Yawn. Likely the Mexican army troops promptly sent there will someday bring a killer suspect forward in chains for a photo op eventually. Or perhaps by the time you read this some cartel might have disappeared this inconvenient guy. Or likely the story will just vanish from the news for months or years, until a convenient happy ending can be found. It's all very likely.

What isn't likely is the stereotyped criminal gang killings fiction we always get force fed to us. This isn't merely some irrational drug crimie out on a personal "rampage." A senior area analyst for the respected International Crisis Group has pointed out: *"There's mounting evidence that a lot of criminal actors are testing the waters to see what they can get away with,"* particularly in terms of taking over state authority in their regions. A Rector of one Jesuit university observed after the killings that Mexico was *"a failed state."*

This isn't a one-mafia-baseball-team deal. Other big criminal capitalist bodies, such as the Mexican state and its own neo-colonial sponsor, the u.s. empire, are heavily invested right with them. By the Mexican police's own admission, the alleged Sinaloa gunman had murdered a white u.s. schoolteacher from North Carolina in 2018, but had been allowed to walk around free and completely got away with it. That was the kind of off-side violent transgression that used to be taboo. The next year he was said by local journalists to have killed a Chihuahua state human-rights activist. Again, he is walking around free and publically sponsoring a local sports team, so can be fairly said to have completely gotten away with it. (And, obviously, he has killed many others, if anyone cared.)

So this shooting down of two local priests is a bold step up, but not out of the question at all. Since then, more violent attacks on the Church have occurred. To help consolidate state power, the drug cartel needs to have demonstrated authority with the local population over what kinds of independent social activity are permissible under their rule and what not. Or, as the International Crisis Group analyst said of the Mexican cartels now: *"They feel they exercise de facto sovereignty."*

Particularly the Sinaloa Cartel, which was visibly among the largest and most powerful cartels, and got that way by almost two decades of covertly working with or for the u.s. government. This is said to have started around 2000 when Humberto Loya, a lawyer who was a top associate and payoff bagman to politicians for then-Sinaloa co-leaders Joaquin "El Chapo" Guzman and Ismael "El Mayo" Zambada, agreed to provide the u.s. government with critical information on other drug cartels in return for immunity for their own lumpen "creative destruction" biz. Lawyers in the u.s. for another Sinaloa figure on trial have also sworn to the court that "Indeed the United States government agents aided the leaders of the Sinaloa Cartel."

Of course, when "El Chapo" Guzman repeatedly embarrassed the Mexican government and became a legendary outlaw prison-escapee figure, they and u.s. national security had to hunt him down by making deals paying off rival gangsters. Cartels, just like legit world corporations, are constantly changing and in transformation, swelling, merging, shrinking, and splintering, concentrating into niches, switching names and business focus. Only, in the lumpen class zone everything happens much faster and with more relentless turnover.

Always the Mexican government tries to maneuver situations where the most publicity-troublesome criminal actors are chased to big fanfare, while other rival criminal groups are left alone to thrive and pay off in the extra space. During the presidencies of Felip Calderon and his successor, the Mexican murder rate actually tripled—while officially 96% of reported crimes got unsolved by the police.

Last winter and spring, "American" shoppers noticed shortages of avocados and then also limes and mangoes—with big price increases—as news came that Mexican drug cartels were trying to move in and take over commercial agriculture exports to the u.s. Governments on both sides of the border and even armed local militias of avocado growers mobilized to take back the towns and highways, which the very violent Jalisco New Generation Cartel defended not only with gunmen but with highway roadblocks and Taliban-style improvised explosive devices on roadsides. Jalisco cartel men even cut off a Mexican army base, which for a while could only be resupplied by air as though it were in remote Afghanistan. Finally, after a long eight-month siege, Mexican army units were able to enter Naranjo de Chila, the Jalisco cartel's stronghold there. The Jalisco "soldiers" simply abandoned their center in Michoacán state and disappeared away for a while.

They usually act to repress a cartel in an area only when there is very bad publicity and they need to lift up their battered image. So it was noticed locally that the Mexican government with its army and police were driving away the Michoacán state's then-dominant Jalisco New Generation cartel, but not other crime factions. In effect, the Mexican army infantry were fighting side by side with the un-uniformed "soldiers" of the ambitious Viagras gang of Jalisco's rival, the United Cartels (who did not give the Mexican and u.s. governments the same public relations headache). By that point, both had been shooting at and besieging the Jalisco forces and their supporters in the town of Naranjo de Chila for months.

For over a decade, these lumpen economic organizations have episodically taxed the avocado crop in different ways, there being billions of dollars at stake. Now they are pushing once again to take it over, setting a high payoff "tax" of 10% at the packaging plants, in some places even taking over farms altogether. Same with limes now, as well as sometimes mangoes and livestock and timber. David Karp, a former *Los Angeles Times* journalist on farm markets and researcher on botany at the University of California at Davis, noticing the trends, wrote eight years ago: *"Criminal cartels now control, to a shocking extent, the growing and packing of much of the Mexican produce on which United States consumers depend."*

The cartels are not young, and in their own way are beginning to take on the bureaucratic sinews that mature businesses need. They always had not simply "soldiers" but also ship's captains and mechanics and logistical planning managers. Now government rural health workers are frightened and some are leaving. Doctors and nurses are worried about being drafted into handling the consequences of prolonged battles and possibly being executed if their cartel patients die on them. Already the cartels put up their own sophisticated telecommunications systems with security in rural areas. They get the telecommunications technicians and engineers by simply drafting them; they usually disappear on their way to work, never to be seen again. There was one telling incident when some gunmen stopped a bus and took two telephone company employees away, but they were the wrong guys: phone company, yes, but not technicians—they did consumer phone bill collecting. Their rejected dead bodies were found soon after. This is like watching a raw capitaloid state of its own kind getting formed from scratch before our eyes.

A program director of a Mexican security research agency commented that with *"mafias"* organized crime is not simply big but has reached into *"a gray zone where you tie legal with illegal, the crime with business and the crime with politics."* Since the cartels *"understand that that they have more power than anyone else, the government or the businesses they extort."* In the wake of the killings of the two and still another priest, a Catholic bishop has called for a new "social pact," which in return for less violence would give the cartels a legitimized voice in deciding Mexico's major political and social questions.

Former Mexican President Calderon, in a speech at the United Nations, said that his earlier attempt to wage a heavily militarized "Mano Dura" or "tough hand" actual war on Mexican drug traffickers—which brought in the regular Mexican army for the first time—as the Bush administration had planned for him, failed because the massive drug economy in the u.s. creates such unstoppable social and political aftereffects swirling through the Global South: *"This allows drug traffickers to create powerful networks and gives them an almost unlimited ability to corrupt; they are capable of buying governments and entire police forces, leaving societies and governments defenseless, particularly in the poorest countries."*

This was clever capitalist propaganda. President Calderon himself is said to have been given $3 million in cash in suitcases via his national security chief, in return for protecting the Sinaloa cartel—this according to the sensational testimony of former Sinaloa lieutenant Jesus "El Rey" Zambada, a u.s. government witness at the 2018 Brooklyn trial of "El Chapo" Guzman. These payoffs included at least one delivery that "El Rey" Zambada himself took part in. The u.s. Department of Justice is also conceding that Calderon's political opponent and successor as Mexican president was even more corrupt and involved with the cartels than he was. Or as one *Wall Street Journal* headline summed it up: "Witness testifies that El Chapo paid a $100 million bribe to ex-Mexican president Peña Nieto." So capitalist pro-u.s. state officials and cartel leaders are much more than "frenemies," because they really do need and benefit from each other even as they still must also play out eroding deadly antagonistic roles in the capitalist system—as though their lives depended on it.

The mega-violent reality fits right into some "The Wire"-type blood drama or "FBI"-type television hoopla. Like the endlessly rebroadcast "tragic" picture here of carelessly dangerous but short-lived violent young men shaped by their intense poverty, caught up in the killing machine of their people's street criminality. This has the seeming of some raw truth, like a Shakespearian tragedy—but really is only a surface frag of truth. It is high-class nonfiction mixed with high-class fiction, an art form made by wealthy advanced capitalism's propaganda specialists with real blood and actual poor bodies offered up for verisimilitude.

What was really moving the earth there is even colder, much more implacable. A reality that capitalism can't let us understand now. Cause at its heart it's not primarily about bloody melodrama, but about capitalism's irreplaceable old nations in free fall, damaged with no repair coming, and the u.s. empire and in this example its Mexican neo-colonial subordinates unable to halt or even slow the descent, just throwing in more and more improvised violent stop-gaps as best they can on the fly.

In case nobody noticed, the u.s. imperial Dept. of Justice has a long-term policy of regularly throwing its top Mexican satraps under the bus, always placing the blame for the massive drug trade and spreading criminal lumpen zone on them. Usually not until they leave office, of course. It is a cover story both for the unwillingness of the u.s. ruling class to stop its always-mounting drug addiction business, and for their implicit claim that u.s. imperial gunmen and detectives and military have to always be policing the neo-colonial world of people of color in the periphery to protect innocent white communities. As though there were innocent white communities, which is the largest criminal fiction of all.

As over the decades the Mexican capitalist ruling class and their state apparatus have gradually shrunk away from society's daily functioning—and moved more profitably outward—the empty space has been taken over by lumpen/proletarian economic organizations with the u.s. empire's tacit agreement. Occupying an important social and economic space, with an improvised and grotesque morphing, part-inside and part-outside of capitalism, Mexican crime cartels carry out many billions of dollars in world trade selling not only drugs of many kinds to illicit North American users, not only agricultural products to u.s. supermarkets, but also industrial goods and raw materials to manufacturers of other countries, such as millions of dollars of enriched iron ore directly from their ports to China.

Most important of all, they step in to supplement the old weakening neo-colonial state with a self-funding and autonomous robotic repressive force with capacities beyond what the FBI, Pentagon, the CIA, or the ruling class actors in Mexico City can do in public. Bullet in the head with that avocado, anyone?

In classic class formations, capitalists are largely free riders on their nation-states. Usually very willing, though, to heavily tax the middle and lower classes to support the state structures such as highways and water systems, the police and military, that allow society to function adequately for their capitalism. But back in the day, some capitalists always understood that they could well afford to contribute in special ways, to strengthen what was really their own society's continued future. Famous capitalists like the steel magnate Andrew Carnegie, the wealthiest man in "America," helped lead the building of the "American" nation's public library system. While in another striking case, Julius Rosenwald of Sears Roebuck paid for the designing and building of over 5,000 basic schools to house New Afrikan formal education over fifteen Southern states, whose "seg" governments would only fund white settler children's school buildings.

There are no longer any Carnegies or Rosenwalds in that old noble patriarch b.s. way, since even billionaires like Gates and Buffet cannot rescue long-neglected and now run-down whole capitalist nations, where everything is worn out and dinged and all inadequate anyway. Even more so in a new onrushing age where according to the International Organization for Migration, by 2050 as many as 200 million refugees will be battering down doors seeking shelter just from rising water levels alone (not counting droughts and floods, desertification, firestorms, failing economies, ethnic and religious genocides, invasions and civil wars). And anyway, big capitalism and the big bourgeoisie can't care that way anymore about whatever place they once came from that's rotting away no matter what—no one is Saran-wrapping their old family condo—since they increasingly are simultaneously both more global and more individualistic in their existence.

We have to get something really reverse to the way most of us are led to understand. Big capitalism gets it that Mexico may be disintegrating just as the u.s.a. is, but from their point of view it is still golden just the way it is. Ruchir Sharma, who manages $45 billion in investments in the Global South as Chairman of International Business for Rockefeller Capital Management, put it this way:

> "In the class of [medium] countries with an average per capita income around $10,000 and a population over 100 million, Russia is a laggard ... The most dynamic is Mexico, which has also produced ten cities of more than a million people since 1985 ... The flowering of second-tier cities in Mexico is intimately connected to the manufacturing centers producing cars and other exports bound for the United States. Among the fastest growing Mexican cities with populations of more than a million, three are in states on the U.S. border: Tijuana, Juarez, and Mexicali. ... In central Mexico, Queretaro is a jack-of-all-trades, making everything from wine to appliances to trucks, as well as offering services from call centers to logistics ... Aguascalientes is home to Toyota's most modern manufacturing plant outside Japan."

Sharma warned investors, however, that the picture on the other side of the peso note is not so crisp. Mexico may have the fifteenth-largest economy in the world, but the Mexican state is bluntly not functional:

> "One clear sign that a state is falling short is when it cannot even collect taxes, a failure that tends to expose both a general incompetence on the part of administrators and a popular disdain for the state. Mexico, for example, collects taxes equal to about 14 percent of GDP. That is quite low for a middle class country, and the lack of revenue is making it hard for the government to maintain law and order or suppress the corrupting influence of the drug cartels. Mexico spends just 0.6 percent of GDP on the military, the second lowest among large emerging countries ..."[20]

At this point, some might ask, why doesn't Mexico take substantial amounts of money from that flourishing big city industrial export economy and use it to fix the rest of Mexico and drive out the cartels? The actual bourgeois world isn't so straight-forward. And for sure the Mexican capitalist ruling class that controls the state isn't going to heavily tax its own self. They would all rather let the present situation just roll on. Which is why it has. And when and if that part of Mexico gets used up, they expect to just move on to the next disposable plastic part of the neo-colonial periphery.

No, in a zombie-world way, the drug cartels and criminal mafias *are* capitalist Mexico's real "military," and its real "police" as well.

As a neo-colony of the u.s. empire, Mexico's 130 million people are a giant reserve army of inexpensive labor to backstop and enrich the u.s. imperial economy. Just a truck ride over the border. And their own small but quite affluent Mexican local ruling class sees no need to be taxed to support a military, since it has no traditional enemies as a country except "America" itself. And the Mexican ruling

class openly feels that it is the rightful task of the rulers in Washington to defend the neo-colony. So it has just enough official army and navy to protect the capital city and hold the industrial centers and gated luxury reserves for its main capitalist families. All the rest can just go to H and blow away. Mexico being a country is not the same thing as it existing as a functioning nation.

It's interesting here in a grim sense to turn to another page, that the Pentagon has warned Congress and the "American" public that there is a danger of them falling behind Russia and China in the next generation of advanced military weaponry. Which is said to be autonomous gun- and bomb-carrying robots flying over or perhaps driving across the battlefield, killing left and right by self-directed AI computer decision-making. That's really scary.

What no one is saying, though, is that they have something like that already, only in less precise but also less expensive flesh form. "America's" forbidden drug cartels and the taboo larger men's criminal street organization culture in Latin America are exactly that. Autonomous and self-aware killing formations of disposable "robots" that capitalists aren't publicly associated with or responsible for, that spread out to gradually cover every town and small city in the countryside. Automatically homing in on and subjecting to lethal investigation any persons trying to cause trouble to the existing social order other than them, whether it be by working against oppression or stopping the destruction of the environment, or anyone for human rights or organizing peasants or workers. Then killing or terrorizing the automatically selected targets into silence.

Best of all from the capitalist viewpoint, these kind of autonomous political killing formations of male "robots" can even be made self-financing by their drug selling, lemonade stands, and community car washes. And it's all "off the books." Can't get better than that.

Although capitalist media and culture never admits it, that is what they already know how to do. Which is why the security apparatus of the u.s. government has always not only used such formations, but has worked in the oppressed zone to create them where they didn't exist. Anywhere the oppressed poor have risen to fight for human rights in the u.s. neo-colonial region of influence in Central America, right-wing mercenary paramilitaries and drug gangs secretly allied to the capitalists and the army have formed to carry out mass killings, assassinations, and cleansing of territory.

In Colombia, a current government-appointed truth commission is trying to finally end the 58-year internal "culture of security," which was taught to Colombian government forces by the CIA, DEA, and u.s. military, and that resulted in hundreds of thousands of deaths in a permanent "cycle of violence." The intelligence chief of the Colombian Army Fourth Brigade provided individual targets for a wave of assassinations of alleged leftists carried out by the Medellin drug cartel. While Western oil companies secretly funded right-wing paramilitary units for "protection," doubtless with the informed but secret approval of key u.s. officials. *"The consequences of this concerted and largely U.S.-driven approach,"* the commission concluded, was a *"hardening of the conflict in which the civilian population has been the main victim."*[21]

This is the same Colombian "tough hands" model that was instituted during the Mexican Calderon presidency by the u.s. Drug Enforcement Agency. Excited at reports of the high tolls of political rebels killed, not just by the army but by paramilitaries and the drug cartels as well, Robert Bonner (Bush's chief of the Drug Enforcement Agency as well as simultaneously head of Customs and Border Protection) urged the u.s.-designed "Colombia model" on President Calderon, and publicly defended his Mexican protégé's actions then and thereafter.

The truth commission has since uncovered that many of those assassinated in Colombia were not doing anything illegal, of course. Which is why they had to be killed "off the books," as it were. More and more of big capitalism's ruling the world as the crisis deepens seems to be "off the books."

As Mexico's export industries are growing and the affluent middle and upper classes associated with that sector grow wealthier, paradoxically the number of Mexicans in extreme poverty only increases. Populist president Andres Manuel Lopez Obrador has deliberately targeted both ends of the spectrum. Programs used to help poor women and children are now being abolished in favor of subsidy programs giving cash to middle- and even upper-class families. While a long-established program that extended the standard half-day in Mexican schools to include a hot lunch and extra classes has been abolished. Formerly it improved children's learning while providing all-day childcare so that women could find employment. A newspaper article notes: "Today 44 percent of Mexicans—nearly 56 million people—are destitute, according to the most recent government data available."[22]

Most ominously, some thousands of communities have in this year's heat wave run out of water. Streams and rivers have dried up in the extreme drought and heat, and groundwaters, in aquifers below the surface, are being exhausted one by one. By Mexican law, factories have priority for water over human consumption. Right now, scarce water is being trucked in to dry neighborhoods and villages every day. This situation has no solution, and is only growing worse.

Kersplebedeb: Which brings us back to the climate catastrophe, and what it might mean for capitalism ...

J. Sakai: Easily the most popular system collapse theory right now, is the spreading climate disaster. This was certainly pushed by James Hansen's increasingly dire messages that the climate crisis is more severe and coming much sooner than even scientists had expected. Before he retired as director of NASA's Goddard Institute for Space Studies, Hansen pioneered the first long-range computer climate modeling, and was one of the world's leading climatologists. He has been called the "father of global warming."

He long years ago warned that increasing dangerous atmospheric CO2 levels had "become an emergency." Almost 14 years ago Hansen said of the eliminating of all coal consumption worldwide by 2029 as the most realistically achievable first real step in the climate recovery process: "This is our one chance." Since then, the bottom line is that nothing has been done except talk and public relations and increased burning of coal. Elizabeth Kolbert, environmentalist and author of *The Sixth Extinction*, says that in ignoring Hansen's prior warning in time, "the planet will be committed to change on a scale society won't be able to cope with." Or as Hansen said: "if you melt all the ice, sea levels will go up two hundred and fifty feet. So you can't do that without producing a different planet."[23]

Most radicals who deal with collapse of the capitalist system, don't predict with the assurance of a Wallerstein or a Collins that it will happen in the range of this date or another. Personally, i have no educated idea whether Wallerstein or Collins are right about their timing of system change. i only am certain that devastating changes beyond what we've ever seen will be happening—and very soon in historical terms.

Kersplebedeb: Are there other writers on this capitalist world-system crisis that you find useful now?

J. Sakai: There are many finally who are making contributions, but i find left political economist Minqi Li helpful because he gives us another angle of vision, since he doesn't share the eurocentric Wall Street, Washington, and London vantage point on the world that is common even in the left, but instead analyzes today's world-system crisis grounded in his China. While he goes vividly into the meaning of the climate disasters predicted by James Hanson, Li also shows how economic class issues are already politicizing and raising up into action masses of Chinese people.

He notes: "In fact, the Chinese economy is already struggling with unsustainable business and local government debt." Since to him the huge bankrupt banks' credit bubble, which is robbing millions and paralyzing the economy, is an assumed fact of Chinese life, just like the Party's ruling dictatorship is. Whether Chinese capitalism's giant bad debt bubble is *politically* sustainable—is another major question, in fact. In China there are already every day illegal protests of the thousands among millions of ordinary people from all walks of life, robbed of their pensions and life's savings and even homes by the corrupt banking bad debt crisis, which is destabilizing their whole economy.

Minqi Li, who learned from the democracy movement and spent 1990–92 in prison there, also points to the political shock absorber of the mass mirage of a future prosperous capitalist middle-class life, a capitalist narcotic which took over a generation of parents and youth—but that to many has now left only the bitterest aftertaste.

"The dramatic increase in college graduates has led to sharp devaluation of their bargaining power in the job market," Li writes. "In 2010, about a quarter of Chinese college students who graduated that year were unemployed. Many college graduates live in slum-like conditions on the outskirts of China's major cities and are known as 'ant tribes' ... Those college graduates who are 'employed' often have to accept a wage that is no higher than that of an unskilled migrant worker. According to a survey by Beijing University, the national average monthly starting pay for college graduates in 2014 was 2,443 Yuan (about 400 u.s. dollars). By comparison, in 2013, the national average monthly pay of migrant workers was 2,609 (about 430 u.s. dollars) ... Since the 1990s, many of China's college graduates have seen their middle class dreams smashed and have undergone a process of proletarianization. To these young people, the promise of a 'free' and prosperous capitalism is no more than empty words." Li ties this to the regrowth of revolutionary politics. "In this context, many intellectuals and college students have been attracted to leftist ideas and become leftist activists."[24]

China probably leads the world in the number of labor strikes and protest demonstrations. Li points out that:

> "The so-called 'mass incidents' (a term used by the Chinese government to refer to a wide range of social protests including strikes, sit-ins, marches, rallies, and riots) increased from about 8,700 in 1993, 60,000 in 2003, to 120,000 in 2008. It is estimated that in recent years, the annual occurrence of massive incidents has stayed above 100,000. According to the data collected by the Chinese Ministry of Public Security, the cases of various forms of the 'social order' violation increased from 3.2 million in 1995, 11.7 million in 2009, to 13.9 million in 2012. In some large-scale mass incidents, tens of thousands of people participated in riots and occupied local governments for days. Assuming that a mass incident on average involves about 100 people, there would be about 10 million Chinese people who are involved in various social protests each year."[25]

Li feels that the capitalist world-system might be even more vulnerable to collapse right now than many believe, because China as the gigantic center of world industrial production, as well as having become a major financial and consumer economy, is more fragile and teetering-on-the-edge than Westerners understand. And that Chinese events could well trigger and then force a systemic collapse of actually-existing capitalism around the globe. Which reminds us that the struggle is always wider than we think.

As a homemade theoryscope on how capitalist world-system breakdown is taking place right now, this has been very incomplete. A quick pencil sketch maybe of parts of its wildly transitioning shape. i had to leave out many, many aspects entirely, just to squeeze this study down to interview size. Somehow rambled into the Mexico thing, which i didn't plan on talking about at all. Was going to explore what has changed so drastically for today's u.s. ruling class—and does the left understand the capitalist ruling class at all? But that got sidetracked totally. So please understand all the limitations here. Think of this as just a kit to jump start the battered family van with.

& Before we go, let's pause around the further question of the *interregnum* a minute. Perhaps one reason the left has been so reluctant to handle the hot event horizon where world-system capitalism is ending, is that we are so uncertain about how to handle the reality of the *interregnum*. Where at first anyway the odds aren't with us in Las Vegas. *"We're not ready yet!,"* lefty thinks to themself. **So i want to talk about it to get used to the idea.**

Once, long ago, there was no *interregnum* in radical thinking—why Gramsci's pocket parable about the delay in a liberated world and the jack-in-the-box appearance instead of fascism had such an impact on us. Capitalism and anti-capitalism were supposed to be intrinsically counter-balanced in a kind of zero-sum game: as capitalism declined, the radical workers' left that was massively opposing them would grow in parallel measure, rising to take the inevitable hand-over as the natural inheritors of society. All neat and happy. Or so early hopeful radical thinkers from Europe's

19th century, who had never seen socialism or for that matter fascism either, believed.

Our actual dirty world picture has little to do with those old silent movies, and is way more frighteningly complicated and challenging, of course. Capitalism as a world-system has been faltering for some time, but there is no guarantee that an anti-capitalist left of any strength will be there immediately to take over from it. It is possible that capitalism will fall into a chaotic confused landscape. That is what I have been talking about here.

Kersplebedeb: This reminds me of passages in the book *Night-Vision*, by Butch Lee and Red Rover, especially the chapter "The Changer and the Changed." In this new twilight reality, what should we be prepared to do? How should we prepare to intervene?

J. Sakai: *Night-Vision* is a prescient revolutionary writing of the late 20th century, and still perhaps the most unsettling one. In "The Changer & the Changed," Butch Lee wrote with a surgical scalpel, cutting away reformism's scar tissue without painkillers, without compromise:

> "But at its essence, the growing chaos of the neo-colonial world order is that many different peoples—armed with conflicting capitalist agendas—have been loosed to fight it out. As transnational capitalism hides behind and backs first one side and then the other—or both—to indirectly use the chaos they see no class interest in containing.
>
> "This chaos is itself a deepening contradiction of the system, one that no one can be certain of riding, not even the ruling class. And on this charged terrain, dis-unity and not unity is the changed strategic need of the oppressed. This is hard to grab, since it goes against truisms inherited from colonial times. And we think that dis-unity is what's spontaneously going on all around us anyway, when it's really an unconscious unity around wrong principles. Old slogans used the picture of unity to make people feel strong: "Sisterhood is Powerful," "Black Unity," "The People United Will Never Be Defeated." But these are dead phrases now, not truths but decaying shells."

And notice that she prefaced the chapter with an acid quotation from the notorious 19th-century revolutionary, the Moor: "The weapon of criticism cannot replace the criticism of weapons."

Often we are all asked, "What should we do?" In the long history of the struggle it is not unusual to be thrown back, to have to restart anew it feels like. Even in the most difficult of times, we have to remember what is basic for us because it is the most practical. To tell the truth. To do the serious and difficult work of learning which truth is key, and then telling it to people who are searching for justice. Which is all there is to do, but is a lot harder than people think. If you assume that things like early 1960s nonviolent civil rights militancy were politically simple, you would be wrong. Often we were thrown into despair because despite the wonderful energy, being on the real offensive for the first time in our young lives, and lots of jail time, we couldn't budge the racist system at all. And all our charismatic often brilliant leaders lied to us, all the time. Dr. King used to blow smoke rings at us regularly, until his final political awakening that he needed to personally redirect the struggle here, from opposing "discrimination" to overthrowing the system of capitalism, which he explicitly named as the problem (and, yes, his personal breakthrough surprised all of us in the struggle, too). That's when they quickly pushed their red button and had him assassinated.

That was painful to learn, but it was the rock bottom truth. Not that the leaders were all evil, but most of the time they didn't know how to proceed without lying. In a capitalist culture, whether on Wall Street or Main Street, "leading" or being the boss is lying as you cover up x and polish up z. The only leader we found to be telling us the truth as fully as he understood it, whether we liked it or not (and largely we didn't like it), was Malcolm. And he was everyone's great teacher. Even today, looking out over a world of so many political movements and struggles, i am not seeing more like him. He was usually rebuked by liberal media and intellectuals for not having a detailed program for ending racism in "America" (an idea that today makes me laugh). He would usually say that his belief was that if you could tell people the truth then they would work out what to do. That isn't the end of our journey, but it certainly has to be the start.

Most things we can't grasp about the *interregnum* yet, but there are significant parts we can start with. Particularly about the two contending political forces everyone expects to see—far-right formations including fascism against the new world working class. Two closely related class forces which the present left more or less knows lots of historical-scholarly things about, but in a practical everyday way knows surprisingly little about.

In the *interregnum*, much of what people say right now won't matter. Because it will be a new environment with unfamiliar terrain, one that will be constantly impressing us with its own demands. Requiring new people self-selected for that go-round.

Each new historical period ruthlessly requires a different generation of rebels, with different abilities and their own specific character suited for their times. After all, the left generation that fought for the "industrial democracy" of politicized mass unionism worldwide in the 1930s, before plunging into the biggest world war ever, was really not the same as the 1960s youth radicals who smoked dope like "Detroit Red" and jammed a monkey wrench into the whole giant machinery of the Pentagon's Vietnam War.

Right now we can see the beginning signs of this system's transition, its breakdown structurally. Most visibly in the old "law and order" which cannot be maintained in the ruleless *interregnum* space between capitalism and its successors. The political left and the political right will not be the only players. Radical upsurges are always signaled and then also accompanied by tidal waves of mass crime and outlaw cultural movements, since the oppressed and everyone else held down sense that the old restraints have torn loose. We aren't the only players on the block, not by far, and in times of change never will be.

The Bolshevik leader Lenin learned that the hard way, luckily to little damage except to his pride and his shoe leather. Working late one night as they often did trying to set up a new regime, Lenin with his bodyguard and a few other comrades drove across the Russian capital in an expropriated nice auto. He had rejected his bodyguard's suggestion that they just crash in communist apartments near their offices, since he wanted to get home. Driving down a deserted street in the dark without traffic, they came to a revolutionary checkpoint. Young "red" fighters manning the barricade waved down the auto, their rifles aimed at the car and its passengers. The communists were peeved that the young "red" guards didn't recognize Lenin's face and were unimpressed with them, and had to haul out their wallets and ID. At which point it turned out that the fighters were not really bolshies after all, but armed bandits—

Soon Lenin and his comrades were walking wearily towards the nearest communist group apartment, as their plush car with the imitation "red" soldiers and their money and their papers and the bodyguard's pistol all roared off into the distance. Understandably angry, Lenin started telling off his bodyguard. Demanding to know why he hadn't used his gun to defend them instead of insisting that they surrender. The bodyguard was pretty angry himself, and promptly tore comrade Lenin a new one. Pointing out that his starting a one-pistol gun battle against a gang armed with rifles would have only gotten them killed. And it was his job to keep Lenin alive, not be a western gunman. Further, that it would have made a lot more sense if Lenin hadn't insisted on the lot of them going all the way across town in deserted streets instead of just bunking at a place comrades had near their offices. Guess he was right sheepish on top of embarrassed, but Lenin had to apologize. You live and you learn.[26]

Late 20th-century globalization reinvented popular piracy of oil tankers and cargo freighters (reaching like 1,000 attacks a year, i believe), but that is overshadowed by what's going on in the streets now. Last winter, business news reported that the commercial losses from urban looters attacking freight trains here were "out of control." As proof, one journalist brought back photos from a Union Pacific rail yard of the mountains of debris left over after the train burglars had gone through everything looking for electronics, brand name clothes, and other choice goods : "... there's looted packages as far as the eye can see. Amazon packages, UPS boxes, unused Covid tests, fishing lures, epi pens. Cargo containers left busted open on trains ..."[27] The National

Retailers Federation estimated these losses from "'organized crime' groups" as high as $1 billion a year, and called for much greater rail policing.

Confess, i got nostalgic when i read that. When you read "organized crime" here you are meant to think the Italian mafia or something, but really in these cases it's more likely bands of New Afrikan and Latino kids usually. Back in the day when we were raising kids on not much money, had an older Asian acquaintance who knew and every month or so dropped by with a few bags of produce he had gotten at work. You know, to stretch our food budget. One day he called, said he had arranged to get us a whole big bunch of vegetables and fruit. Only i'd have to come by his job after ten that night with a car, so he could load my trunk with bags of grapefruit and oranges, tomatoes and lettuce, til it looked like a grocery store (which it did).

My friend did the graveyard shift at one of the Union Pacific freight yards, where stuff from California came in (i had worked at a yard, too, but different railroad down on the South Side). i showed up of course, and he showed me around. i asked him if giving us all this stuff was a risk, and he said nobody would even notice or care. Showing me some rail cars that were already half empty.

He explained that you can't speed with a long, zillion-ton train of loaded heavy rail cars without a lot of braking once you get into the city. The risk is too great. So your freight train is going only maybe 5 miles an hour as it very slowly winds through poor neighborhoods getting ready to come to a safe stop in the yards. Bands of teens run alongside the train, trying to break into the cars and climbing in, quickly searching for really good stuff like televisions and jeans. If a rail car had new washing machines they'd gladly try a few of that, too. Good cash stuff on the streets. Which they could ease off to the track side, then if necessary come back with a borrowed truck and vanish with into the night. They only had brief windows of time to get into each rail car and do whatever and jump out. If they ran across oranges or veggies they might take some to sell and a bag or two for mom and the neighbors, but it's not really that valuable to them or to the railroad.

Not simply crime, but the amount of fearless transgressive activity right now, is more than i've ever seen since the 1960s. It is like a torrent from a fire hydrant that's shoving everything around before it. If anything, the police and capitalist media are frantically trying to downplay it as much as they can. Mostly, it isn't "political" of course—and too much of it is anti-social—but it all definitely stepped up a whole level on the streets after George Floyd. It's the big dance.

In the same way of edging outside the lines, women here after the second disaster knifing Roe v. Wade to death by the Supreme Hate Court, were inspired both by the generation-changing novel, *The Handmaid's Tale,* and by the 1960s underground "Jane" women's abortion collective in Chicago, and started small unlegal groups to quietly provide medication abortions wherever they are. On their own, desperate women are going around their state laws and using internet resources to illegally "self-manage" abortions. No one is saluting the flag anymore first thing in the morning. (The first great abortion disaster was enacting Roe v. Wade itself, which temporarily granted u.s. women abortions only so as to rebind with looser chains their obeisance to the principle that born women may not do anything with their bodies without patriarchal permission.)

The full meaning of "Jane" and the twin abortion disasters remains unspoken even now by the actually-existing left, because too many still don't get it. Or don't want to get it. Let's dial the clock backward to the raw situation we grew up and lived in, where abortion was outlawed and policed and imprisoned and "always" had been. One thing no one ever says, i guess because it is "dirty" talk, is that in those backward, unscientific days in the A-bomb 1940s and polio vaccine 1950s and moon rocket 1960s, is that many, many thousands of women here needed abortions all the time. Always have. This was civilization without "the pill" yet,

JUNE 9th: "I Shot Andy Warhol": Review of the Reviews, Group rap on Valerie Solanas, 'The Scum Manifesto' & 'Manhating'

JUNE 16th: Father's Day report on fathers • Men fighting Misogyny

JUNE, JULY, AUGUST: 'Politics of Orgasm' • Mothers Day II: single mothers rap continues • Feminist Generation Gap • Riot grrrls • Street Harassment • Deconstructing 'Women's Studies,' more...

Always: Music, Humor, Group Raps, W'min's History, Radical Feminist Classics remember. (As Butch used to say triumphantly when "the pill" arrived: "Freud was wrong—for women, *chemistry* is destiny!") But except for rare public statements adding up to nothing, the postwar u.s. imperial left politely ignored the issue in a manly way. Keeping both respectable and legal. It was much more important to them to demand public support for the steelworkers' strike or some such issue, of which the then-existing left had a truckload.

On the surface. Below that, in hidden daily life, the desperate need for and massive illegality and fear around abortions churned lives across the left just as in the larger body of society. If you were wealthy or even just very affluent, of course, no prob. Airplane off to Mexico or many other warm and sunny tourist places for a legal abortion vacation. (One of the fav Mexican doctors for that among progressives was an old radical friend of the great artist Diego Rivera, whose large house and clinic was informally a gallery for his patients of many of Rivera's paintings).

In those old days, the Communist Party, while fading fast, was still the 800-pound gorilla in the room, whose membership and sympathizers even controlled some AFL-CIO unions and were a majority of the anti-capitalist left. Although the Party never said so publicly, women in and around its ranks who got in trouble could on an individual basis quietly find Party doctors who would arrange abortions. Knew women who did that, gratefully.

People today somehow assume that because the women's "Jane" collective was in operation in the 1960s, that women in Chicago had that covered. You only wish. Although "Jane" eventually had done thousands of abortions, as a small secretive and illegal outfit, of course relatively few women in Chicago knew about them even as they edged more and more into the daylight to spread the rebellion. My comrade Butch knew in a casual movement way some of the "Jane" women, but of course didn't know their secret. In part because she was older and in different currents in the left. Women she unknowingly knew who were in "Jane" were like white university student activists, who tended to be straight and to live on the North Side (even if they went to the University of Chicago southside). Those who were less reputable, coming out of the South Side Black rebellion and the street drug culture, as Butch did, were less likely to be with that crowd.

That doesn't mean that women not in that know never got knocked up or needed any less abortions. Abortions were a real issue for women in and around the left back then, a need as immediate and personal as a next meal and a place to lay your head and safety from violence. In our stream of young South Side non–Communist Party, non-respectable rebels back then and there, if you needed an abortion people knew of two options (certainly there were more than two around, but illegally dangerous as it was different groupings had different contacts, just like with copping a gun or scoring dope).

One was the "next day" guy. Who had a very small shabby storefront on 63rd street in the "ghetto." He was not any doctor or nurse, just a middle-aged Black man, and for $80 he would give you a really foul smelling drink you had to take on the spot, and keep it down which was not always easy as it didn't taste any good either. But it worked, women swore, if you went to him no later than the next day after sex.

Usually you were dealing with the need much later than that. For that you needed a real doc, and the one we knew of then was way down south of Chicago near Galesburg. He was an old hostile white country physician, who didn't make any pretense of respecting the women who came to him. It was all about the greenbacks, and for $400 he would do a quick "D&C" with tools old style ($400 was real numbers back then, like you could get an okay used Ford or Chevy or Plymouth with it). You had to call him for an appointment first and immediately take the one and only he gave you. His phone number was the real secret, and he questioned you to feel safer that you weren't setting him up. Though he was never nice or "professional." He was doing a profitable crime he loved to scumbag women he despised, and he didn't even try to cover that up. Maneuvering in desperation outside the law isn't as romantic as idealists sometimes like to picture it.

But the thing with illegal contacts is that sometimes you can't locate them for a while or ever again. My comrade Butch had a young friend, not an intellectual but around the left because she was an outcast, too. Very poor and a high school student—and suddenly preg by a guy she didn't love and with a family that was breaking up and telling her she was on her own. And Butch couldn't find any resource we knew about, except the CPUSA doctors. Who paradoxically because they had maneuvered within the medical system so successfully, ran into a wall in this case. They were used to on the sly arranging completely legal medical abortions in hospitals—but couldn't do it with that girl, since as a family-less minor the legal hurdles were too big. She had the kid, then lost the kid since she tried but couldn't earn enough working crap jobs to support them with no regular child care anyway. Had to drop out of school, and by the laws then she could never return to public school. Salvaging her life alone after such loss was a tough piece of work, and in some ways though she did it, she always moved with the scar of that bitter oppression.

This experience wasn't uncommon. You are probably wondering why i am giving all these old details? It is to show how control or not over abortion was real and material to women's practical lives in a threatening way around the left back then. That was the majority experience in society, not a brilliant breakthrough like "Jane." Which is why the reformist men's left ducked and dodged it all as too dangerous in all senses of the word, as completely as they could. Here is the first lesson: we don't ever need a left like that again. It's too late for that. It is not even openers in the wild card game of replacing capitalism with a liberated human world-system.

For generations, women in and around the left had to deal with the need for their women's safety—including abortions and the constant haze of men's violence—completely informally on their own. Their lives and all women's lives weren't judged as needing "political" struggle. Whether communist or socialist or anarchist, the left's priorities didn't include that at all. Yes, we all know of brave left women earlier in history who spoke out as exceptions. But Butch's point which she later blew her stack about a lot was, why couldn't the anti-capitalist left have made that kind of illegal underground work for women the first priority, the main thrust of reorganizing the culture. Not in the 1960s, which was too late, but starting decades before like in the 1930s say.

Her point was that whether it was a "Jane" or a communal subversive day care and school replacing bourgeois "education," or women's dead-secret armed patrols outside the law, women must sooner or later organize themselves to make or provide and control the heart of what they need in society. "Jane" wasn't just part of a hallway towards a Roe v. Wade, but something alternative and much better, much richer in her eyes. If revs don't understand that lesson, which people's struggle itself repeats for us in various ways and forms over and over, we are trying to climb a stairway but tripping on the first stair. To find the future the oppressed need to liberate us all, we need to move towards the danger. Not easy to do, for sure.

The whole 1960s shakeup against the "American" status quo wasn't only directly fighting the state in terms of anti-war and anti-racism, and cultural rebellions from dope to gender to music. They were heralded by a wave of unafraid outlaw activity of all kinds, including straight-up rude crime both good and evil. That's what we are experiencing right now. Rough change of all kinds is coming, and the left will grow out of that, too

the end

Marginalized Notes / Monday Nov. 28, 2022

Like most interviews, this discussion was never researched in the first place. It reflected whatever current news and talk was bouncing off my own thoughts and long memories. When i needed a fact or a name spelled out, like everyone else i just quickly went to the internet pantry. Didn't even think of endnotes, since others could just google things like i did. A few times, it became convenient to use an old book or a clipping file from my bookshelves, but that wasn't much and i didn't worry about it.

That was when i hadn't planned on anything past the present Part 1. But after delays going to press during the pandemic, and my trying to answer continued questioning from my editor, Karl K., led to adding an even longer Part 2—and using specific sources on facts more heavily not simply my memory.

(BTW at the same time, discovered that some of the sources of my facts had up and disappeared themselves. Just ran away into the forest of knowing. i couldn't re-find several internet sources i had earlier used.)

Anyway, my editor has always liked source notes whether endnotes or footnotes, arguing that giving people leads where they can read an author's sources more extensively on their own, is a real help to some readers. Finally, he wore me down and i've tried to note sources if only in incomplete ways, particularly in Part 2. Good luck in the hunt.

1. Mikhail Bakunin was obviously an important revolutionary figure in starting revolutionary anti-capitalism, and although much maligned and dismissed by Marx and Engels in a way that wasn't truthful, he did lead a life much of which sounds like it was from an adventure novel. Wanted to list and comment on where i had found my facts about his life, so i went back to the suburban public library where i had found and read three biographies of the Russian revolutionary—only to find that all were now unavailable. Asking about them, i was told unofficially by

one library worker after a computer search that all three were really missing, had probably been stolen. Wasn't that just like something that would happen to the footloose rebel? And, no, i was told, they were not being replaced, because that was futile since some kinds of books were just always being stolen. Hmm, not sure if that is a good thing or a bad thing, but it is frustrating.

2. Roxanne Dunbar-Ortiz. *Outlaw Woman. A Memoir of the War Years, 1960-1975.* City Lights Books, 2001. Pages 198–200.
Incidentally, during the anti–Vietnam War struggle days i had met both women involved in that political clash of wills at that GI coffeeshop, and had even worked with one. Both were respected in the movement then, and i recall hearing on the anti-war grapevine about their disagreement at that Army base town—and how the one later came out and crossed over to women's liberation work. So Dunbar-Ortiz wasn't just making up that great story.

3. Rosa Brooks. *How Everything Became War and the Military Became Everything.* Simon & Schuster, 2016. Pages 318–320; Alison Bowen. "Easing the Path to Owning A Home." *Chicago Tribune* November 22, 2020. For poverty problems among young u.s. military families in the time of coronavirus and job losses in off-base civilian communities, see: Jennifer Steinhauer. "For More Military Families, Losing a Job or School Lunch Means a Search for Food Aid." *New York Times.* December 17, 2020.
Unlike most sources used here, this *How Everything Became War* book was an international bestseller that made an unlikely state policy star out of a professor of international law. Rosa Brooks was both a former advisor for Human Rights Watch and once the member of a top secret Pentagon committee which gave the final yes or no to individual u.s. assassinations of young Muslim activists. In her latter role Brooks rose to being a senior counselor to the u.s.

Deputy Secretary of Defense for Policy (she still lectures soldiers as an adjunct at the Army's West Point Modern War Institute). *How Everything Became War* never does explain its title subject, of course, but the book was so popular in the Establishment and warmly recommended by a number of top u.s. generals because it intellectually massages the growing contradictions in "America's" cancerous military-civilian relationship, from a soothingly white liberal humanitarian but loyally pro-imperialist viewpoint.

4. "FTA," short for "F—K The Army," was the great all-purpose anti-brass graffiti among u.s. Army troops then in the 1960s–70s, with it inked onto the front of many thousands of helmets in 'Nam (not usually taken up in other u.s. services, especially among Marines, who used their own graffiti phrases incorporating the slang dis "The Green Machine").

5. H. Bruce Franklin. *Crash Course. From the Good War to the Forever War.* Rutgers University Press, 2018. Pages 264–267. Franklin was widely followed, envied, admired and resented on the West Coast during the anti-war 1960s. As a controversial Stanford professor, his breakthrough literary criticism which insisted on raising up as important then-banned or marginal genres, such as criminal prison writings and science-fiction, had a wide effect. He was more immediately one of the main radical anti-war activists in the Bay Area. Finally burning out as one purist national leader in the birth of u.s. Maoism, a failed period of his life he later wrote off as a self-delusional fever. He retained his basic anti-capitalist view of u.s. society, though. Much of this memoir of his own capitalist war (he was a frontline air force veteran) and anti-war is shocking material with a positive jolt. Though to be clear, it's not about the u.s. revolutionary left.

6. Alan Greenspan and Adrian Woolridge. *Capitalism in America: A History.* Penguin Press, 2018. Page 84. This is a different kind of history of "America." Stripped down and perhaps easier to read, the legendary former longtime chairman of the Federal Reserve Board and his co-author, the political editor of *The Economist*, explain the u.s.a. primarily in terms of business investments, profits, and developing the capitalist class economy. Minor things like the rise of the Klan and lynchings, as well as changes in presidential politics, receive only brief lines to help frame the passing times as direct capitalist activity holds center stage. In its own way, a very cold-blooded but telling exposition of how "America" was made into a great-but-now-declining economic empire. The blame now, according to the conservative authors, is the "encrusting" suffocation of liberal state benefits like Social Security, which bestow automatic income on the masses without their having to work every day or risk anything. Charming.

7. Ibid. Pages 88–89.

8. Gabriel Kolko. *Main Currents in Modern American History.* Harper & Row, 1976. Pages 26–29.

9. Daniel Bergner. "Open Minds." *The New York Times Magazine.* May 22, 2022.

10. See: statista. "leading construction equipment manufacturers in 2020 based on global market share"; iSeekplant. "TOP TEN HEAVY EQUIPMENT COMPANY MARKET SHARES."

11. Greenspan & Woolridge. op cit. Page 14.

12. Shane Goldmacher. "Drop in Small-Dollar Donations Alarms G.O.P." *The New York Times.* July 27, 2022.

13. Ilona Andrews. *Blood Heir.* Nancy Yost Literary Agency, Inc, 2021. Page 77.

14. David Brooks. "The G.O.P. Is Getting Even Worse." *The New York Times.* April 23, 2021.

15. This quotation is often seen right now, but almost always attributed to the left critic Fredric Jameson. As in it being described as "the famous Jameson quote" on one popular Goodreads page. Not that there's any mystery about H. Bruce Franklin's work, but Jameson is so much more "hip" and "in" right this moment to the shoddy white reformist intellectuals.

16. Sally Rooney. *Beautiful World, Where Are You?* Farrar, Straus and Giroux, 2021. Pages 43–44.

17. Immanuel Wallerstein, Randall Collins, Michael Mann, Georgi Derlugian, Craig Calhoun. *Does Capitalism Have a Future?* Oxford University Press, 2013. Pages 57, 65. For a good browse, try his paperback selected works, which include not only some highlights from his world-system theory but also short writings on subjects such as race and ethnicity, the bourgeois as concept and reality, and liberalism: *The Essential Wallerstein.* The New Press, 2000.

18. Wallerstein, Collins, Mann, Derluguian, Calhoun. op cit. Page 35.

19. After the June 2022 slaying of the two Catholic priests, i took out one of my files of press clippings on the Mexican crisis. While these are separate news stories on different events in the crisis, they really are interconnected, and i urge anyone interested in diving deeper into the situation to simply read them all together. It's like an extended magazine article:

Natalie Kittroeff and Oscar Lopez. "Catholic Church Joins Mexico's Critics After Murder of 2 Jesuit Priests." *The New York Times.* June 25, 2022 ;

CBS News. July 6, 2022. 10:06 am. "Bishop proposes 'Social Pact' with drug traffickers to tackle violence in Mexico";

Maria Abi-Habib. "In Mexico, Farmers Are Caught in Middle of Drug Cartels Turf War." *The New York Times.* May 5, 2022;

David Agren. "Witness testifies that El Chapo paid a $100 million bribe to ex-Mexican president Peña Nieto." *Washington Post.* January 15, 2019 at 7:34 p.m. EST;

Noah Hurowitz. "El Chapo Trial: Witness Alleges Presidential Bribes, Cartel Brutality." *Rolling Stone.* November 21, 2018. 12:54 PM ET;

Randal C. Archibold. "In Mexico, a Growing Gap Between Political Class and Calls for Change." *The New York Times.* December 13, 2014;

David Karp. "Is the Lime an Endangered Species?" *The New York Times.* May 30, 2014;

Jose de Cordoba. "Bloody Struggle Erupts Over Avocado Trade." *The Wall Street Journal.* February 1–2, 2014;

Santiago and Jose de Cordoba. "Executive Slaying Sparks New Fears." *The Wall Street Journal.* January 11–12, 2014;

Ginger Thompson, Randal C. Archibold and Eric Schmitt. "Hand of U.S. Is Seen in Halting General's Rise." *The New York Times.* February 5, 2013;

Mary Anastasia O'Grady. "The Real Victims of Mexico's Drug War." *The Wall Street Journal.* November 12, 2012;

Jose de Cordoba. "Trial Exposes Odd Ties in Mexico Drug War." *The Wall Street Journal.* January 7–8, 2012. (contains Mexican Attorney General Office's color map of different drug cartel areas at that time).

SPECIAL NOTE: Look up if you are interested some of the many internet articles on drug cartel officer Jesus Zambada

Niebla as well as Bush regime security official Robert Bonner (especially his op ed on Mexico in the New York Times).

20. Ruchir Sharma. *The Rise and Fall of Nations: Forces of Change in the Post-Crisis World.* W.W. Norton & Co. 2016. Pages 141, 193–194.

21. Julie Turkewitz and Genevieve Glatsky. "Soul-Searching Report From Colombia's Truth Commission." *The New York Times.* June 29, 2022; Phil Klay. "America's Ongoing Secret Wars." *The New York Times.* May 29, 2022.

22. Maria Abi-Habib and Oscar Lopez. "Plight of Mexico's Poor Worsens, Despite President's Promises." *The New York Times.* July 18, 2022.

23. Elizabeth Kolbert. "The Catastrophist." *The New Yorker.* July 27, 2020.

24. Minqi Li. *China and the 21st Century Crisis.* Pluto Press, 2016. Pages 33, 95, 137.

25. Ibid. Page 182.

26. Lenin never wrote much about his own life, particularly in the chaotic time when the revolution was going on, so this isn't something i read about (my best friend seized my set of the collected works anyway, when we moved into separate places and divvied up the bookcase). This great story of Lenin getting held up by stick-up guys posing as red guards was told to me by an old trotskyist, as part of the mostly unwritten lore of the marxist-leninist movement. i was young and not in his faction of the left, but he tried to wise me up anyway. He said it came from a French socialist who had gone to Russia to work with Lenin and his communist international and was a first-hand witness. Much later, that French comrade published his own memoir, parts

of which were translated into English and circulated in the movement here. Was struck by the story so much that i kept asking questions about it, to get that older comrade to repeat the tale so i could remember it best i could. Can't prove the facts, but in some dusty old sectarian journal or zine from the way past i think it was passed on.

27. Dani Romero. John Schreiber. "LA freight train looting 'out of control' as thieves worsen supply chain bottlenecks." Yahoo/finance Wed, January 19, 2022. 6:47 AM.

Settlers: The Mythology of the White Proletariat from Mayflower to Modern

J. SAKAI

978-1-62963-037-3 • 456 PAGES

$20.00

Settlers is a uniquely important book in the canon of the North American revolutionary left and anticolonial movements. First published in the 1980s by activists with decades of experience organizing in grassroots anticapitalist struggles against white supremacy, the book soon established itself as an essential reference point for revolutionary nationalists and dissident currents within the predominantly colonialist Marxist-Leninist and anarchist movements at that time.

Always controversial within the establishment Left, *Settlers* uncovers centuries of collaboration between capitalism and white workers and their organizations, as well as their neocolonial allies, showing how the United States was designed from the ground up as a parasitic and genocidal entity. *Settlers* exposes the fact that America's white citizenry have never supported themselves but have always resorted to exploitation and theft, culminating in acts of genocide to maintain their culture and way of life. As recounted in painful detail by Sakai, the United States has been built on the theft of Indigenous lands and of Afrikan labor, on the robbery of the northern third of Mexico, the colonization of Puerto Rico, and the expropriation of the Asian working class, with each of these crimes being accompanied by violence.

This new edition includes "Cash & Genocide: The True Story of Japanese-American Reparations" and an interview with author J. Sakai by Ernesto Aguilar.

ALSO FROM KERSPLEBEDEB

Basic Politics of Movement Security

J. SAKAI & MANDY HISCOCKS

978-1-894946-52-0 • 68 PAGES

$7.00

There are many books and articles reporting state repression, but not on that subject's more intimate relative, movement security. It is general practice to only pass along knowledge about movement security privately, in closed group lectures or by personal word-of-mouth. In fact, when new activists have questions about security problems, they quickly discover that there is no "Security for Dummies" to explore the basics. Adding to the confusion, the handful of available left security texts are usually about underground or illegal groups, not the far larger public movements that work on a more or less legal level.

During Montreal's 2013 Festival of Anarchy, J. Sakai gave a workshop about the politics of movement security, sharing the results of typical incidents of both the movement's successes and the movement's failures in combating the "political police" or state security agencies. He also discussed the nature of those state sub-cultures. This booklet contains a transcript of that talk, and of the subsequent lively question and answer period, along with several after-the-workshop observations by Sakai.

Mandy Hiscocks comes at the topic from her personal experiences organizing against the 2010 G20 Summit in Toronto. In this in-depth interview, reprinted from the radical Canadian political journal *Upping The Anti*, Hiscocks describes how her political scene and groups she worked with were infiltrated by undercover agents over a year before the summit even occurred. Hiscocks spent a year in prison as a result of these experiences, shortly after this interview was conducted.

ORDER FROM WWW.LEFTWINGBOOKS.NET

The "Dangerous Class" and Revolutionary Theory: Thoughts on the Making of the Lumpen/Proletariat

J. SAKAI

978-1-894946-90-2 • 301 PAGES

$24.95

J. Sakai's ground-breaking, *The "Dangerous Class" and Revolutionary Theory: Thoughts on the Making of the Lumpen/Proletariat*, is our first major exploration of this most controversial and least understood "non-class" in revolutionary politics. It is an attempt to unknot the puzzle. It encompasses the threads of criminality as well as gender, of breaking social boundaries and eating the bitterest of class politics.

The "Dangerous Class" and Revolutionary Theory starts with the paper of that name, on the birth of the modern lumpen/proletariat in the 18th and 19th centuries and the storm cloud of revolutionary theory that has always surrounded them. Going back and piecing together both the actual social reality and the analyses primarily of Marx but also Bakunin and Engels, the paper shows how Marx's class theory wasn't something static. His views learned in quick jumps, and then all but reversed themselves in several significant aspects. While at first dismissing them in *The Communist Manifesto* as "that passively rotting mass" at the obscure lower depths, Marx soon realized that the lumpen could be players at the very center of events in revolutionary civil war. Even at the center in the startling rise of new regimes. Like his was at times almost a post-modern understanding.

The second part of the book includes the detailed paper "Mao Z's Revolutionary Laboratory and the Role of the Lumpen Proletariat." This, too, is ground-breaking work. If the major revolutionary theory we have about the lumpen was first roughly assembled in 19th-century Europe, these ideas weren't put to the test then. As Sakai points out, the left's euro-centrism here prevented it from realizing the obvious: that the basic theory from European radicalism was first fully tested not there or here but in the Chinese Revolution of 1921–49. Under severely clashing political lines in the left, the class analysis finally used by Mao Z was shaken out of the shipping crate from Europe and then modified to map the organizing of millions over a prolonged generational revolutionary war. One could hardly wish for a larger test tube, and the many lessons to be learned from this mass political experience are finally put on the table.

In addition, there are also two lively Addendums: The first is an informal correspondence, a back and forth of questions raised by an early draft of *The "Dangerous Class" and Revolutionary Theory*, between the book's editor and J. Sakai. It starts with the question of how to place the traditional gay community in this?

The second Addendum is a reprint of J. Sakai's 1976 covert intelligence paper, "U.S. Experiment Using Black 'Gangs' to Repress Black Community Rebellions" (circulated under the earlier title "The Lumpenproletariat and Repression"). There is both an extensive Foreword explaining the politics and circumstances that led to this paper, as well as an Afterword explaining how the education paper was used and some critical reaction to it.

Night-Vision: Illuminating War and Class on the Neo-Colonial Terrain

BUTCH LEE & RED ROVER

978-1-894946-88-9 • 264 PAGES

$17.00

bell hooks: "*Night-Vision* was so compelling to me because it has a spirit of militancy which reformist feminism tries to kill because militant feminism is seen as a threat to the liberal bourgeois feminism that just wants to be equal with men. It has that raw, unmediated truth-telling which I think we are going to need in order to deal with the fascism that's upon us."

A foundational analysis of post-modern capitalism, the decline of u.s. hegemony, and the need for a revolutionary movement of the oppressed to overthrow it all.

KER
SPL
EBE
DEB

Since 1998 Kersplebedeb has been an important source of radical literature and agit prop materials.

The project has a non-exclusive focus on anti-patriarchal and anti-imperialist politics, framed within an anticapitalist perspective. A special priority is given to writings regarding armed struggle in the metropole, the continuing struggles of political prisoners and prisoners of war, and the political economy of imperialism.

The Kersplebedeb website presents historical and contemporary writings by revolutionary thinkers from the anarchist and communist traditions.

Kersplebedeb can be contacted at:

Kersplebedeb
CP 63560
CCCP Van Horne
Montreal, Quebec
Canada
H3W 3H8

email: info@kersplebedeb.com
web: www.kersplebedeb.com
www.leftwingbooks.net

Kersplebedeb

www.ingramcontent.com/pod-product-compliance
Lightning Source LLC
Chambersburg PA
CBHW050643270326
41927CB00012B/2846